What Your Colleagu

M000299842

A superb book. Full to the brim of practical, workable ideas. Sharratt and Fullan exude love and compassion for all students everywhere, reinforcing that they all deserve the best educational experience, irrespective of circumstance or context. It also reminds us to look at faces first, data second, in the pursuit of achievement for all. Powerful and persuasive, this book speaks directly to the importance of focusing on global education now more than ever.

—Alma Harris
Emeritus Professor, University of Swansea
Wales, UK

A rich tapestry weaving together data, student identity, and informed professional judgment. Sharratt and Fullan have provided a context for the use of student data to move from an aspiration that all children can learn to an accountable set of actions to ensure that all means all. Putting faces on the data requires knowing the whole learner, including their identity, community, and lived experience.

—Cathy Montreuil
Deputy Minister, Department of
Education and Early Child Development
Nova Scotia, Canada

Unlocking the capacity of each student remains the essential work of all teachers and leaders. This new edition expertly provides an elaborated and contemporary focus on how to enhance school performance through identifying and understanding the abilities, passions, and potential of our next generation of innovators and problem solvers.

—Jim Watterston
Dean, Enterprise Professor, Education
Systems, The University of Melbourne
Victoria, Australia

Sharratt and Fullan's 2012 work was a catalyst for progress in Queensland public education, leading us out of a "teacher-led/data-driven" binary into a new era characterized by deep understanding of our student and community needs, grounded in evidence. New perspectives in this edition reflect contemporary research and case studies, updated parameters, and provocations around emerging global challenges.

—**Sharon Schimming**
Deputy Director-General, State Schools,
Department of Education Queensland
Queensland, Australia

A book starts with blank pages, has within it a lovely apparition and a sense of beauty waiting to be imprinted so that potential readers can then make interpretations about what they see. There is no immaculate perception when interpreting data, but there are multiple meanings tied to beautiful faces. Sharratt and Fullan paint the pictures, sculpt the beauty of the meaning of data, and dive deeply into the interpretations and implications. A work of art, indeed.

—**John Hattie**
Emeritus Laureate Professor, University of Melbourne and
Co-director of the Hattie Family Foundation
Victoria, Australia

This is our forever work.

—**Gerard Mowbray**
Director of Education, Diocese of Maitland-Newcastle
New South Wales, Australia

My journey as a school and system leader has run parallel to the 10 years of *Putting FACES on the Data*. As a school leader, it helped me learn that the only way you lift outcomes—whether for a class or a school—is child by child. This ensures that we have a line of sight to what each child and school needs to improve student outcomes. Thank you from every child who has been "given a face" in a class, school, and system across the world.

—**Leanne Nixon**
Deputy Secretary, School Performance North
New South Wales, Australia

This book changed the way our system views data and how collectively a shared understanding of data literacy brings accountability to the forefront. There is no system improvement without "Putting FACES on the Data"!

—**Kate O'Brien**
Director of Education and Research Sydney Catholic Schools
New South Wales, Australia

It is great to have a 10th anniversary edition of *FACES*! This book changed our understanding of how to promote improvement in our work with teachers and leaders in Chile. It taught us what to look for in the process of learning, what data is relevant to collect, and how leaders become learners with their teachers. *FACES* taught us that focus for collaboration and professional learning is all about putting each student's achievements at the center of our conversations!

—**Isidora Recart**
Executive Director, Fundación Educacional Arauco
Santiago Región Metropolitana Chile

In this fast-paced world, work that is relevant ten years after its first edition speaks to its durability. Each part of this book can be found in the work we do—I see data Walls and I hear conversations about assessment and how it drives instruction. This book guides our work with practical examples, clear explanations, and guidance. Thank you to Lyn Sharratt and Michael Fullan for continuing to make *Putting FACES on the Data* relevant and valuable to all educators!

—**Elaine Lochhead**
Chief Superintendent, Seine Rover School Division
Manitoba, Canada

Lyn Sharratt and Michael Fullan clearly articulate the complexity of change and the necessity to understand the 14 Parameters by providing an insightful resource using case studies to provide an indisputable pathway to system improvement. This is a must read for every system leader, school leader, and teacher leader. Their work has been pivotal in my work as a system change leader in both Manitoba and Alberta and is even more important coming out of a global pandemic.

—**Michael Borgfjord**
Chief Superintendent, Pembina Hills School Division
Alberta, Canada

This powerful book provides the missing links between intention and action. Educators want to see every student succeed in learning and in life. The challenge is to reform the system to deliver on broader and deeper goals while also engaging each student on a pathway to their "best possible, most richly imagined future." This book is a beacon of hope that honors the work of all teachers and leaders by making sense of the improvement journey in classrooms, schools, and systems.

—**Mary Jean Gallagher**
Assistant Deputy Minister (Rtd.), Ontario Ministry of Education
Ontario, Canada

NEW 10th ANNIVERSARY EDITION Putting

FACES

on the Data

NEW 10th ANNIVERSARY EDITION Putting

FACES
on the Data
WHAT GREAT LEADERS AND TEACHERS DO!

LYN SHARRATT • MICHAEL FULLAN
FOREWORD by SIR MICHAEL BARBER

A JOINT PUBLICATION

Inspiring Educational Leaders

THE PROFESSIONAL LEARNING ASSOCIATION

A SAGE Publishing Company

FOR INFORMATION:

Corwin

A SAGE Company

2455 Teller Road

Thousand Oaks, California 91320

(800) 233-9936

www.corwin.com

SAGE Publications Ltd.

1 Oliver's Yard

55 City Road

London EC1Y 1SP

United Kingdom

SAGE Publications India Pvt. Ltd.

B 1/I 1 Mohan Cooperative Industrial Area

Mathura Road, New Delhi 110 044

India

SAGE Publications Asia-Pacific Pte. Ltd.

18 Cross Street #10-10/11/12

China Square Central

Singapore 048423

President: Mike Soules

President and Editorial Director: Monica Eckman

Senior Acquisitions Editor: Tanya Ghans

Content Development Manager: Desirée A. Bartlett

Editorial Assistant: Nyle DeLeon

Project Editor: Amy Schroller

Copy Editor: Deanna Noga

Typesetter: C&M Digitals (P) Ltd.

Proofreader: Dennis Webb

Cover Designer: Gail Buschman

Marketing Manager: Morgan Fox

Printed in Canada

Library of Congress Control Number: 2022941043

This book is printed on acid-free paper.

MIX
Paper from
responsible sources
FSC® C011825

22 23 24 25 26 10 9 8 7 6 5 4 3 2 1

In every block of marble, I see a statue as plain as though it stood before me, shaped and perfect in attitude and action. I have only to hew away the rough walls that imprison the lovely apparition to reveal it to the other eyes as mine see it.

—Michelangelo, 1475–1564

CONTENTS

For additional resources,
please visit the book's companion website at
resources.corwin.com/faces.

LIST OF FIGURES
AND TABLES

PREFACE

Statistics are a wonderful servant and an appalling master.

—Hopper and Hopper (2009)

There are certain fundamental questions that plague educational practice, none more perplexing than: How do we know specifically THAT something has been accomplished; exactly HOW was it carried out; and WHAT should we do to make it better the next time? To make it more complicated, how can all this be done in times of constant upheaval?

It turns out that when people make changes in dynamic times, they must also build the capacity to continue to make changes. The good news is that *when they learn to change* in "changing times" *they also build their capacity to keep on changing.* In this edition we once again show how to focus on the details of essential changes even when *everything* is changing around us.

"FACES" is a metaphor. It was difficult enough in 2012 to get the best fix on the personalized performance of hundreds of thousands of students, but it became possible as we got a better fix on the goals, the means of implementation, and the nature of outcomes of desired reforms in literacy, numeracy, and high school completion. Ontario had just come off a successful decade of increased capacity and performance of its 5,000 schools and 72 districts in its public school system. We were able to make wide-spread and in-depth observations of positive changes across Ontario.

Now it is incredibly more difficult to get that same sort of system fix or perspective on performance because the learning goals go beyond the important basics into "deep learning" such as 6 Global Competencies (character, citizenship, collaboration, communication, creativity, and critical thinking) in our work. And COVID has dramatically imposed itself, simultaneously stopping education systems in their tracks, causing them to pivot continuously between remote, hybrid, and classroom models of learning and creating cracks and gaps where major innovations (in assessment, for example) may seem more obvious. We are producing this *FACES* edition before the full consequences of COVID play themselves out. We are doing so because getting the important basics right and finding ways to ensure deeper learning can occur are vitally important to educators, to students, and to us.

In this 10th anniversary edition of *FACES*, we go deeper in the quest to balance and integrate two critical aspects of school improvement that look like they can't be brought together: On the one hand is the question of how to personalize data for all students so that each is treated as a real person and helped to learn according to their own individual needs; on the other hand is the question of how to do this for 100,000 students at a time without losing the human touch. *FACES* does just this, honoring and helping educators work with the individual and giving educators the tools to learn how to make the changes in their own practice, thereby improving the system.

We are fortunate to have Sir Michael Barber "playing along" in real time tackling the same issues. Sir Michael was the architect of Tony Blair's British reform of "literacy and numeracy" that began in 1997. It was during this time and into the first decade of the 2000s that Sharratt (with Fullan as an external consultant) developed the fundamentals of FACES in York Region, Ontario, with its 150+ schools. Sharratt and Fullan have worked together and independently in the two decades of this century to develop the ideas and practices of FACES initially in Canada, the United States, the United Kingdom, Australia, and eventually in more than 20 countries. It is this fully extended work that we report on in this anniversary edition.

In Chapter 1, we set the context and mode, via Case Studies, of how we and others use data to create impact, a practice we carry through every chapter. Chapter 2 examines what we found from our key research questions. Then we focus on assessment (Chapter 3) and instruction (Chapter 4), the inseparable conjoined twins. In Chapter 5, we examine the leadership required to make balanced and integrated systems work. Finally, in Chapter 6, we consider ownership—who is responsible and accountable for putting FACES on the data.

We have always recognized that *practice drives practice*, or more accurately *best practice drives better practice*. All our work—small and big examples—is based on close partnerships with practitioners, ranging from students to policy makers. We believe that this *action pact* force will take off within the next year given the pent-up frustrations in society and in schools.

We are excited to publish our new edition in real time alongside these developments. Even better, we are again accompanied by Sir Michael Barber who wrote the foreword to our first edition in 2012. As if it were on cue, Sir Michael has just published his own major set of lessons in a magnificent book, *Accomplishment: How to achieve ambitious and challenging things* (2021). His chapters on "Getting Ready" and "Getting it Done" are compatible with our book. We are incredibly fortunate to have Michael join us in this anniversary edition.

It is time to put our new FACES forward as we have found the *wonderful servant* for which the Hopper Brothers yearned—10 years on!

FOREWORD

The challenges facing humanity in the immediate decades ahead are more profound than ever—climate change, biodiversity loss, the need for an ethical basis for the rapid developments in AI and genetic engineering, and the continuing threat that, with the nuclear proliferation, one of the many conflicts around the world could turn nuclear. I'm not naïve enough to think that improved education alone could resolve these mega-challenges. But I believe strongly that none of them can be solved without improved education, not just for a few but for everyone. And it's not just about improvement either; it's also about broadening and deepening what we consider to be a good education; broadening because we need people arriving at adulthood with wide horizons and a global perspective; deepening because depth of understanding and empathy are more important than ever. For most of human history, for good or ill, it was assumed that as long as an elite was well-educated they could do the deep thinking for everyone. In a world with approaching 9 billion people all making decisions, day after day, that materially affect the future of humanity, it will no longer do.

That is why I wrote my recent book *Accomplishment: How to achieve ambitious and challenging things* (2021). The aim was to identify and describe the pattern that enables great accomplishment whether for individuals, organizations, or governments. It is also why we need this outstanding new edition of Lyn Sharratt's and Michael Fullan's book *FACES*. The dramatic changes required in education won't be brought about by seventy-word sentences or rhetoric or speeches or even books. Success depends on getting the detail right; on tracking the data to know whether we are on track student by student and school by school; and on remembering, as Sharratt and Fullan constantly remind us, that every number has a face, a name and a personal history.

As they argue at the outset of this revised edition, to succeed we educators need to examine three very demanding questions: How do we know THAT something has been accomplished? Can we explain HOW it was accomplished? And WHAT do we have to do to make it even better next time? Answering these questions rigorously drives continuous improvement and unlocks innovation. Only by checking constantly and then acting where there are problems will we be able to ensure we make the necessary advances.

As we attempt these huge tasks, only by checking rigorously and constantly and then acting where there are problems, will we be able to ensure we make progress. Just as important, this will ensure that when we find ourselves succeeding, we can learn and apply the lessons. As they argue elsewhere, in the twenty-first century and beyond, "the learning is the work, and the work is the learning."

In this new edition of their classic, Lyn Sharratt and Michael Fullan have performed a vital service for progressive education reformers around the world. They demonstrate more deeply than ever that good data and good teaching go together and that success is only possible, if in fact they do. For many years, a powerful strand of the culture among educators has been skeptical about data, sometimes even rejecting the need for it altogether. Great teaching, in this view, is about inspired individuals walking into a classroom and, through force of personality and knowledge of subject, engaging the students who happen to be in there. And, of course, we can all remember in our own lives teachers who did exactly this, so it's a story we're inclined to believe.

Moreover, the argument continues, the data are at best limited and out of date; worse still, the argument concludes, given that so much of what makes great education great is hard to measure, the data force a reductionist perspective on schools and turn teachers into technicians.

Sharratt and Fullan demonstrate convincingly the flaws in this perspective. There will always be uniquely inspired teachers who rise above the mere mortals around them, but what the authors show here is that if we want whole systems to succeed with every child—which, as I'm arguing here, is indeed the challenge of the twenty-first century—then we need collective capacity; and collective capacity involves teachers in each school and between schools engaging in serious conversation of what good teaching looks like in diverse circumstances and how it is achieved. For these conversations to be successful, evidence is required; and if the evidence is to go beyond the anecdotal, then good data are essential. Above all, Sharratt and Fullan demonstrate the vital two-way street between assessment and instructional improvement.

Of course, any data in any field have their limitations and learning from the data requires insight, analysis, and imagination. Data alone rarely make clear what needs to be done. They provide the context for decisions. As Dave Brailsford, former legendary head of UK Cycling, put it, "The data inform, they don't decide." For teachers, good data put the "informed" in informed professional judgment; they make possible the kind of aspirational informed professionalism that insists that however good a school or system was yesterday, it can and should always strive to be better tomorrow.

What makes the argument in this book so powerful is the continuing emphasis of the authors on putting FACES on the data, repeatedly reminding us that the numbers represent real children and young people striving to make the most of themselves as they prepare for an uncertain future. This perspective applies not only at the level of the classroom and the school, but also at the level of the district and the state or province as well.

In my own experience of bringing the data to bear on domestic policy priorities at No. 10 Downing Street or with the governments I've worked with around the world, I tried always to remember that, however aggregated the data, they represent real lives. For example, back then every 1 percent increase in the reliability of trains represented a million extra journeys that started and finished on time; every 1 percent increase in children reaching the standard in English or Mathematics at age 11 represented 7,000 more children ready to succeed in secondary education; reductions in drug abuse represented so many family tragedies avoided; and so on.

Sharratt and Fullan bring this perspective to bear excellently not least because, in addition to writing with great insight about education, both have direct experience in education reform as system, government, and university advisors in a number of countries. They have participated in reforms that are exemplary and incorporate a powerful focus on building principals' and teachers' capacity—they know that data without capacity-building cannot make the required difference and also that the combination can be transformative. As this revised edition of *FACES* shows so clearly, using the data at every

level in combination with capacity-building is a critical ingredient of successful whole-system reform.

I wholeheartedly recommend this book for every educator, wherever they are in the world, who wants to master using data to drive up performance, who understands that every child, every FACE, needs to count and be counted and, above all, believes in the power of education to create a sustainable future for humanity.

—Sir Michael Barber
Former Head of the Delivery Unit in No. 10 Downing Street and
Author, *Accomplishment: How to Achieve Ambitious and Challenging Things* (Penguin 2021)

ACKNOWLEDGMENTS

We know that it takes many people to produce a book that will be a meaningful contribution to the educational research literature. All the folks involved in the production of this book are too numerous to mention; however, there are some who deserve special mention for their yeoman-like efforts.

One such person is **Jim Coutts**, an educator himself and a successful businessman, who not only edited the manuscript but also contributed to the content and the data analyses in a big way! Thank you, Jim, for your positive ways of supporting the writing, for being there through the good and bad times of writing a book, and especially for helping make it happen!

We want to thank **Claudia Cuttress**, a very creative designer who always willingly added a personal and professional touch to the manuscript and helped record our research data, as well.

Thank you to **Michelle Sharratt**, Co-Ordinator, Curriculum and Instructional Services, York Region District School Board (formerly Pre-Service Co-Ordinator, University of Toronto, Canada), who shared her outstanding teaching expertise and helped add the current realities in teaching and learning to our work, making it even more precise and meaningful.

Thank you **Jill Maar**, former principal of Armadale Public School, a vibrant, thoughtful instructional leader and good friend, who is always focused on all students' achievement.

And thank you to **James Bond**, former principal of a Manor Park Middle School, who went out of his way to share with us his intentional leadership to ensure that *all* students in his school are achieving.

We thank **Denyse Gregory**, independent researcher, who diligently put unwieldy raw data into a categorized format we could then think and write about cogently.

Christine Ward, former instructional consultant from Scotland, thank you for your invaluable help not only in asking our research questions during your cooperative learning and leadership sessions, but also in highlighting the great practitioner stories from teachers across Scotland to add to our database.

Thank you, **Peter Hill**, former CEO of ACARA, for his wisdom and patient determination that we should understand how NAPLAN in Australia works and who is continuously improving data delivery in a timely, meaningful way.

Thank you to the **507 educators** who filled out our research placemat for this extensive data collection. We appreciate that you came from all over the world to lend your voices to this manuscript. We asked you to participate from across the United States, Scotland, Canada, and Australia. Your practitioner voices made a huge difference to our work—thank you, sincerely, on behalf of *all* children.

And, finally, thank you to the **authors of the case studies and narratives**, whose eagerness and commitment to tell their improvement stories illuminated the concepts that we were trying to convey in the manuscript. On many occasions, these authors highlighted for us, through example, the importance of being specific where students' achievement is concerned. Nothing was too challenging for these authors in writing about their important and creative work.

Finally, it is crucial to have a great publisher. Our sincere thanks to Tanya Ghans, senior acquisitions editor at Corwin; Desirée A. Bartlett, content development manager; Nyle De Leon, editorial assistant; Amy Schroller, project editor; Deanna Noga, copy editor and the rest of the crew at Corwin, who were always gracious, constructive, creative, and caring about our book that we affectionately and proudly call *FACES*.

ABOUT THE AUTHORS

Lyn Sharratt is a practitioner and researcher working in remote and urban settings worldwide. Lyn is an Adjunct Professor at the Ontario Institute for Studies in Education, University of Toronto, Canada; an Honorary Fellow at University of Melbourne, Australia; an author consultant for Corwin Press; an advisor for International School Leadership with the Ontario Principals' Council; and consults internationally, working with system, school, and teacher leaders at *all* levels in Australia, Canada, Chile, New Zealand, the Netherlands, Norway, the United Kingdom, and the United States. Lyn focuses her time and effort on increasing each student's growth and achievement by working alongside leaders and teachers to put FACES on their data, taking intentional action to make equity and excellence a reality for ALL students.

Visit www.lynsharratt.com for articles, video clips, and podcasts; on Twitter: @LynSharratt; on Instagram: lyn_sharratt; and on LinkedIn where Lyn owns the "Educational Leadership" LinkedIn group made up of 100,000+ members.

Lyn's authorship includes *Realization: The Change Imperative for Deepening District-Wide Reform* (with Michael Fullan); *Putting FACES on the Data: What Great Leaders Do!* (with Michael Fullan); *Good to Great to Innovate: Recalculating the Route, K–12+* (with Gale Harild); *Leading Collaborative Learning: Excellence* (with Beate Planche);

CLARITY: What Matters MOST in Learning, Teaching and Leading (International Best-Selling Education Book in 2020); and *Putting FACES on the Data: the 10th Anniversary Edition* (with Michael Fullan).

Lyn is proud of the recent co-development of the CLARITY Learning Suite (CLS)—a web-based collaborative Professional Learning opportunity that mirrors the text, *CLARITY*. Lyn and her team believe that *everyone's a leader*, thus CLS provides guidance to Learning Leaders on how to do this work of system and school improvement—together—to make a difference for all students. Visit www.claritylearningsuite.com.

 **Michael Fullan**, OC, is the former Dean of the Ontario Institute for Studies in Education and Professor Emeritus of the University of Toronto. He is co-leader of the New Pedagogies for Deep Learning global initiative (www.npdl.global). Recognized as a worldwide authority on educational reform, he advises policy makers, local leaders, and school communities in helping to achieve the moral purpose of all children's learning. He served as Premier Dalton McGuinty's Special Policy Adviser in Ontario from 2003–2013. Fullan received the Order of Canada (OC) in December 2012. He holds five honorary doctorates from universities around the world.

Fullan's latest books are *Coherence: Putting the Right Drivers in Action* (with Quinn); *Deep Learning: Engage the World Change the World* (with Quinn, McEachen); *Dive Into Deep Learning: Tools for Engagement* (Quinn, McEachen, Fullan, Gardner, & Drummy); *Surreal Change* (autobiography); *Core Governance* (with Davis Campbell); *Nuance: Why Some Leaders Succeed and Others Fail*; *The Devil is in the Details: System Solutions for Equity, Excellence, and Well-Being*

(with Gallagher); and *Spirit Work and the Science of Collaboration* (with Mark Edwards).

Fullan and his team currently work on *system transformation* in education in several countries globally. For more information on books, articles, videos, and podcasts please go to www.michaefullan.ca.

CHAPTER 1

From Information Glut to Well-Known FACES

Introduction

Two decades ago we concluded that what mattered most in accomplishing school success on a large scale was *focus*. That holds today, and we add to focus the importance of alignment and coherence across schools in a system, state, or nation.

Too many competing priorities came and went; systems became both fragmented and constantly overloaded. So we did begin to focus—on literacy and numeracy, for example, first in the York Region District School Board, then in Ontario as a whole system, and indeed in our work around the world. It paid off in results, as we shall see, but we discovered something even more important in the course of this work. To focus best, leaders and teachers need to combine their *technical expertise* with strong *emotional connections* to what they are looking at. The key is how to make important things personally important to individuals on both cognitive and affective grounds. FACES is about personalizing the individuals we FACE daily: students, teachers, leaders, parents and community members; being transparent, inclusive, and collaborative with each one. FACES is about doing something to ensure the sustainability of focused System and School Improvement practices that are evidence-proven. FACES is about the right factors for improvement, at the right time with the right resources in place. FACES is our "forever work" (G. Mowbray, Director of Schools, Diocese of Maitland – Newcastle).

It is not just the sheer volume of information that is daunting. It is the unfocused form in which the data arrive—can you imagine a devoted teacher becoming excited (or not) about the latest electronic report that serves up scores of seemingly irrelevant disaggregated statistics? Our colleagues Hargreaves and Shirley (2006) say that teachers are "data-driven to distraction." They have data all right, but it comes in waves of indigestible, dehumanized information. We say, as do Hargreaves and Shirley, that teachers' actions need to be "evidence informed," but more than that, they must be moved and inspired by the data and helped to pinpoint the action that will be effective. Teachers and school leaders need, in short, to be able to put FACES on the data and to know what to do to help individual children unobscured by their statistical masks.

What matters to most teachers is their children, their humanity— what we have called their FACES. We asked over 500 teachers and administrators, "Why should we put FACES on data?" One teacher said playfully, "Because they are so damned cute." True enough for Kindergarten, but overall our answer is "Because it is so damned important." We need to care for students' well-being, but we also need to help them get better at the one thing that can serve them for life: their day-to-day learning.

As well as the need to connect to students emotionally, teachers need the technical skills to be able to diagnose and act on their students' learning needs. In other words, teachers need to be knowledgeable experts about each student. Altogether, this is a tall and demanding order because effective teachers need to combine emotion and cognition in equal measure. Weaken either one of these links, and the learning possibilities collapse.

In New Pedagogies for Deep Learning' (NPDL) (Quinn et al., 2020) FACES become more complex because we are addressing both cognitive and noncognitive qualities in the form of the 6Cs (character, citizenship, collaboration, communication, creativity, and critical thinking). In the NPDL scenario, we are assessing the 6Cs as outcomes; we give some examples of how this works with the 14 Parameters in Chapter 6.

Toward Well-Known FACES

In this 10th Anniversary Edition, we distill what we have learned about getting to the human side of learning, while focusing on the knowledge base and expertise required to achieve deep and widespread positive learning outcomes. It is essential not just to discover a passionate teacher here and there but rather how to generate emotional commitment and effective assessment practices that inform instruction on very large scale—for whole systems. To do so we do need data, but we need to generate and use it in ways that make individual students come alive in the minds and actions of teachers and leaders. In the past 10 years, we and our colleagues have learned even more about how to do this.

We know that lessons may be learned from leaders who have created and sustained district-wide improvement, lessons about the importance of uncommon persistence in the face of competing priorities, unfailing attention to the details of implementation, hard-nosed decision making regarding where best to allocate scarce resources, encouraging ego-free leadership, and focusing ongoing attention on evidence about what is working and what needs to be modified. Leading educational reform in your state, district, school, or division is not for the faint-of-heart, the impatient, or those who are easily distracted. This book offers critical and detailed lessons for those aiming to help schools do a better job on behalf of their students, lessons learned from those who, through sustained focus, are achieving state, district, school, and student success across the globe.

Within the structure of each chapter, readers will find "Deliberate Pauses" that offer opportunities to reflect on questions the chapter may raise. In addition, we include in each chapter at least one "Narrative From the Field," stories that outstanding teachers and leaders have shared with us about emotional connections or cognitive insights they have gained into a student's or a teacher's FACE. Finally, throughout the book we integrate current case studies of real schools, districts, whole states, and nations that have achieved success and where we have more stories to tell or examples to provide, we use QR codes to take you to these other resources.

Deliberate Pause

- How useful have your data been?

- Of all the data available, which are most critical to enabling emotional connections to or cognitive insights about each FACE?

- Which data are missing?

- Instead of using data, do leaders at every level "hope for" exceptional instructional practice within the confines of the mysterious black box known as the classroom? **(Hope is not a strategy when considering the growth and achievement of each learner.)**

- Give examples from your data that demonstrate you know that every student is learning to their maximum potential.

A growing body of work has pointed to the use of data to inform decisions concerning the level of students' growth and achievement made by states, school districts, school administrators, teachers, and the broader community. However, one could say that a "faceless glut" of data is both a political and a systemic pathological problem facing educators almost everywhere.

With so much information available, can politicians and education leaders, who want to raise achievement standards and have the will to do so, determine the *right* mix of simple-to-read yet deeply informative data to overcome the inertia of the achievement status quo in their jurisdictions?

At the state or regional level can education system leaders find a proven, *how to* solution to drive observable growth and achievement? If they find a solution, how can they ensure that every student learns, that every teacher teaches like a Master Teacher such that all schools within their systems become high performers and therefore are responsible and accountable for the funding dollars they receive as well as achieving their social-moral imperative? Can they sustain the focus on the solutions that work and not be distracted by the next new thing? Let's see what's out there that might answer these questions.

We have worked in many different states, regions, and districts across the globe on full implementation or what we are calling "collective capacity-building to increase all students' growth and achievement." We examine here what it means to "put the FACES on the data"—the powerful notion of how to go deeper within focused assessment, by harnessing the value of only relevant data sources that tell teachers what to teach next for each student (the very next minute), and doing so in a way that connects the emotions and the intellect of teachers and students.

An example of getting the right data and using it to direct student achievement is that of Luis, a boy in 11th grade—out of the classroom more often than in, due to highly disruptive behavior. Every week, often on a daily basis, he was suspended for rude, uncontrollable, aggressive behavior. He had been forced to change districts and schools many times. Not knowing what to do next, the vice principal at his latest school, in search of a deeper cause, recommended that Luis's literacy skills be assessed. The results presented at an in-school case management meeting (see Chapter 4) showed that Luis was reading at a second-grade level. His teachers and his parents were shocked and disbelieving. His father said, "It's not true. Luis reads his texts every day in the car on the way to school." (Luis had been banned from riding the school bus.) Luis had been covering up and faking it for several years, acting out or withdrawing because he was being asked to read texts way beyond his level of competence.

After several case management meetings, it was decided that Luis would meet Miss Andrews, the high school's literacy coach, every day after school for a focused *word study* (see Glossary) and reading comprehension strategies lesson. Miss Andrews gradually built rapport and trust with Luis and at the same time determined that Luis was attempting texts and recreational reading (such as *Harry Potter*) that were well beyond his skill level and that he couldn't do his in-class work or homework. Being frustrated, Luis acted out belligerently, to the puzzlement of his teachers, who later began to avoid interacting with him.

Over the next few months, after school, demonstrating patient work with Luis, Miss Andrews brought Luis to reading and writing, gradually increasing his competence and confidence. When Miss Andrews "chunked" high-interest, low-vocabulary texts with Luis, the words became sentences and the sentences in paragraphs had meaning for Luis. And in class? Luis's teachers learned to modify

his written assessments, using simpler words that Luis could understand, and his scores rose gradually to grade level. Luis, and everyone around him, experienced much less frustration as a result. Now
Luis reaches for a newspaper each morning, and not only does he
look for the hockey scores, but he also reads the front page because
he likes to learn about what's going on in the world. This is the story
of a tragic situation in which a simple data-driven analysis, ongoing,
supportive Case Management Meetings, and intervention resulted
in a positive ending.

How many Luises and Vickys (see Narrative From the Field below)
fall through the cracks? It is not good enough to catch the odd Luis
and Vicky here and there. We must catch each and every student,
each and every teacher. *FACES is about humanizing the teaching of
each student optimally and having the expertise and tools in place sys-
temically to make that possible for ALL students.*

Narrative From the Field

This teacher didn't think her sixth-grade student, Vicky, could learn.
After several weeks of working in cooperative learning groups and
rotating roles within groups, Vicky, who has communication challenges
and specific learning needs, was given the role of reporting to the class
what her group had done. The teacher was quite anxious about Vicky's
ability and how she would manage, so the teacher gave the groups the
opportunity to pass the reporting to another child in their group if the
child selected didn't want to do it. When it came to her group's turn,
the group endorsed Vicky. She stood up and then clearly and confidently
told the class what her group had done. After this, Vicky regularly shared
her learning and ideas with her groups and her class. The story of Vicky
challenged the teacher never to doubt a student's ability but to support
each, to recognize each student's work and worth, and to become even
better informed by "listening" to the data presented in the actions of
other students in supporting each other.

—Linda Forsyth, Deputy Head Teacher,
Perth and Kinross Council, Scotland

We begin by discussing the *14 Parameters* (see Glossary), a system
and school improvement strategy that identifies the drivers and
keys to implementation that has now been replicated in many

jurisdictions worldwide. With the inclusion of a strong literacy-numeracy and critical thinking strategy, schools and districts that have deployed this approach have reached and sustained success. We integrate the NPDL focus into this plan, including the question of how to teach and assess the noncognitive qualities (character, citizenship, and the like). We also speak about how the use of student achievement data is a powerful tool for improvement at every level—especially if improvement is noted and monitored on the basis of drilling down into that data to individual student names and FACES in individual classrooms.

Deliberate Pause

- How many students (in your state, network, school, and classroom) can read with fluency and *comprehension* (see Glossary) by the end of Grade 1? How do you know?

- How many of your Grade 7 to Grade 10 students cannot read the texts used at their grade level or write to the expected level of the curriculum standards?

- How many students are bored or otherwise disengaged?

- How does the support of students in a group enable the learning of others in the group?

How the 14 Parameters Came to Be

In the book *Realization,* we discussed the 14 Parameters, the key drivers that we have found to be important for schools, districts, states, and nations to become places where high student growth and achievement are expected and delivered year after year by energized staff teams of true professional educators. To summarize, when Bill Hogarth, director of education for the York Region District School Board, in Ontario, stated that all children will read by the end of Grade 1, a literacy initiative was launched within the district's seventeen lowest performing schools, as determined by results of the Education Quality and Accountability Office (EQAO—see Glossary) standards-based assessment for Grades 3, 6, 9, 10.

We draw frequently in this book on EQAO data. It should be noted that the level 3 and 4 threshold represents a very high standard which includes higher-order thinking skills and requires a student to achieve a score of at least 70 percent to meet the standard.

Of 150 schools in York Region at that time, seventeen found a small staffing allocation within their overall staffing allotment, sufficient to have half-time literacy coaches in each school. There were two caveats concerning the role and the Professional Learning (PL) provided by the district: (1) The literacy coach had to be a respected, valued teacher selected from the school staff; and (2) the principal and the literacy coach had to attend monthly district PL sessions together.

The initiative became known as the Literacy Collaborative. It was driven by the Literacy Steering Committee, which comprised the superintendent of curriculum (Sharratt), curriculum coordinators, an appointed system literacy principal, and selected principals from the field, to get feedback from the field about the implementation progress of each school. The Literacy Advisory Committee—composed of the elected chair of the board, Bill Crothers; director of education, Hogarth; two field superintendents; Sharratt; an elementary and secondary principal representative; and the literacy principal—strategically guided the initiative.

After one year, district scores began to improve with literacy (broadly defined to include Critical Thinking in every subject area) as the priority; the scores from the initial seventeen Literacy Collaborative schools outperformed both state and other district schools (see Figures 1.1 and 1.2). In year 2, the seventeen schools again outperformed the others. When we examined the seventeen schools more closely, we found that nine of the seventeen were able to align and sustain their work on improvement. We called these "high-focus schools." The figures show that in years 3, 4, and 5, the nine "high-focus" schools advanced their level of achievement. Scores for the eight "low-focus" schools were inconsistent because they could not maintain their focus on the specific practices to increase all students' achievement. What factors differed between the high- and low-focus schools to affect scores as they did?

To determine why nine schools improved so dramatically while the other eight started well but failed to sustain their performance, we analyzed the annual reports from the seventeen schools and interviewed leaders and teachers involved in the Literacy Collaborative to learn which schools had incorporated the literacy coach and

PL monthly sessions more fully and how they had done it. The nine high-focus schools (see Figures 1.1 and 1.2) that did especially well were initially among the lowest performing schools in the district, yet they moved beyond the state and district averages in a relatively short time and sustained their achievement levels. The explanation for better performance in our view lies in more carefully focused attention to the details in each of 14 improvement areas, or what we call the 14 Parameters (Sharratt & Fullan, 2009). It turned out, as we have since found time and again, that it is not mere acceptance or endorsement of an idea or practice that counts but rather *engaging consistently and relentlessly in the actions that cause implementation.*

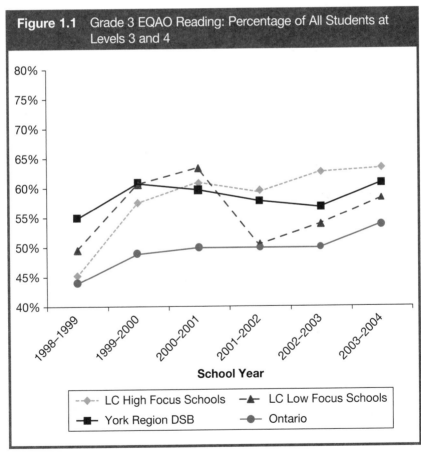

Figure 1.1 Grade 3 EQAO Reading: Percentage of All Students at Levels 3 and 4

Note: A Level 3 score means the student has met the minimum standard of 70 percent, and a Level 4 score means the student has exceeded the minimum standard.

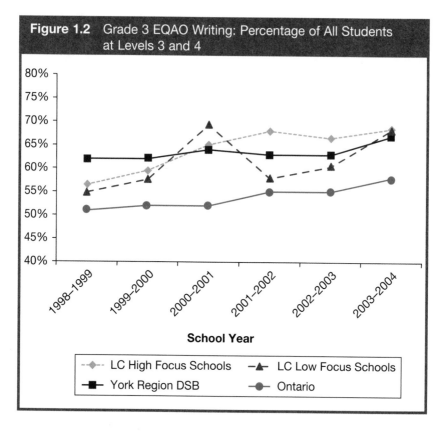

Figure 1.2 Grade 3 EQAO Writing: Percentage of All Students at Levels 3 and 4

Understanding the reasons for the gains, the district launched the 14-Parameter-based program broadly, K–12, by incrementally expanding the Literacy Collaborative. The low-focus schools refocused on increasing *all* students' achievement through intentional assessment and instructional practices. Over time, the remaining elementary and secondary schools in the district followed and began to impressively raise their students' achievement results.

The factors we studied, *the 14 Parameters, are in effect the nitty-gritty of deep and sustainable collective capacity-building of teachers and leaders to teach all students.* Think of the 14 Parameters as the specific reform strategies that—in combination (and over time, as the organization progresses to greater implementation of the 14 Parameters)— "cause" classroom, school, district, state, and nation improvement. The 14 Parameters are listed in Figure 1.3. A self-assessment tool that can be used to track progressive implementation of the 14 Parameters is provided in Appendix A.

We now know a great deal more about the 14 Parameters—the fourteen drivers of reform and practice in successful school districts—and are even more convinced of their validity and efficacy. First, we learned and understood that effective change reform to increase student achievement involves precise planning and detailed work. We know that to improve student achievement individual school leaders must actively (by being present in the learning) and diligently work to raise their school's assessment in each of the 14 Parameters.

Second, from our initial results and further use of the 14 Parameters in other jurisdictions across the globe, we developed a detailed self-assessment implementation tool (Appendix A). Schools, districts, and states have used this tool on a regular basis to determine how well they "stack up" against the 14 Parameters of successful systems, schools, and districts. Often the results of a system or school staff's self-assessment has become the outline of their purpose-built school improvement plan—specific to each school's needs and against which progress can be measured by the school (see "Collaborative Inquiry," in Chapter 4).

Third, when we get some schools in a district to move ahead using the 14 Parameters, we know we have a critical mass of instructional leaders who will lead to an almost inevitable tipping point toward system and school improvement for every school and for every student in the jurisdiction We also know that reaching this point will cause some people in leadership positions to deviate from the plan—"too much work," "not my interest," "not my school," "we've done it"—being excuses and complaints they will use to distract motivation and remove resources from achieving the system's planned reform. So, currently, many systems have developed a "No Excuses" mantra. With ongoing monitoring of all assessments used purposefully to inform instruction and to select resources needed, leaders must ask key questions (see previous sample questions in Deliberate Pause) and confront factors that stand in the way of deep implementation and of ongoing sustainability.

Fourth, the work can be and has been replicated successfully across contexts, as we illustrate throughout this book using new case studies from several jurisdictions in which we are currently working (Authors' Note: The original case studies are found in QR Codes in each chapter). We know that learning how to succeed in implementing every Parameter, with fidelity, is the ongoing, relentless and collaborative work of education leaders and teachers. It is not surface beliefs that matter; it is focused commitment, making tough resource allocation decisions, drilling down to put FACES on the relevant data, and staying the course that matter, no matter what pressures or new concepts the unfocused distracters might launch.

Finally, we learned that new approaches are needed to increase the specificity of teaching and the opportunity to learn. Although it is ideal to use student assessment data to tailor individual student learning, school performance data must also be used to define the precise and intensive support for instructional improvement that is needed in each school. In other words, not only must teachers differentiate student instruction by using various forms of student achievement data to inform the instruction, but system and school leaders must also use student achievement data to differentiate support to teachers and middle leaders whose tracked student achievement scores represent the need for targeted PL sessions.

Only a laser-like focus on daily student progress will enable leaders and teachers to put the FACES on the data so that they can improve instruction for all students—**our ultimate vision**—our moral imperative. Not coincidentally, such an approach can improve teachers' and leaders' professional lives. As well, it should be noted that system leaders put the FACES on their data, too.

Figure 1.3 The 14 Parameters of System and School Improvement

1. Shared beliefs and understandings
    a. All students can achieve high standards given the right time and the right support.
    b. All teachers can teach to high standards given time and the right assistance.
    c. High expectations and early and ongoing intervention are essential.
    d. All leaders, teachers, and students can articulate what they do and why they lead, teach, and learn the way they do. (Adapted from Hill & Crévola, 1999)

2. Embedded Knowledgeable Others

3. Quality assessment informs instruction

4. Principal as lead learner

5. Early and ongoing intervention

6. Case management approach

7. Focused Professional Learning at staff meetings
8. In-school meetings—collaborative assessment of student work
9. Book rooms of with "just-right" books and multi-modal resources
10. Allocation of system and school budgets for learning
11. Collaborative Inquiry—a whole-system approach
12. Parental and community involvement
13. Cross-curricular literacy connections
14. Shared responsibility and accountability
    a. We all own all the FACES!

Source: Sharratt (2019, p. 11); Sharratt and Fullan (2005, 2006, 2009, 2012).

Integrating New Pedagogies for Deep Learning (NPDL)

FACES ultimately discusses, teaches, and endorses the technical expertise underlying assessment and instruction. Initially, we began the school improvement work during which we developed the 14 Parameters by focusing on what would improve literacy and numeracy practices. We have moved past that to the 14 Parameter Framework that supports all subjects and all curricula with leadership at the core of each Parameter. In this edition of *FACES*, we are not able to systematically introduce NPDL. The best way to think about it is to say that if the focus was on Deep-Learning outcomes, the 14 Parameters would serve to strengthen the NPDL goals: implementation of the 6Cs and corresponding pedagogy (Fullan et al., 2018; Quinn et al., 2020). **The 14 Parameters and NPDL are symbiotic, they indeed work well together (see Chapter 6, The Integration of Our Work).**

Self-Assessing Against the 14 Parameters

A crucial issue with any new implementation is to have all staff buy-in to the vision, the intended learning and the ultimate goals. One school did just that by assessing their practice against the 14 Parameters as found in Figure 1.4. It demonstrates the actions staff members took to make changes in practice. Importantly, by doing

(Text coninued on page 28)

Figure 1.4 St Bridget's Primary School Audit Against the 14 Parameters

Parameter	Audit of Things We Are Already doing
1 **Shared Beliefs and Understandings** 1. All students can achieve high standards given the right time and the right support. 2. All teachers can teach to high standards given time and the right assistance. 3. High expectations and early and ongoing intervention are essential. 4. All leaders, teachers, and students can articulate what they do and why they lead, teach, and learn the way they do.	✓ Having high expectations of students ✓ Making adjustments for students with additional needs ✓ Providing ongoing intervention ✓ Developing Personalized Learning Plans (PLPs) for students who require additional support and/or receive funding as part of the Nationally Consistent Collection of Data (NCCD) ✓ Parent Support Group Meeting (PSGs) for those students where a PLP has been prepared ✓ Creating a whole-school approach (e.g., Spelling, Writing, Inquiry, Religious Education)

Parameter	Audit of Things We Are Already doing
	<ul><li>Designing a Mentorship Program for all graduate (new and early career) teachers</li><li>Supporting teachers with Professional Learning Goals</li><li>Assisting with students' assessments</li><li>Acknowledging and utilizing each other's strengths and expertise</li></ul>

2 Embedded Knowledgeable Others

These **Knowledgeable Others** are instructional coaches who have time purposefully scheduled during the school day to work alongside classroom teachers, supporting focused work on assessment that informs instruction.

Knowledgeable Others must have strong interpersonal skills to build relational trust while co-laboring with teachers.

Parameter	Audit of Things We Are Already doing

Audit of Things We Are Already doing

☑ Assessing using pre- and post-assessment in Spelling, Numeracy, Comprehension

☑ Giving one-on-one feedback and instruction based on incorrect response(s) to assessment questions

☑ Giving and Getting Descriptive Feedback from the student

☑ Setting individual goals with students against the Success Criteria

3 Quality Assessment Informs Instruction

- Evidence-proven, high-impact practices, like using ongoing assessment data that differentiate instruction, are embedded in the planning for daily, specific subject classes where every lesson features a literacy skill and teachers embed **assessment for and as learning** practices to inform their next steps for instruction.

- **Gradual Release and Acceptance of Responsibility** (GRR) model to ensure precision in practice.

Parameter	Audit of Things We Are Already doing

Audit of Things We Are Already doing

- ✓ Co-constructing a Data Wall
- ✓ Conducting Learning Walks and Talks
- ✓ Crafting specific Professional Learning for all staff as identified through their Annual Review Meetings (ARMs) and/or informal feedback
- ✓ Studying; Masters of Educational or Instructional Leadership
- ✓ Being part of The Learning Collaborative (TLC) in Melbourne Archdiocese Catholic Schools (MACS) – Eastern Region

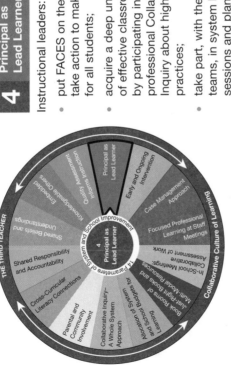

4 Principal as Lead Learner

Instructional leaders:

- put FACES on the data and take action to make a difference for all students;

- acquire a deep understanding of effective classroom practices by participating in ongoing professional Collaborative Inquiry about high-impact practices;

- take part, with their leadership teams, in system learning sessions and plan how they will replicate the learning back in their schools,

- conduct Learning Walks and Talks daily in classrooms.

Parameter	Audit of Things We Are Already doing

Audit of Things We Are Already doing

✓ Communicating between Learning Support Officer (LSO) and Classroom Teacher

✓ Implementing a strategic reading intervention program via the Early Reading Intervention Knowledge (ERIK) program

✓ Learning About Letters and Sounds Program

✓ Working in partnership with external providers (e.g., Occupational Therapist, Psychologist, Speech Therapist)

✓ Timetabling for an LSO to provide additional support via one-on-one and small-group sessions

5 **Early and Ongoing Interventions**

- Individual student need is determined by the ongoing scrutiny of a variety of assessment data.

- A structured, collaboratively planned approach by all teachers (e.g., classroom, special education, Reading Recovery, English language learner, and support teachers) is necessary to design and deliver units and lessons with an integrated co-teaching approach to supporting all students.

Parameter	Audit of Things We Are Already doing
### 6 Case Management Approach Putting FACES on the data using the case management approach is a two-pronged process: 1. **prevention:** the co-construction of Data Walls allows staff members to stand back and discuss student's areas of need, to set targets, and to decide what is possible for each FACE, and 2. **intervention:** case management meetings (CMMs) in which a teacher presents one student at a time, through a work sample, to a problem-solving forum focused on supporting the classroom teacher with a recommended instructional strategy to try. 	✓ Co-constructing a Data Wall ✓ Conducting regular Case Management Meetings ✓ Conducting PSGs for those students where a PLP has been prepared ✓ Meeting regularly for Teacher Moderation of student work ✓ Monitoring student progress and constant follow up with the Classroom Teacher

Parameter	Audit of Things We Are Already doing

Audit of Things We Are Already doing

- ✓ Holding specific and focused staff meetings on learning goals we as a school want to achieve
- ✓ Using staff as learning resources for each other
- ✓ Developing a common language of precise classroom practice
- ✓ Understanding that data comes from many sources
- ✓ Assessing a strong culture of learning

7 Focused Professional Learning at Staff Meetings

Using meeting times for Professional Learning builds teacher and leader **collective capacity** and develops a common language across all learning areas.

Starting with data, teachers who are Knowledgeable Others and leaders together provide the Professional Learning needed at staff meetings, at division meetings, and during Professional Learning Community (PLC) time (see Chapter 3), modeling a culture of learning—the Third Teacher— that reflects clear expectations about precision in practice.

Parameter	Audit of Things We Are Already doing

Audit of Things We Are Already doing

✓ Developing differentiated learning strategies and tacks

✓ Making time for PL conversations about students who may be underachieving

✓ Scheduling writing moderation within and across year levels to ensure moderation is consistent and provides Descriptive Feedback

✓ Grouping students is fluid and based on ongoing formative assessment

✓ Spelling across the school where students are assessed and complete tasks at their ability level

8 In-School Meetings— Collaborative Assessment of Work

It is often noted that the greatest variation in teaching in a system is not between schools; it is between classrooms in the same school. To reduce that variation, evidence of learning through student work samples is used in regular, ongoing co-teaching conversations in which teachers collaboratively determine:

- how to sharpen their use of assessment data, every minute, to drive precise instruction; broaden their individual and collective instructional repertoire;
- challenge assumptions in a respectful way;
- improve immediate Descriptive Feedback strategies;
- move students from one level of work to the next and beyond expectations.

Parameter	Audit of Things We Are Already doing

Audit of Things We Are Already doing

✓ Using Leveled Readers and Guided Reading texts (built a Reading Room)

✓ Ensuring technology is integrated into the school day using Chromebooks 1:1 so each student across the school has access to a Chromebook from Prep to Year 6

✓ Providing access to Interactive TVs and iPads to engage students and support their learning

9 **Book Rooms of "Just-Right" Books and Multi-Modal Resources**

Resources that support differentiated instruction are compiled and organized in a multimedia room or resource center for teachers' access to just-right, just-in-time resources.

These high-quality, multi-modal resources reflect the diversity of the community, meet a range of abilities and needs, and address a range of student interests.

Parameter	Audit of Things We Are Already doing
10 **Allocation of System and School Budgets for Learning** Principals and leadership teams intentionally allocate budget items for resources that address instructional needs revealed by school and classroom assessment data. Leaders can articulate why they are doing what they are choosing to do. Equity of outcomes for all learners is assured through budget resourcing (human and material) to support learning and learners. 	⟩ Distributing staffing allocation based on student need ⟩ Ensuring that needed support of student learning is timetabled ⟩ Funding the purchase of online whole school literacy and numeracy resources to engage and support student learning such as Reading Eggs, Literacy Planet, and Matific

Parameter	Audit of Things We Are Already doing

Audit of Things We Are Already doing

> Developing whole school approaches (e.g., Mappen which is evidence-based resources linked to the curriculum and used for Inquiry and the curriculum)

> Capabilities (e.g., Sound Waves which is an Australian spelling program; Seven Steps to Writing Text; creating a planning template for Religious Education for all teachers to utilize and populate, which is common to all staff)

> Conducting Annual Review Meetings for all staff for goal setting and evaluation of practice and performance

> Setting individual learning goals with students based on data and Success Criteria

11 Collaborative Inquiry —A Whole System Approach

Every system or school meeting begins with a review of data, searching for the impact of actions taken on previously identified issues. Questions about the data are the basis of SMART goals. Collaborative Inquiry (CI) questions follow and are developed by system leaders, principals, and groups of teachers to test pedagogical approaches they feel will enable instruction to elevate student achievement to meet their collective SMART goals. Development of CI questions is deliberate using a structured, collaboratively planned approach; it is not left to system teams or schools to independently create their own processes because "being systematic" counts.

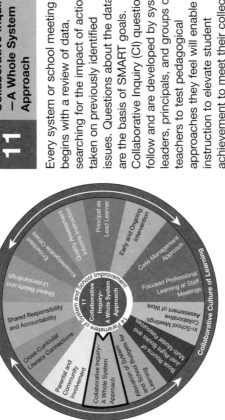

Parameter	Audit of Things We Are Already doing

12 Parental and Community Involvement

Research indicates that parent and community involvement increase all students' achievement. Schools build strong relationships with parents by keeping them informed about their children's progress and by involving them in the why and how the school is teaching literacy skills, for example, in every subject area. Parents, caregivers, and the broader community are helped to understand how they can support their children and are continuously invited to provide input into annual system and school plans for improvement.

Audit of Things We Are Already doing

- ✓ Reporting to parents
- ✓ Holding Parent-Teacher interviews
- ✓ Conducting Meet and Greet sessions at the beginning of each year for parents to provide information about their child to the classroom teacher
- ✓ Holding PSGs for students where a PLP has been prepared
- ✓ Preparing PLPs for students who require additional support and/or receive funding as part of the NCCD – keeping in touch with parents through email, text messages, newsletters, website with *upschool* where education and well-being content is provided to support parents with their child's learning
- ✓ Establishing Parent Helpers and Parent Volunteers (e.g., Parishioners and Rotary Members who support our students during the literacy block by listening to them read and asking them comprehension questions)
- ✓ Communicating with parents via platforms such as Skoolbag and Operoo
- ✓ Encouraging Home Reading

Parameter	Audit of Things We Are Already doing
	✓ Integrating Religion into literature used in Reading Groups ✓ Developing Inquiry linked via Mappen (which is evidence-based resources linked to the curriculum and used for Inquiry and the Capabilities as well as other curriculum areas)

13 **Cross Curricular Literacy Connections**

Assessment data determine what literacy skills each student will need to develop in order to access a subject's curriculum content; however, teachers in all content areas can further students' achievement by modeling the skills, sharing in the making of meaning, guiding students toward independence, and monitoring their independent work using the Gradual Release and Acceptance of Responsibility model in all subject areas.

Parameter	Audit of Things We Are Already doing
14 Shared Responsibility and Accountability

Everyone is responsible and accountable for every learner within and across schools in a district and a state. That is, everyone knows and can clearly articulate the system, school, and classroom priority because SMART Goals and CI questions are aligned, clear, precise, intentional, and published.

Everyone sees himself or herself as responsible for achieving the goals and accountable for the learning that results from their implementation.

 | ✓ Co-constructing and using a whole-school Data Wall

✓ Being aware of students in the school with additional needs (e.g., watching out for certain students on the playground)

✓ Holding regular Case Management Meetings across the school year levels

✓ Discussing how to support students with additional needs.

✓ Streaming spelling across the schools. Where students are assessed and complete tasks at their ability level rather than their grade level

✓ Involving whole-school approach to improvement (principal, teachers, Learning Support Officer, volunteers) in our focus on Spelling determined by our school's data |

this gap analysis with staff they got all teachers' buy-in to make deliberate refinements to their practice, *as data drives instruction.*

Based on the Audit of the 14 Parameters, St. Bridget's set their Future Learning Goals, as follows:

We will:

- Use the Data Wall more consistently to identify which students require early and ongoing intervention (Parameters #1 and #5) as well as to inform Case Management Meetings (Parameter #6).

- Continue to increase staff capacity and confidence around deconstructing Learning Intentions (LI) and co-constructing Success Criteria (SC) (Parameters #3 and #13). This will be achieved through allocating time in a staff meeting each week for a teacher to share their LI and SC with the staff for feedback. Also, to help build capacity in co-constructing SC, staff meeting time will be used for staff to practice co-construction of SC together (Parameter #7).

- Timetable Learning Walks and Talks with teachers and leaders walking in classrooms together to look for evidence of students' growth and achievement (Parameters #4 and #14).

- Develop all teachers as "Knowledgeable Others" (Parameter #2). This will be achieved by providing a coach to work closely with teachers to set individual goals, to plan, model and observe strong classroom practice (Parameters #7 and #10). Our focus moving forward is around differentiated instruction in the classroom.

- Review assessment literacy across the school to ensure it is still high quality and is being used to inform instruction and ultimately improve student outcomes (Parameters #3 and #13).

With the template as the guide to action, St. Bridget's was able to focus on corresponding action and in turn assess their progress and impact.

- Students now have a greater understanding about what they are learning, what success looks like for them, and how to articulate this.

- By being part of the Teaching and Learning Collaborative and through the partnership the Melbourne Archdiocese Catholic

Schools has developed with Dr. Lyn Sharratt, we have access to evidence-based, relevant, and effective Professional Learning (PL) and a framework for school improvement.

- As a direct result of the PL provided, we have been able to increase staff capacity across the school. We know this as we hear a common language of improvement developing among teachers and students; the 5 Questions for Students are displayed in every classroom (see page 101); staff meetings begin with data and focus on learning not operational issues; teachers are more open to improving their practice and we have seen genuine changes embedded across the school. It is evident that our teachers believe they can have a positive impact on student outcomes therefore demonstrating high collective teacher efficacy (Robyn Thomson, Principal, St. Bridget's Primary School, Balwyn North, Victoria, Australia, personal communication, January 2022).

Practice Aligns in Systems and Schools

In many ways, the implementation of the 14 Parameters mirrors Sir Michael Barber's (2011) "Deliverology," which we referred to at length in the first edition of FACES. Deliverology is about having a plan and making it happen. For a discussion of Deliverology, click on QR Code 1.1. In the discussion that follows, we speak more to our message of measuring and assessing how individual schools, districts, and states are performing and we speak to how we feel that putting the FACES on the data is a win-win strategy that creates changes in assessment and instruction and in achievement levels. This ultimately results in a culture of success for students and education professionals—a culture in which all stakeholders can be proud to participate and in which stakeholders *want* to perpetuate.

QR Code 1.1: Deliverology Parallels

We learned in our initial study, and subsequent work has reinforced the idea, of the overarching value of quality leadership at every level and, in particular, at the school level. The successful schools in our research were led by principals, vice principals, and part-time literacy coaches who understood and were committed to the specifics. We discovered that "Leadership MATTERS"! For example, in the successful schools we initially studied, and now in new, highly successful schools we continue to find, the following:

1. School leaders clearly understand the model and, most important, live the shared beliefs and understandings (Parameter #1) and shared responsibility and accountability (Parameter #14) in the design.

2. School leaders clearly understand that they need to attend to ALL the components of the 14 Parameters.

3. School teams did constant self-evaluation, striving to align beliefs and understandings among the principal, literacy coach (Parameter #2), teacher-leaders, and special education resource teacher as the leadership team who worked with all staff. This involved *accountable talk* (see Glossary) and corresponding action, with each other and with teachers, in an ongoing way—during the school day.

4. School leaders did not let staff or other program "distracters" divert their energies and focus—they stayed the course toward students' growth and improvement—holding their nerve until improvement results were realized—**no matter what!**

We discuss further, in Chapter 5, the specifics of what it takes to put the FACES on the data as an instructional leader. At this point, let's put more flesh on the concept by considering a system case study.

A System Case Study

A. Context

The Diocese of Wollongong was established in 1952, extending across the four regions of Illawarra, Macarthur, Shoalhaven, and Southern Highlands of New South Wales, Australia. There are twenty-nine primary schools, eight secondary schools, and one K–12 school with an overall enrollment of 19,445 students. Of the student population there are 3.9 percent Aboriginal Torres Strait Islander (ATSI), 34.3 percent Language Background Other than English (LBOTE), 8.1 percent English as an Additional Language/Dialect (EAL/D), and 1.3 percent Students With a Disability (SWD).

The Diocese has experienced huge growth especially in Shellharbour, Dapto, and Macarthur. It is incredibly diverse with urban, regional, and rural schools and a wide range in socioeconomic status (SES), in ethnic diversity and in rapid population growth, which all make planning and resource allocation difficult.

B. Background: Why improvement was needed?

In 2014, senior leaders undertook comparisons with other Dioceses' data identifying that Wollongong had room for improvement. They found schools operated independently and there was little or no collaboration within and between schools. Due to very limited data sources, staff had little access and very few opportunities to own system or school data. There was also a focus on PL being held at a system level that did not always address school, staff, or student needs.

In 2015, the Director of Schools determined that the Service Delivery to schools needed to undertake a structural reshaping with a focus on school improvement, and thus created a model of K–6, 7–12, and Specialist Support K–12 areas with a system leader in each of the three areas.

In 2016, senior leaders from Wollongong approached Sharratt to work alongside them in what ultimately became known as the *Collaborative Leadership Improving Learning* (CLIL) work. CLIL was actively supported with consistent and ongoing commitment from the Director and Senior Leadership Team. These CLIL members attended ALL the initial input sessions with Sharratt, including the initial Sunday meeting in student vacation time, and meetings prior to each of her CLIL sessions. Their commitment to the work with FACES and CLARITY was palpable.

A CLIL Strategic Plan was developed so that the system would have a consistent, strategic approach to the roll out and implementation of this system-wide approach to improvement. The CLIL Strategic Plan set timely and realistic expectations. Principals and school staff undertook PL opportunities that developed their understanding of the 14 Parameters (Sharratt, 2019; Sharratt & Fullan, 2009, 2012). Principals were acknowledged for their initial and ongoing support of CLIL.

Schools readily recognized and acted on the system commitment of budget allocation to this research-proven approach that enabled each school to have:

- ✓ an Instructional Coach (IC);
- ✓ PL opportunities with Sharratt;

(Continued)

(Continued)

- ✓ teacher release time for Collaborative Professionalism; and
- ✓ the development of a system Education Officer role to lead and oversee the CLARITY work.

Teachers with capacity and credibility in schools were able to step into the Instructional Coach role knowing they had the ongoing support of their principal, School Leadership Team, and system personnel.

C. Focus on Improvement

The system embraced Parameter #1: Shared Beliefs and Understandings. It was determined that there would be a whole-system approach to improving student learning outcomes. Their strategic intention was that:

- ✓ System data would show and sustain improvement in student learning outcomes (Parameter #14).
- ✓ There would be a systematic and consistent approach to identifying and addressing student learning needs.
- ✓ The 14 Parameters would become part of the vernacular and ongoing practice across the system, developing a common language of improvement.
- ✓ School Improvement Services would model the implementation of the 14 Parameters at every opportunity.
- ✓ The Learning Progressions in the curriculum expectations would be used for the monitoring and tracking students' growth and achievement (Parameters #3 and #13).
- ✓ Schools would be student-centered, focusing on ALL students' development, growth, and achievement (Parameters #1 and #14).
- ✓ There would be high expectations for every student and whole-system access to school and system data (Parameters #1 and #6).
- ✓ Each school would have an Assessment Schedule and Plan according to Literacy and Numeracy Policy that included system-purchased assessments (Parameters #9 and #10).
- ✓ The system and schools would have Data Walls that would be current and regularly maintained and would conduct regularly scheduled Case Management Meetings (Parameter #6).

✓ CLIL would be a priority in system planning and budgeting (Parameter #10).

✓ The CLIL approach would build staff capacity to teach ALL students (Parameter #6).

✓ Every primary and secondary school would have a part-time IC based on the student population (Parameter #2).

✓ PL in each school would be focused on, and determined by, school/staff needs based on relevant data (Parameters #7 and #8).

✓ The principal would be expected to attend PL and lead the 14 Parameter work with the support of the School Leadership Team that included the IC (Parameters #2 and #4).

D. IMPACT

The impact of CLIL is apparent across the system, within individual schools and classrooms.

1. From a System Perspective

The impact is tangible. Leaders and teachers now have a common language based on the 14 Parameters and schools now have a consistent approach to the improvement of student learning outcomes. This approach to CLARITY is based on

✓ Quality Assessment,

✓ Quality Pedagogy, and

✓ Data Literacy.

Relevant system data sources are monitored on a System Data Wall. There has been a notable improvement in system data since 2017. The delivery of PL is no longer one size fits all; it is directly related to school data and improvement priorities. Relevant documents, such as system policies and procedures, now reflect CLIL and the 14 Parameters. School Improvement K–12, purposely models the 14 Parameters as the whole system moves to improving student learning outcomes collaboratively.

A Project Officer role has been created to support the CLIL Education Officer in building the capacity of School Leadership Teams in the areas of Data Literacy, Strategic Planning, and the ongoing development of Collaborative Professionalism.

(Continued)

(Continued)

Time is a precious commodity. Two full-day Principal and Assistant Principal Meetings are dedicated each year to the School Improvement Agenda. There has been a restructuring of School Improvement Primary Service meetings where all personnel meet twice a term with agendas directly relating to PL and Collaboration time, with only one session for General Business.

Significant system resources have been allocated to schools to support Early Learning and the growing number of students who are identified as EAL/D. Multimedia resources have been developed to support staff with current research and PL around pedagogy and expected practices.

2. From a School's Perspective

Each school's improvement journey continues to be captured in the School Review and Improvement (SRI) Plan that is strategic, data-informed, Principal-led, and leadership-driven.

Schools now have a whole-school approach to improving student learning outcomes using the 14 Parameter Framework where all staff have shared beliefs and understandings (Parameter #1) and are responsible and held accountable for ALL students (Parameter #14). The IC role (Parameter #2) allows for a focused approach to improvement in student learning outcomes, by ICs working alongside leaders and teachers. Their work is aligned with each school's Improvement Plan.

All schools maintain a current, physical Data Wall related to their improvement journey. Student learning is monitored and tracked during regularly held Case Management Meetings (Parameter #6).

School budgets now have a more strategic focus on improving student learning outcomes (Parameter #10). Schools now operate in geographic networks, known as Learning Collaboratives. The Learning Collaboratives are supported by the CLIL Education Officer and ICs. There are five Primary Learning Collaboratives of six schools each of whom are also supported by two School Improvement Primary Education Officers. The eight secondary schools form a single Learning Collaborative and the K–12 school operates across two Service Areas.

The Assessment and Instruction Framework (Assessment Waterfall Chart, Sharratt, 2019, p. 124) is a critical part of our pedagogy across the system and is evident in every classroom (see Chapter 3).

All schools undertake the Collaborative Inquiry processes and share their data results, successes and challenges once each year at a System

Collaborative Inquiry Symposium (The Learning Fair, Sharratt, 2019, pp. 39–41).

Schools now allocate resources to "The Third Teacher": Leaders and teachers constantly evaluate the use of their learning spaces and furniture to maximize the benefits of this change in pedagogy.

3. From a Classroom Perspective

Staff Collaboration is now seen as an important component of this relentless focus on pedagogy; staff utilize the system funding for Collaborative Professionalism. Eight half days were allocated to PL based on staff feedback. As a result, each classroom teacher is allocated these days to meet and collaborate to analyze and interpret student data to refine practice.

The learning space, known as the *Third Teacher*, is where students access support in their learning through clearly displayed Learning Intentions, co-constructed Success Criteria, and "Bump-It-Up Walls" (see Chapter 3). Classroom furnishings support individual student developmental needs and the opportunity to implement the Gradual Release of Responsibility Model.

Learning Walks and Talks (LWTs) have become part of the common practice, allowing teachers to seek and provide feedback. It is noticeable that classrooms now have less *teacher talk* and more student voice, with students being able to answer the 5 Questions of LWTs (Sharratt, 2019, pp. 59–65).

The IC is visible in classrooms as they mentor, work alongside, and upskill classroom teachers.

4. Leadership Lessons Learned

Leaders and teachers have learned significant lessons along the way in implementing the "Putting FACES on the Data" approach:

1. The need for ongoing support and visibility of the Director and System Leadership Team is ensured by having an aligned, clear, and focused direction that is captured in the Strategic Plan and is frequently articulated by leaders.

2. School leadership roles and the capacity of the principal and School Leadership in implementing and sustaining the FACES and CLARITY work is not to be taken lightly. There is a critical

(Continued)

(Continued)

need to provide **time** for ongoing feedback within the school and across the system.

3. Facilitate embedded budget decisions that enable staff to be given **time**, during the school day, to engage in Collaborative Professionalism, such as Case Management Meetings—both regularly scheduled at system and school levels is critical.

4. The need for system staff to have an understanding of the importance of the 14 Parameters and their links to sustained school improvement is like lightning and thunder, you cannot have one without the other.

5. Key is the critical importance of the selection and ongoing development of the IC to enable them to build teacher capacity in all schools. There is a necessity for a clear role description for the IC that is relevant to the school context and data.

6. Sustainability is ensured when the system has a strategic plan to address issues related to staff turnover.

7. Collaboration and feedback opportunities within and between schools must be mirrored within and between system service teams to ensure alignment of the work.

8. Strategic planning around a *small number of priorities* must be highlighted.

9. A system role, with inclusion at decision-making tables, is necessary to lead, oversee, and sustain the CLIL work.

5. Did It Work?

In NAPLAN Assessments (see Glossary), 2021, Years 3 and 5 students in the Diocese are above the State Mean in nine of the ten domains assessed.

Year 3:

Students remain above the State Mean in ALL Domains (Reading, Writing, Spelling, Grammar and Punctuation, and Numeracy).

Year 5:

Students are now above the State Mean in four out of the five domains assessed. Numeracy has increased 3.8 points since 2019, the best

Numeracy result in Year 5 since the beginning of the NAPLAN assessment in 2008 (Noel Henry Head of School Improvement Services—Primary; and Kay Blundell Senior Professional Officer School Improvement Services—Primary Diocese of Wollongong, New South Wales, Australia, personal communication, October 26, 2021).

Success breeds success as illustrated by this impressive case study of system-wide improvement. Being able to share increased student achievement results on school and system assessments was an enormous boost to staff and the broader community in the Diocese—a valuable validation of all staffs' conscientious commitment to "doing something positive" for ALL students. It certainly appears that patience, endurance, compassion, and putting FACES on Data Walls will continue to be needed for Wollongong to stay the course. As we said about Simcoe County and Brechin Public School in the first edition (Sharratt & Fullan, 2009, p. 12; see QR Code 1.2), we can say again about the Diocese of Wollongong, the entire system knew they were on the right track! Hand in hand with success was a very real willingness to take risks to change structure and refine practice always highlighting our notion that "learning is the work."

QR Code 1.2:
Simcoe
Case Study

Deliberate Pause

- What is your plan for improvement—how do all staff commit?

- What resources do you have available to implement this focused work?

- Do you have instructional coaches (Knowledge Others [KOs]) in every school—primary and secondary?

- Are your instructional coaches offering added value to the PL of principals, leadership teams, *and* teachers?

- What lessons learned from the Wollongong Case Study apply to your context?

Narrative From the Field

An audible silence struck the conference room. He had just shown the assembled school district administrators and principals the standard testing data they knew so well, but with a twist that changed their comfort level. He translated the cold district data showing the percentage of students falling into the "below standard" and "meets minimum standard"—data each member of the audience could repeat by rote—into very challenging new school performance data highlighting the precise number of student FACES each year who failed to reach the minimum standard. They could see the number of students who failed in their group of schools, and they could see how many failed in their own schools.

She picked up the pieces. She showed how first one school district, then another, had used the 14 Parameter approach, and how they adopted the concerted, determined but inclusive leadership style that focuses on managing available resources to transform student achievement results. She showed them that this combined process—implementation strategy and leadership style—built "capacity" in the process. This collective capacity-building was successful because it improved student achievement results and also produced higher classroom teacher satisfaction measures—realization was occurring. The conference room silence was broken by the buzz of very real and keen interest. They got to work.

So far we have had only a taste of what it means to move from a page of statistics to the flesh, blood, and destiny of individual students. And we have shown that it can be done for all students in a school and in a district, region, or diocese. In Chapter 2, we go deeper to demonstrate the power of putting FACES on the data. Then in the rest of the book we work through the heart of our model—the integration of assessment, instruction, leadership, and ownership.

CHAPTER 2

The Power of Putting FACES on the Data

In education systems, moving toward goals defined by our shared beliefs and understandings starts with collaboratively structured plans based on shared specificity and consistency of good practice across all classrooms in all schools—without imposing it (which we know doesn't work). But which practices are so impactful that they become non-negotiable, expected operating norms in every classroom? How do we ensure these practices are in fact delivered in every classroom? If we believe that every child can learn and has the right to learn, then we need to determine that every child has learned.

To optimize classroom teacher effectiveness, we need to know on a continuing basis that every child is learning by implementing ongoing assessment and by incorporating that information about each child's learning into daily instruction. This process—assessment becomes instruction—should become a non-negotiable practice. If we believe all teachers can teach if supported with the right resources and Professional Learning, we need to offer them rich, easy-to-use inputs, including putting the FACES on the data, so that they can do what it takes to reach the goal of every student learning. Doing so is the system's responsibility to the students and it is necessary to guarantee every teachers' right to teach like an expert.

Genesis of the Dialogue
With Educators

From research and experience we know that when teachers understand how students are performing, that knowledge enables them to present or to ask more appropriate questions. However, there are so many forms of information, so many types of data available, and so many students in our classes that sometimes teachers become bewildered, in the sense that if they knew what information was important, and how to cut through all the other "stuff," they would more readily know what to do in their classrooms with each of their students. "If only I could put FACES on the data" is a comment we have heard dozens of times in working on system-wide implementation and on approaches to improve student growth and achievement.

Starting with this notion of the "faceless glut" of data, we approached hundreds of professional educators with whom we were working in the United States, Canada, the United Kingdom, and Australia for their views on three questions and to gather examples or stories we could share. These are the questions we asked:

1. Why do we put FACES on the data?

2. How do we put FACES on the data?

3. What are the top three leadership skills needed to put FACES on the data?

When and How We Asked
the Research Questions

In group sessions we had the cooperation of and received input from 507 educators from across the globe. We used a Placemat format to gather the data (see Appendix B) and gave the participants time to provide open-ended responses to the first two questions and to reach consensus on the third question. Participants included directors of systems, superintendents of regions within systems, principals, vice principals, curriculum consultants, instructional coaches, support teachers, and many classroom teachers.

We were delighted with the response—not one of the 507 respondents lacked for definite opinions! In this chapter, we discuss and display the general findings from the three questions. The details from question 1 follow in this chapter. Question 2 is answered in depth in Chapter 3 (Assessment) and Chapter 4 (Instruction). The top three leadership skills as defined by practitioners are examined in Chapter 5.

In reviewing the responses, we noted a number of broad generalizations with implications for communicating the importance of using data correctly and with impact at varying levels within an organization. In sum, messages must be target specific—which sounds parallel to the importance of understanding student data, doesn't it?

Table 2.1 displays the number of responses received to each question. These are the generalizations we noted from the data:

1. The questions received very different numbers of responses.

2. Respondents understand and report a broad range of reasons for putting FACES on the data.

3. Respondents often used the 14 Parameters (Sharratt & Fullan, 2009, 2012) or other common language that clustered readily.

4. Respondent groups provided approximately 2.2 responses per person for question 1, showing their interest in the *humanity* aspects of putting FACES on the data.

5. Respondent groups provided approximately the same number of responses per person for question 2 as for question 1, showing they had definite opinions about and viable experiences in putting FACES on the data.

6. Participants (placed into small groups, usually of four) were asked to reach consensus on the top three leadership skills before responding to question 3. As a result, the overall number of responses to question 3 is many less than for questions 1 and 2.

Table 2.1 Number of Responses Received for Each of the Three Questions Asked

Question	Question Asked	Number of Responses	Percentage of Responses
1	Why do we put FACES on the data?	1,102	43
2	How do we put FACES on the data?	1,095	43
3	What are the top three leadership skills needed to put FACES on the data?	369	14
	TOTAL:	**2,566**	**100**

Research Findings: Question 1

Research question 1 (Why do we put FACES on the data?) had 1,102 individually crafted responses, which when clustered, fell into four categories: human-emotional, instruction, assessment, and ownership. Figure 2.1 demonstrates that 46 percent of responses focused on the human-emotional connection to the question, 29 percent of the responses focused on the connection to instruction, 13 percent focused on the ownership connection as the reason for putting FACES on the data, and 12 percent focused on the assessment connection for putting FACES on the data. The pattern of these responses confirms the theme of this book—putting FACES on the data. What excites and motivates humans, teachers all the more so, is emotional connections to other humans with respect to current life situations. In fact, when you take this connection and incorporate *instruction*—both values on the human condition—fully 75 percent of respondents identified with **this core moral purpose.**

The responses grouped into each of the four clusters are shown in Table 2.2. Each identified cluster may have had dozens of unique responses, which have been reduced to exemplars of thinking and expression. We believe most educators and parents will understand and relate to these clustered responses.

Table 2.2 displays the summary phrases for clustered responses collected for question 1. Once listed, summary phrase items were totaled within the clusters and ranked by the number of mentions underlying each. The ranking appears in the right-hand column and is for the entire collection of items, as opposed to representing rankings within each cluster. Line items with similar ranking were scored as ties with the subsequent ranked line item skipping one numbering position to accommodate the tie.

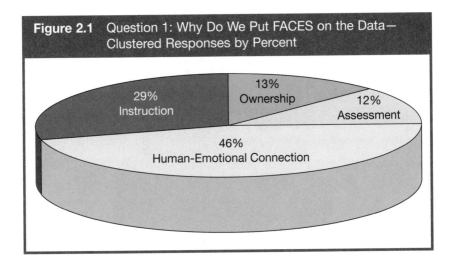

Figure 2.1 Question 1: Why Do We Put FACES on the Data— Clustered Responses by Percent

Table 2.2	Question 1: Why Do We Put FACES on the Data?—Items in Clustered Responses	
Cluster	**Responses**	**Rank**
Human-Emotional	Add a personal, human, emotional element	1
	Encourage all system, school members to make the work personal, motivating, meaningful	3
	Identify areas of need for individual students	4
	Make our work about the real students	5

(Continued)

(Continued)

Cluster	Responses	Rank
	Know all your students	6
	Be engaged with, make connection to learners	11
	Support individual growth	14
Instruction	Align teaching strategies	2
	Specify strategies required for improvement	6
	Ensure success for all—no one gets left behind	12
	Base teaching on student aptitudes and interest	13
	Support effective teaching practices	15
	Bring moral purpose to our work	16
	Engage students in the teaching and learning process	18
	Inform curriculum decisions and resource allocation	21
	Set goals for future instruction	26
Ownership	Promote shared responsibility for student success, collective responsibility, commitment	8
	Promote accountability	9
	Make a connection with the parents	23
	Use the research to guide the practice	25
Assessment	Understand if the processes and strategies we are using are having an impact	10
	Identify students who are struggling and require additional supports	16
	Find, measure, and celebrate success	19

Cluster	Responses	Rank
	Target those students who may require special strategies to achieve curricular learning goals	20
	Identify possible groupings of students with like needs	22
	Look for trends (e.g., socioeconomic, cultural, family circumstances, English language learners)	24

The human-emotional connection was the highest overall ranked cluster. Five of its seven line items fall into the top ten of all mentioned responses. Instruction and ownership each have two in the top ten, whereas assessment has one in the top ten, and that is number 10.

Responses from the 507 respondents define **our why** by indicating that putting FACES on the data helps them

- Know the students (personal, human-emotional element; encourage colleagues to make the work personal; make our work about the real students; know your students)

- Plan for them (align teaching strategies, specify strategies required for improvement)

- Ensure everyone knows they are responsible or "own" **all** students (all are our students, promote accountability)

- Assess progress widely and for individuals (understand if the processes and strategies we are using are having an impact)

Figure 2.2 represents graphically the item distribution in response to question 2: How do we put FACES on the data? Table 2.3 summarizes the 1,095 individual responses from the 507 respondents. Gathered into three clusters, the data set is a collection of 19 topics that themselves are compilations of like-responses. The uses of data fall into three clear categories that we would call assessment oriented, instruction oriented, and learner-identity oriented. If, as a teacher, you combine these three orientations, you come pretty close to becoming *a teacher of choice, one who can effectively help ALL students learn.*

As seen in Figure 2.2, the overall split of responses among assessment, instruction, and knowing the learner were 36 percent, 39 percent, and 25 percent, respectively. Respondents provided the largest number of responses for the first item—assessment *for* learning and assessment *as* learning to determine the next steps in learning—over 220 responses. Respondents were the next most responsive in the instruction category—collaborative use of evidence gathered for group input, those opportunities taken when teachers bring all their evidence of student work to grade meetings, co-teaching meetings, or to special group meetings designed specifically to discuss instructional challenges (see discussion of case management meetings and co-teaching in Chapter 4).

Figure 2.2 Question 2: How Do We Put FACES on the Data—Clustered Responses by Percent

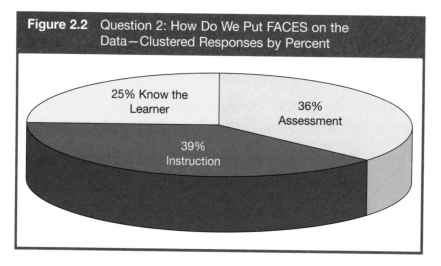

Table 2.3 Question 2: How Do We Put FACES on the Data?—Items in Clustered Responses

Cluster	Responses	Rank
Assessment	Assessment of learning and to determine next steps in learning—tracking walls	1
	Collect, monitor data to track students' progress on intervention program over the year	5

Cluster	Responses	Rank
	Goal setting—clear, identified goals for individuals and classrooms for a period of time	9
	Assessment results used to identify groups of like abilities and specific learning strategies	10
	Assessment to develop profiles of need for individual students	16
	Data analysis to determine trends, patterns among students, classes, and groups in the school	19
Instruction	Collaborative use of evidence gathered for group input	2
	Discussion of specific student work in school teams to discover new strategies with teacher	3
	Adapt styles of teaching to match styles of learning as evidenced in data	6
	Identify *target students* for interventions—usually bottom three students in the class	10
	Identify *marker students* whose work samples are brought regularly to grade or team meetings: usually an underperforming, at level, and above level student in each class	12
	Celebrate successes at every stage of learning; assume all students will have success	15
Know the Learner	Engage students (e.g., in making decisions about what to learn and mode of assessment)	4
	Build meaningful relationships using information about the learner to build trust, confidence	7

(Continued)

(Continued)

Cluster	Responses	Rank
	Get to know each student's learning style and interests to capture their attention	8
	Have all student's teachers look at the student's full-work portfolio to understand whole student	13
	Use photos everywhere; ensure no student name goes unknown; highlight all who need help	14
	Believe in Parameter #1—all students can learn if all teachers understand the data-driven strategies	17
	Engage parents in dialogue early, often; be sincere in offering them ideas, asking for their help	18

Balancing the two notions of assessment to lead instruction and data that can enlighten a group of teachers about a student's performance is the concept that putting a FACE on the data can inform the teacher and other staff about a student sufficiently that they can begin to form a working relationship with that student. *Respondents feel that the more a teacher can know about each learner, the greater the opportunity to break through, to create trust, and to show the teacher's respect for every student.*

Within the assessment cluster, responses included the following:

- To *set goals so that teachers can prepare lessons* and break lessons into learning style segments to match what their class data sets say

- To *identify trends in learning or low levels of learning* coming from other grades or classes or from communities within classes

Within the instruction cluster, responses included the following:

- To *identify and target students early for interventions* and for potential ongoing monitoring by others

- To be able to *adapt teaching styles to learning styles* as noted in the various forms of assessment done in class during the early part of the year and in an ongoing manner

Knowing the learner responses can be divided evenly among the following:

- Learning everything a teacher can about every student to *build a positive environment* for all students

- Using technologies like digital photography and video to *name the student* so that as many staff as possible can know as many students as possible, especially those in their divisions or in classrooms next door, again, to provide a positive learning environment for all FACES

- *Knowing the parents* and having them *become learning-teaching partners* with the student and the teacher, as their influence can be (should be) very powerful and positive

As shown in Figure 2.3 and Table 2.4, the respondents clearly identified three critical leadership skills. Responses were spread more evenly across these clusters than they were for questions 1 and 2. This even spread of importance may have been due to the collaborative manner in which the small (usually four-person) groups produced their lists of the top three leadership skills. Respondents talked to key elements of leadership theory: vision, leader-learner, and preparation of and participation in a sustainable, purposeful working environment or culture. They want someone who

- Will know what to do (*knowledge and understanding of impactful practices, is professional; is an effective manager of resources, the structure, time, human resources available; is a teacher but is leading, as lead learner, modeling continuous improvement*)

- Is visible and gets people moving in the same direction (*involved in meetings, with the data, in Professional Learning sessions—leading and learning, communicates consistent messages precisely in words and follow-through actions, someone who everyone sees because they are visible in classrooms*)

- Leads for the long term (*builds and sustains strong relationships to foster trust, positive environment of trust, is a committed advocate for the learner, and shares responsibility for each student's progress*)

The respondents clearly value leaders who will work with them through instructional conundrums they may have with students, because when those students succeed, the teachers and often the whole staff will have learned new skills together to apply at other times. *Using data to lead, modeling collective capacity for collaboration, and empowering through shared leadership were other key skills that respondents noted* (discussed in more detail in Chapter 5).

All these findings corroborate what we know about effective leaders (for example, principals). Above all, they *participate as learners* in helping teachers figure out how to make instructional improvements. **Leaders who participate do learn** and are appropriately named *learning leaders*. Their "know-ability" "mobilize-ability," and "sustain-ability" get stronger as they learn. They become more effective and more appreciated for being so.

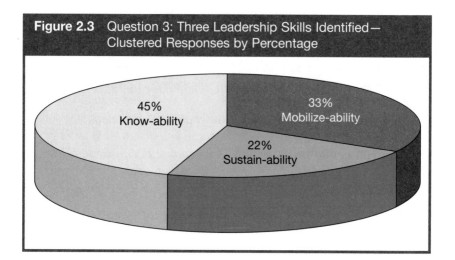

Figure 2.3 Question 3: Three Leadership Skills Identified— Clustered Responses by Percentage

45%
Know-ability

33%
Mobilize-ability

22%
Sustain-ability

Table 2.4 Question 3: Three Leadership Skills Identified—Items in Clustered Responses

Cluster	Responses—Skill Items Defined	Rank
Know-ability	Knowledge and understanding of impactful practices, professional	1
	Having a strong, compelling message	4
	Effective management of resources, structure, lead organization to gather data, meetings, accountability	6
	Effective management of human resources; looks after well-being of the team	9
	Capacity building for collaboration, empowering through shared leadership, recognizes contributions	10
	Leader as "lead learner," why this, why now, modeling continuous learning	11
Mobilize-ability	Instills collaborative culture focused on shared values	2
	Effective communication skills, delivering clear consistent messages	3
	Ability to motivate and inspire others	11
	Being involved and visible— in meetings, with the data, in Professional Learning	11
Sustain-ability	Building and sustaining strong relationships to foster trust	5

(Continued)

(Continued)

Cluster	Responses— Skill Items Defined	Rank
	Creating positive environment of trust and encouragement, nonthreatening	7
	Committed to advocate for learners, to shared goal that each student's progress is a shared responsibility	8

Clustering the Parameters

The graphs in Figures 2.1, 2.2, and 2.3 show how the research data allow us to cluster the 14 Parameters from our previous work in *Realization* (Sharratt & Fullan, 2009) into four big ideas that we call *improvement drivers*. To zero in on putting FACES on the data, these are the things that impactful leaders and teachers do. These four drivers are underpinned with our foundational belief in Parameter #1— the answer to question 1: all students can learn and all students have a right to learn, as discussed in this chapter. Table 2.5 organizes our thinking about how we take the research data, weave in our previous research work with the 14 Parameters, and unfold the story in the remaining chapters in this book. We are now in a position to answer clearly the question, why do we put FACES on the data?

Why Do We Put FACES on the Data?

In every block of marble I see a statue as plain as though it stood before me, shaped and perfect in attitude and action. I have only to hew away the rough walls that imprison the lovely apparition to reveal it to the other eyes as mine see it.

—Michelangelo, 1475–1564

Revealing "the lovely apparition" is our work. Adding a human-emotional element to our work is what makes teaching "the noblest of all professions"—and also the most complex yet motivating and meaningful. Feedback from teachers and leaders across the world defined our work as making connections with learners to find FACES in the data and then to make "statues of exquisite beauty appear from sometimes rough-hewn stone." Not only in the answers to question 1 but also in the answers to questions 2 and 3, **the common theme of knowing learners as real students with real-life stories emerges**. Comments such as "know the child—grow the child" call us to place students at the center of what we do in teaching and learning, *making data today become instruction tomorrow for each one.* In considering leadership skills needed to do just that, respondents mentioned the importance of tying leadership decisions to the instructional core and monitoring that moral purpose in every school, believing that every student has the right to be known, literate and successful. This book is about finding "the lovely apparition" and being the best we can be to carve and create real people.

Table 2.5 Four Drivers Answer Our Questions

Research Question	Drivers	Clustered Parameters	Chapter
1. Why do we put FACES on the data?	Our moral imperative: All students can learn and have the right to learn.	Parameter #1: Shared Beliefs and Understandings: • All students can learn • All teachers can teach • Early and ongoing intervention and high expectations are critical • Teachers, leaders, and students can articulate why they do what they do	2

(Continued)

(Continued)

Research Question	Drivers	Clustered Parameters	Chapter
2. How do we put FACES on the data? Part 1	1. Assessment	Parameter #5: Early and Ongoing Intervention	3
		Parameter #6: Case Management Approach (a) Data Walls	
		Parameter #8: Collaborative Assessment of Student Work	
2. How do we put FACES on the data? Part 2	2. Instruction	Parameter #3: Assessment that Informs Instruction	4
		Parameter #2: Embedded Coaches	
		Parameter #6: Case Management Approach (b) Meetings	
		Parameter #9: Centralized Resources	
		Parameter #13: Cross-Curricular Literacy and Critical Thinking Connections	
		Parameter #11: Collaborative Inquiry	
3. What leadership skills are needed?	3. Leadership	Parameter #4: Principal Leadership	5
		Parameter #7: PL at Staff Meetings	
		Parameter #10: Budget Allocation to Strategic Resources	

Research Question	Drivers	Clustered Parameters	Chapter
4. Where does this happen?	4. Ownership	Parameter #12: Parent and Community Involvement	6
		Parameter #14: Shared Responsibility and Accountability	

Of course, Michelangelo was being disingenuous. He had to bring out the best in the marble. He had to carefully chisel it to display its magnificence. This is what teachers and leaders do. *They unleash and stimulate what students are capable of becoming.*

Similarly, Sir Ken Robinson (2009) writes about a teacher finding Gillian Lynne's lovely apparition:

> Someone looked deep into her eyes—someone who had seen children like her before and knew how to read the signs. Someone else might have put her on medication and told her to calm down. But Gillian wasn't a problem child. She didn't need to go away to a special school. She just needed to be who she really was. (p. 4)

How Do We Drill Down to Find "the Lovely Apparition"?

When first faced with a mass of student achievement data or state-provided information on populations related to school districts, most of us would rather look for something else to do. Our shared beliefs and understandings are based on a simple foundational beginning— all students can learn—and the capstone, our realization that we are all responsible and accountable for the learning of each and every student in our system or school. So how do we make the right choice—do we get the coffee or break down the data?

Some educators are really good at breaking down the data, but most are not trained or experienced at chipping away the marble in their system reports—they haven't been shown how to imagine there might be a "statue" in there. What follows is a look at how some of the more complicated information provided, such as by state or district authorities, may be chipped away to provide a glimpse at what is happening in the district or system, or the network, or even at the school level.

We have been privileged through our consulting at every level in nations, states, systems, and individual schools to meet and learn from exceptionally fine state and system analysts—often incredible teachers who have become quite expert in data use because early on in their careers they really wanted to know what they needed to do to understand how to help "all our kids learn." What follows then is our look at some tables, adapted from various systems with which we have worked, that provide a glimpse of the statue from different vantage points around it.

To Be, or Not to Be (Good): That Is the Question

We will not become involved in the debates over whether standardized testing is good or bad, or whether or not the data posted on websites are too detailed or invasive. Our only interest here is in what the data sources say about the students in a system or in a system's schools and how these data can best be used (1) to stimulate further improvement and (2) to satisfy the public that the system is in strong working order.

We are interested in numbers related to scoring levels, particularly at minimum standard or below minimum standard to reveal the statues (that is, the FACES) in our midst. Our interest arises from the fact that a student who starts in Grade 1 at a minimum standard with a minimal literacy level will likely never recover from that start throughout their entire education. Students who start below minimum standard in their first assessments will likely continue to barely pass throughout elementary school and will most likely not graduate from secondary school—all because they did not learn to read with fluency and comprehension by the end of Grade 1.

We work here with some charts from various jurisdictions. Beginning with Table 2.6 are the standard assessment results for a group of schools we call Bear Paw Schools, a group of schools within a district that we call Small System. The results are for four assessment years (grades). The values shown for our Bear Paw Schools are the percentages of the population of Year 3 students who were at or below minimum standard. The trend is for these values to increase: the percentage of students at or below minimum standard across assessment Years 3, 5, 7 reaches its highest point in Year 9. The percentage of students performing at the lowest two bands (that is, at or below minimum standard) increases each year. Compared to other schools in Small System, Bear Paw Schools actually performed about the same in Years 3, 5, and 7; in Year 9, they performed better than other schools in the system, with fewer students in the bottom two bands.

Now let's put some FACES on these bits of data!

Table 2.7 causes us to take more notice, given that these data are the actual numbers of students who were at or below minimum standard. Notice that the number of students in the bottom two bands increases from Year 3 to Year 9. We learned that there is a slightly anomalous dip in Year 7 due to changes in student enrollment; however, the trend, spiraling downward, is unmistakable. Students started slow in Year 3, and because they had not learned to read proficiently in Year 1, the values continued downward to Year 9. The trend continues across all domains assessed.

Table 2.6	Percentage of Students in Bottom Two Bands at Bear Paw Schools				
	Reading	Writing	Spelling	Grammar and Punctuation	Math
Year 3 Bear Paw Schools	**11**	**5**	**15**	**14**	**12**
Year 3 System	12.7	6.3	14.9	14	12
Year 5 Bear Paw Schools	**18**	**16**	**21**	**18**	**16**
Year 5 System	17.9	15.4	22.3	17.6	16.3
Year 7 Bear Paw Schools	**13**	**18**	**18**	**20**	**12**
Year 7 System	15.4	20.2	20.6	18.7	17

(Continued)

(Continued)

	Reading	Writing	Spelling	Grammar and Punctuation	Math
Year 9 Bear Paw Schools	**20**	**34**	**21**	**19**	**17**
Year 9 System	*26.6*	*35.7*	*24.4*	*25*	*22.9*

Is the fact that 120 actual FACES are underperforming in reading in Year 9 all that bad? Table 2.7 shows that the 120 students came from a pool of 593 who were assessed from Bear Paw Schools. To Small System and to Bear Paw Schools, the number of FACES underperforming was deemed to be unacceptable. **And they have done something about it because they know the FACES.**

More graphically, if staff from Bear Paw Schools were not engaged in a major reform initiative that called for intervention using assessment data and specific instruction for all students, we could say that their results would probably not improve over the years to come. If that were the case, we could assume that a mythical cohort made up of the test year classes in Years 3, 5, 7, and 9 could represent an actual class traveling through Bear Paw Schools (Table 2.8). Looking at proficiency, we can see how the numbers of those who are assessed as doing well would dwindle—again, all things being equal and with no interventions occurring.

Table 2.7 Number of Students in Bottom Two Bands at Bear Paw Schools

	Reading	Writing	Spelling	Grammar and Punctuation	Math
Year 3 Bear Paw Schools	**78**	**37**	**106**	**100**	**84**
Year 3 System	*302*	*151*	*354*	*333*	*286*

	Reading	Writing	Spelling	Grammar and Punctuation	Math
Year 5 Bear Paw Schools	**112**	**107**	**144**	**120**	**105**
Year 5 System	*416*	*360*	*523*	*413*	*379*
Year 7 Bear Paw Schools	**87**	**121**	**121**	**134**	**80**
Year 7 System	*330*	*438*	*446*	*405*	*370*
Year 9 Bear Paw Schools	**120**	**201**	**125**	**112**	**99**
Year 9 System	*554*	*750*	*511*	*523*	*475*

Table 2.8	Number of Students Assessed in Bear Paw Schools in the Years Shown				
	Reading	**Writing**	**Spelling**	**G and P**	**Numeracy**
Year 3 Bear Paw Schools	722	719	724	724	725
Year 5 Bear Paw Schools	678	678	674	674	668
Year 7 Bear Paw Schools	666	671	671	671	666
Year 9 Bear Paw Schools	593	599	596	596	592

Another way to portray and use data from a specific grade or year over time is simply to stack them, year over year in order. Tables 2.9 and 2.10 are from a single district in Ontario, Canada. You can stack the years across the whole district or just in one school to read the trends. The Education Quality and Accountability Office (EQAO) standard is for 75 percent of students in any grade assessed to be at Level 3 or Level 4. The percentages shown refer to the percentages of students who had reached Levels 3 and 4.

The Grade 3 scores in Table 2.9 are not good—in any domain assessed—75 percent of students at Levels 3 and 4 is the expectation. There has been a slow improvement trend. However, scores were well below state averages in every year shown—at no point did Ontario County as a whole reach standard. Now look at Table 2.10.

Table 2.9 Percentage of Ontario County Grade 3 Students at EQAO Levels 3 and 4, 2000–2009

	EQAO Assessment		
School Year	**Reading**	**Writing**	**Math**
1999–2000	50	48	49
2000–2001	50	52	58
2001–2002	50	54	58
2002–2003	49	60	54
2003–2004	49	58	52
2004–2005	52	65	62
2005–2006	58	70	66
2006–2007	64	70	69
2007–2008	65	71	68
2008–2009	62	70	70

Table 2.10 Percentage of Ontario County Grade 6 Students at EQAO Levels 3 and 4, 2000–2009

School Year	EQAO Assessment		
	Reading	Writing	Math
1999–2000	50	48	49
2000–2001	53	53	50
2001–2002	55	55	52
2002–2003	55	57	50
2003–2004	57	58	54
2004–2005	65	63	58
2005–2006	67	67	61
2006–2007	67	67	58
2007–2008	70	72	62
2008–2009	72	72	65

Table 2.10 shows improvement in Grade 6 since assessment began. However, although the Grade 3 and Grade 6 reading scores were almost identical in 2000, the Grade 6 reading scores climbed much more rapidly and steadily toward standard than did the Grade 3 scores. In fact, Ontario County started its own internal improvement program for literacy in 2007, followed by outside consulting in 2009. In some districts, reviewing these two simple charts would lead to questions about the quality of instruction and the quality of the "new" internal intervention program in the primary grades (Years 1–3). *Is it possible that senior leadership did not pay attention to the potential for improvement? Were there shared common beliefs and understandings? Did anyone "own" the need to increase student achievement?* Yet there was some notice of the need for improvement, at least by the junior-grade (4–6) teachers, that created the positive variance in grade improvement over the primary improvement. Why the difference at the junior level?

One way to project future performance is to review same-student assessment results across the full spectrum of years assessed (the Cohort Data). Where assessment has not been in place long enough to do this, you might look at all the years and domains assessed and assume that the results could represent a mythical cohort moving through all assessment years. You might assume that you can project future results, but that, of course, would be a mistake. Planned interventions to rectify what you have seen and other unplanned factors will make differences, too. The exercise, however, does add **a sense of urgency**. Would the declining assessment results in Figure 2.4 be an accurate prediction of what would happen in a larger system? Can this downward spiral in assessment results be stopped? Can it be corrected?

Whereas Figure 2.4 represents a mythical cohort, what follows in Table 2.11 is a longer-term look at a large system's actual assessment data to see if a downward spiraling might be accurate for a larger system, too. And if it is accurate, are there ways to halt the downward trend?

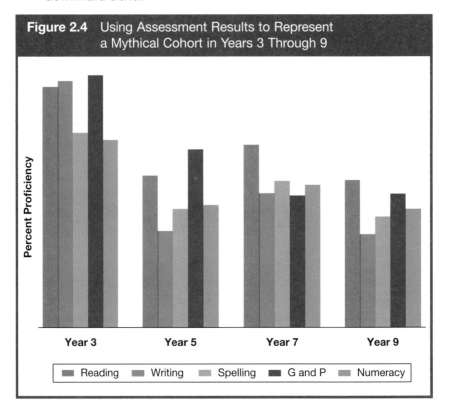

Figure 2.4 Using Assessment Results to Represent a Mythical Cohort in Years 3 Through 9

In Table 2.11, the Ontario County student data have been arranged into a cohort report to show the percentage of students who meet EQAO standard (75 percent is the expectation) and the actual number of students who *do not meet* the standard. Now the trend data of Tables 2.9 and 2.10 are really apparent and screaming out for interpretation and action by the district's senior leaders. The average population of the Grade 3 and Grade 6 classes across Ontario County during the years shown for cohorts was 5,000 students in Grade 3 and 6,000 in Grade 6. This is not, strictly speaking, accurate; however, it is close enough to illustrate the power of showing class progress, from which some strong conclusions can be drawn for planning purposes.

Table 2.11 shows the progression of the same students in six cohorts with several interesting differences between Grade 3 and Grade 6 assessments in reading, writing, and math:

- In every cohort the difference between Grade 3 and Grade 6 reading scores is at least +7 points, with the greatest difference being +18 points. This represents increasing scores by the same students, which can be attributed only to **strong junior-school instruction targeted to each FACE**.

- Grade 3 reading results increased very slowly after the introduction of the EQAO assessments, such that by the sixth year of EQAO assessments only 58 percent of students met standard, whereas the Grade 6 teachers managed to increase the percentage of reading scores at Levels 3 and 4 from 57 percent to 72 percent in the sixth year of assessment. Why would it have taken so many years to improve Grade 3 reading levels? Ontario County argues that, because of high immigration, it is impossible to have higher primary scores. Many districts worldwide refuse to accept the argument and apply high-impact classroom teaching practices and matching strong intervention programs to have had at least 80 percent of their Grade 3 students achieving at or above expectation (that is, at Levels 3 and 4).

- Writing scores improved in both Grade 3 and Grade 6; however, Grade 6 continues to outperform Grade 3. Again, the same children are learning more in Grades 4, 5, and 6, while neither Grade 3 nor Grade 6 assessment results are at state standard (75 percent) at this point.

Table 2.11 Ontario County Same-Student Cohort Performance

Percentage of Students Below Standard (Not at Levels 3 and 4)

Cohort 1 in		Reading	Writing	Math
Grade 3	2000–2001	50	52	58
Grade 6	2003–2004	57	58	54
Cohort 2 in		**Reading**	**Writing**	**Math**
Grade 3	2001–2002	50	54	58
Grade 6	2004–2005	65	63	58
Cohort 3 in		**Reading**	**Writing**	**Math**
Grade 3	2002–2003	49	60	54
Grade 6	2005–2006	67	67	61

Number of Students Below Standard (Not at Levels 3 and 4)

Cohort 1 in		Reading	Writing	Math
Grade 3	2000–2001	2,500	2,400	2,100
Grade 6	2003–2004	2,580	2,520	2,760
Cohort 2 in		**Reading**	**Writing**	**Math**
Grade 3	2001–2002	2,500	2,300	2,100
Grade 6	2004–2005	2,100	2,220	2,520
Cohort 3 in		**Reading**	**Writing**	**Math**
Grade 3	2002–2003	2,550	2,000	2,300
Grade 6	2005–2006	1,980	1,980	2,340

Percentage of Students Below Standard (Not at Levels 3 and 4)

Cohort 4 in		Reading	Writing	Math
Grade 3	2003–2004	49	58	52
Grade 6	2006–2007	67	67	58
Cohort 5 in		**Reading**	**Writing**	**Math**
Grade 3	2004–2005	52	65	62
Grade 6	2007–2008	70	72	62
Cohort 6 in		**Reading**	**Writing**	**Math**
Grade 3	2005–2006	58	70	66
Grade 6	2008–2009	72	72	65

Number of Students Below Standard (Not at Levels 3 and 4)

Cohort 4 in		Reading	Writing	Math
Grade 3	2003–2004	2,550	2,100	2,400
Grade 6	2006–2007	1,980	1,980	2,520
Cohort 5 in		**Reading**	**Writing**	**Math**
Grade 3	2004–2005	2,400	1,750	1,900
Grade 6	2007–2008	1,800	1,680	2,280
Cohort 6 in		**Reading**	**Writing**	**Math**
Grade 3	2005–2006	2,100	1,500	1,700
Grade 6	2008–2009	1,680	1,680	2,100

- Math results started low for both Grades 3 and 6 and have improved only slowly at Grade 3, with a similar slow and small improvement in Grade 6. It is not just language literacy that requires attention, but mathematical literacy, as well. Note: Math results continue to disappoint on the Grade 9 assessment for those students selecting applied rather than academic math, with only 40 percent of students in applied math achieving standard.

Let's look again at the mythical cohort. The answer to the question posed—will low test results continue to decline as the cohort advances through school—is no, provided there is focused assessment that informs instruction beginning in Kindergarten to identify the FACES who require early support.

In Bear Paw Schools, senior leadership has engaged powerfully and involved everyone in the system, developed an agreed-upon set of principles (beliefs and understandings), supported everyone in ongoing PL, engaged the emotional connection of FACES across the system, and shared cognitive insights of teaching and learning across the system. Their ongoing cohort results are moving ahead rapidly toward **all** students achieving. Bear Paw Schools will not be satisfied with mediocrity—all FACES will count.

FACES in Secondary School

Once you establish the habit of seeing behind the statistics, powerful new strategies come naturally. A case in point is Ontario's Student Success Strategy. By using a personal, focused approach on a large scale, Ontario had been able to increase its high school graduation rate from 68 percent to 81 percent in six years across the 900 secondary schools in its school system. The basis of the program is the strategy whereby each of the 900 schools has on staff a "student success teacher" whose job it is to help the school identify students who are on the margins (at-risk and vulnerable) and take action with each student. We have written elsewhere about the details of this program (Fullan, 2010a), but here we wish to report a recent spinoff.

As the schools and the system got in the habit of paying personal attention to students, one of the central leaders thought to identify on a system level how many students entered Grade 11 but did not graduate one year later. They identified 7,000 students who got as far as Grade 11 but dropped out before graduating. A simple and direct program—let's call it FACES—was developed quickly. The central leaders contacted the seventy-two school districts in the Ontario system and gave them the lists of dropouts for each school. They then provided a small amount of money to each school and suggested that the schools hire recently retired guidance counselors to track down each student and figure out what it would take to invite them back to complete their program. Of the 7,000 students, 3,500 returned, most of whom graduated. Our point is that personalization programs—FACES, for short—do not occur spontaneously, but the effects of a simple realization about the numbers of FACES, even on a large scale, can be dramatic.

The focused work in the Eastern Region of the Melbourne Archdiocese Catholic Schools (MACS) reflects the specificity of practice occurring in the region and in one school within that region. Improvement just doesn't happen by chance, as this case study demonstrates. Improvement happens because leaders and teachers "work on the work together" to see the big picture and to be all over the detail.

MACS Case Study: Evidence-Proven IMPACT!

Staff in MACS Eastern Region, Australia, believe in collaborative communication and precision-in-practice. "They are strongly committed to PL at the school and system levels to improve ALL students' life chances," says Regional General Manager, Marwin Austerberry.

From 2017 until the present, Austerberry and her team have worked with Sharratt, even through the pandemic lockdowns and re-adjustments, to implement the essence of *Putting FACES on the Data* (2012) and *CLARITY: What Matters MOST in Learning, Teaching and Leading* (2019) as displayed in Figure 2.5. The vision, culture of learning and operating norms were all developing well when COVID hit; Austerberry and her unified, multidisciplinary team sustained the plan.

(Continued)

(Continued)

Figure 2.5 Bringing Together *Putting FACES on the Data* (2012) and *CLARITY: What Matters MOST in Learning, Teaching, and Leading* (2019)

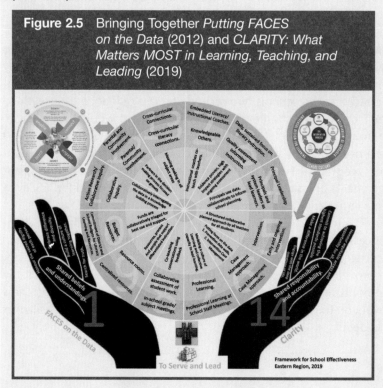

They call their work "The Learning Collaborative" (TLC). All system and school staff members have stayed the course, first in the calm and since 2020 through crises, and have begun to experience the results for which they planned. Here is a glimpse at their successes as noted by Austerberry:

"In the MACS Eastern Region, Victoria, Australia, there is a Regional support structure for the FACES work alongside Sharratt. The Regional Leadership Team meets twice per term, School Effectiveness consultants provide timely and ongoing support, Knowledgeable Other/Literacy/Math/Secondary consultants feature ongoing support of schools' priority areas and dedicated Religious Education Consultants continue the focus on catholic culture within the 94 schools in the Eastern Region.

"It is critical that we have embraced a multidisciplinary approach," says Austerberry, "that involves dedicated time each term with

Primary and Secondary schools, to strengthen the 14 Parameters work, including a Case Management Approach (CMA) in the Regional Office (as well as in schools) to advance our schools' ongoing growth and achievement."

Their multidisciplinary team acts as a Guiding Coalition that has a strong focus on collaborative communication, a commitment to PL and a culture of learning together at a school and system level that supports the "full flourishing of students" (Horizons of Hope: An Education Framework for the Archdiocese of Melbourne, 2018).

Outstanding outcomes have resulted from this precision-in-practice, such as:

- ✓ a shared language across the system and schools;
- ✓ shared beliefs and understanding using the non-negotiables of Parameters #1, #6, and #14;
- ✓ teachers and leaders increased data literacy (Parameter #6); and
- ✓ shared responsibility and accountability for owning ALL students' FACES (Parameter #14).

These outcomes were evidenced in all schools through the adaptation of enabling structures and processes, such as:

- ✓ development of Data Walls and resulting Data Conversations (Parameter #6);
- ✓ Case Management Meetings, to interrogate students work and give specific feedback to teachers and school leaders (Parameters #6, #3, and #13); and
- ✓ Learning Walks and Talks by system, school and teacher leaders (Parameters #1 and #14).

Evidence of Improvement

All schools systematically use the 14 Parameters of System and School Improvement to self-assess how they are progressing and to determine their next steps in learning based on the analysis of their school data. Figure 1.3 displays the 14 Parameters (Sharratt, 2019; Sharratt & Fullan, 2012) that have been embedded in every one of their schools as a self-reflection tool.

The work of one Eastern Region school, St. Bernadette's the Basin, is highlighted here although many other schools could have been chosen. St. Bernadette's leadership team has worked with Sharratt to drive change and innovation throughout many aspects of the school improvement journey using the 14 Parameters as the self-assessment lens to increase all students' achievement. St. Bernadette's leaders unpacked the Parameters with staff to identify areas within the school that showed strength and those that could be improved to enhance student learning. Staff selected, in a consensus-building, safe process, Parameter #7: PL at school staff meetings and Parameter #11: Collaborative Inquiry to focus on, in addition to the non-negotiables of Parameters #1, #6, and #14.

Figure 2.6 Teachers Collaborating to Make Meaning

As shown in Figure 2.6, School Improvement Meetings were focused on consistent approaches to assessment that informs instruction across the school with collaboration and co-construction being central to the outcome of Parameter #1: Shared Beliefs and Understandings.

Teachers undertook Collaborative Inquiry (Parameter #11) regarding how The Third Teacher (the learning environment) might support students. The school acknowledges parents as the first and most important teacher whilst the classroom teachers are the second teacher. The third teacher is the classroom environment with learning walls of deconstructed Learning Intentions (LIs), co-constructed Success Criteria (SC), anchor charts for learning support, and Bump it Up Walls (BIUWs; see Glossary) with anonymous pieces of student work, in every subject area, on display with feedback forms for self-assessment.

Figure 2.7 below shows St. Bernadette's hyperlinked graphic in preparation for Zoom calls with Sharratt in 2020. These calls produced evidence of improvement in the three areas that school leadership teams prioritized as the outcome of this work: Parameters #1, #6, and #14.

As noted in Figure 2.7, this whole staff approach focuses continuously on Parameters #1, #6, and #14—the non-negotiables in building shared beliefs and understandings plus increased clarity of expectations of students' growth and achievement. Teachers strove to achieve professional capacity to instruct all students across all subject areas. As one teacher reported, *"We not only survived the pandemic, but we have excelled because of the 14 Parameters and the agreements we had in place as a result of using them as a lens for continuous improvement."*

What data informs their practice?

St. Bernadette's began their Data Wall immediately upon engaging with the work of the TLC, following an initial webinar with Sharratt titled: *From Assessment Schedules to Data Plans.* They then developed their staff agreements and *"we used CLARITY, the text, as a Methodology."*

To ensure consistency and focus, the staff developed a team approach to writing improvement across the school, focusing on Parameter # 8, Collaborative Assessment of Student Work (CASW). The CASW process (Sharratt, 2019, pp. 283–285) was co-constructed as a step forward in strengthening curriculum knowledge and in engaging with

Figure 2.7 Hyper-Linked Learning Journey Map, St. Bernadette's

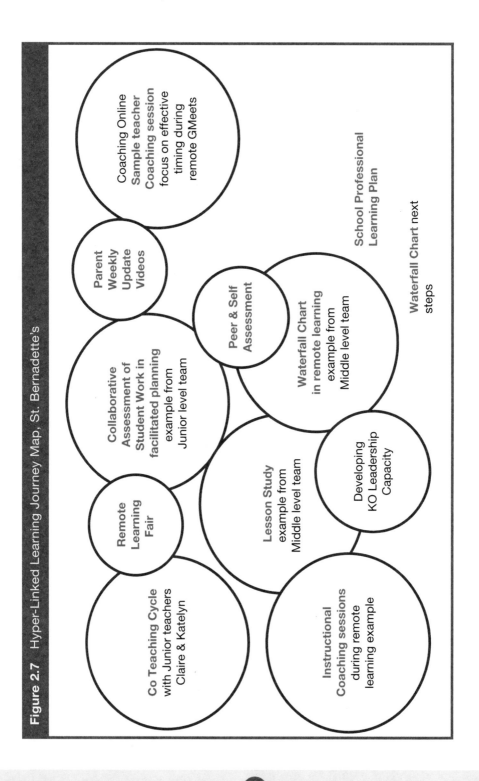

each other using the progressions of learning and student work. From this they developed a standard approach to assessment that would provide student direction and feedback on their work. They utilized BIUWs, anchor charts, goal setting, and regular/frequent conferences on students' next steps in learning. They strengthened their approach to CASW that now sits within a framework of modeling, sharing, collaborative assessing, and mentoring using student writing as the driver of changed teacher practices in the classroom.

Impact!

NAPLAN results show impressive growth in student outcomes at St. Bernadette's, due to the focused work of leaders and teachers. The Top 2 Bands of NAPLAN assessment from 2018 to 2021 indicate an increase of 15 percent more students in Year 3 Reading and 9.5 percent more students performing in the Top 2 Bands in Year 5 Reading, and a reduction to ZERO of students performing in the Bottom 2 Bands in Years 3 and 5 Reading.

Similarly, in Year 3 Writing, students in Top 2 Bands increased by 9 percent and by 17 percent in Year 5. The percentage of students in the Bottom 2 Bands of Writing decreased to ZERO in Year 3 but increased by 3 percent in Year 5—establishing Writing as St. Bernadette's continuing priority school-wide.

This impressive trend in Reading and Writing in Years 3 and 5 is an indication of improvements because of the shared approach designed and implemented by all teaching staff.

Leaders and teachers at St. Bernadette's indicate their impressive impact has been due to the following:

- Established weekly CASW (Parameter #8)

- Strengthened deep knowledge of the key components of the Assessment Waterfall Chart (Chapter 3, Sharratt, 2019, p. 124) to build an expert teaching force (Parameter #3)

- Motivated Students now view and discuss their data helping them consider their next steps—using the five Questions of Learning Walks and Talks (Sharratt, 2019; Sharratt & Fullan, 2012) to

(Continued)

(Continued)

Figure 2.8 IMPACT at St. Bernadette's

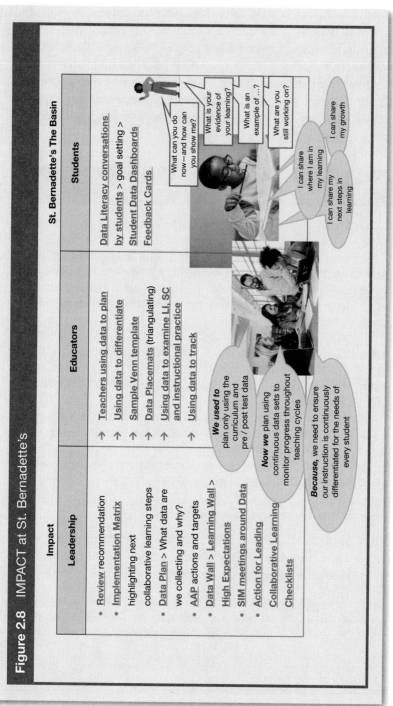

Source: Jennifer Kennedy, Deputy Principal and Learning and Teaching Leader, MACS. educators image by SDI Productions/istock.com; student image by katleho Seisa/istock.com; teacher image by Ponomariova_Maria/istock.com

determine students' ownership of their learning and improvement (Parameters #1, #6, and #14)

- Regularly held writing workshops across all subject areas and year levels (Parameter #13)

- Increased excitement and motivation from students and their teachers who are now empowered to co-learn (Parameters #1 to #14—celebrating ALL small and large wins)!

AND all this has been rolled out during a pandemic in the country/state that has had the greatest number of days in lockdown and remote schooling across the globe.

Recently on an Instagram episode of FACES Friday with Lyn Sharratt, Marwin Austerberry, and Karilyn Gumley answered the question, "What particular knowledge gained from the CLARITY work was having an impact in the 94 schools that have been collaborating with Sharratt since 2017?"

Austerberry and Gumley discussed the impact of:

- seeing the data (on Data Walls), owning it and taking action;

- embedding of the non-negotiables: Parameters #1, #6, and #14;

- modeling by doing at the system level what they expect schools to be doing: co-constructing a system Data Wall, conducting regular system Case Management Meetings and taking action as a team

- developing a common language

- putting FACES on their data through routine PL offerings and

- stepping back to encourage and enable others to step up and continue the work.

(Marwin Austerberry, Regional General Manager; Karilyn Gumley, Teaching and Learning Coordinator; Peter Steward, Principal; and Jennifer Kennedy, Deputy Principal and Learning and Teaching Leader, MACS Eastern Region, personal communication, January 2022.)

The success in MACS Eastern Region has been due to the regional team's clear improvement vision that they share continuously and model consistently. As demonstrated in the St. Bernadette's case study, all field and central staff live the values and strengths of the *leadership abilities* in Chapter 5 and demonstrate clarity in all aspects of leadership behavior, which is key to making the entire enterprise of a school or system work best and become a Learning Organization (Sharratt, 1996).

Leaders in Learning Organizations, like those in the Eastern Region, are *consistent, persistent, and insistent* in knowing, expecting, and seeing effective, high-impact practices in every school, in every classroom, that have a positive impact on ALL students (Sharratt, 2019). As Harris and Jones (2020) write about leadership in crisis:

> *There is no neat blueprint for leadership in such times; and, no predetermined roadmap, no simple leadership checklist of things to tick off. There are only highly skilled, compassionate and dedicated education professionals trying to do the very best they can and to be the very best they can be.* (p. 246)

System Leaders, like Marwin Austerberry and Karilyn Gumley and school leaders, like, Peter Steward and Jennifer Kennedy, use their positional power to model what it takes to lead in calm and crisis and to demonstrate their expectations. They constantly seek out and encourage the learning from and the power of new influencers within their system and school. Leadership influence has a trickle-down effect. With these senior system and school leaders "out in front" throughout COVID, everyone else (who are also leaders), have had to step up, to show deeper caring and to develop and/or exhibit their competence toward all students' learning and all teachers' teaching.

St. Bernadette's and all other schools in MACS Eastern Region have continued their drive toward equity and excellence for all students by emulating Austerberry's and Gumley's *consistent, insistent, and persistent* style. They are following their lead in seeking out and celebrating the remarkable moments in their schools and, like them, school leaders, like Steward and

Kennedy, are learning to never lower their expectations for all learners' growth and achievement. Through this crisis, these leaders have been rewarded with very positive results for holding their nerve and staying the course, the course to success for ALL students and teachers.

We conclude this chapter with a practical leadership matrix adapted by South East Region (SER) leaders in Queensland that draws on the 14 Parameters and the Learning Conditions (Clarity, Depth, and Sustainability) from NPDL. SER is a large, diversified school district of 124 primary schools, 36 secondary schools, and 3 K–12 schools with demanding needs and changing demographics, situated on the Gold Coast in Australia. The leadership and school teams have embraced the FACES and NPDL work. Their priorities include

- Improve academic achievement for all students

- Lift the performance of their top students

- Improve reading and writing for all students

- Improve Year 12 certification rates

- Close the gap for Aboriginal and Torres Strait Islander students

- Improve the participation and achievement of students with disability

- Prepare to implement the new Queensland Certificate of Education (QCE) system

- Enhance the learning opportunities of rural and remote students

Figure 2.9 demonstrates SER's current thinking about moving forward together in the FACES work to reach their moral imperative of every student succeeding. SER leaders have adapted an explicit leadership model that we have highlighted in two of SER's schools— a Secondary Case Study of Cleveland District State High School in Chapter 4 and of Wellington Point State High School in Chapter 6.

Figure 2.9 The Dynamic of Leadership Impact

SER Dynamic of Leadership Impact

PRE-CONDITIONS	CLARITY	DEPTH	SUSTAINABILITY
Begins with: • Knowing all students • Shared Vision, Beliefs & Understandings • Creating & prioritising structures, tools & processes that drive behaviour • Principals sharing research & modelling/leading collaborative processes • Protocoled data analysis (four square approach) • Collective sense of urgency **Becomes:** • Partnerships in learning • Targeted Professional Learning at Staff Meetings • Allocation of System & School Budgets for Learning & equitable resourcing • Establishing opportunities for collaboration in school time • Distributed instructional leadership through evolving structures, tools & aligned processes **Evidenced by:** • Open communication • A common language • Professional learning teams with operating norms & schedule • Protocols enabling collaborative decision-making • Principal as Lead Learner • Parent & community consultation & communication including Literacy focus	**Begins with:** • Aligning resourcing (human, material etc) with determined actions • Understanding how Quality Assessment Informs Instruction • Learning about the Third Teacher & learning environments • Responding to learning needs commencing with collaborative learning design cycles **Becomes:** • Assessment Literate Learners • Precision in pedagogy • Agreed practices for Learning Walks & Bumping-it-up • Collaborative Assessment of Student Work – in school moderation • Collaborative inquiry in the classroom – deepening learning through investigating pedagogy • A culture of trust and transparency **Evidenced by:** • Answers to the five questions for teachers & students • Demonstrations of practice & demonstration classrooms • Planning processes or learning design cycles incorporating the Assessment & Instruction Waterfall or BAA • Student voice • Connection with school community as partners regularly informing and responding to questions and concerns	**Begins with:** • Co-constructing & embedding a two-pronged Case Management Approach (data walls & case management meetings) • Utilising KOs to support CMMs & teachers enacting actions resulting from the CMMs • Learning about & prioritising Learning Walks & Talks **Becomes:** • Shared Responsibility & Accountability within schools • Embedding Learning Walks & Talks & feedback loops sharing trends & patterns with staff to co-design next best learning moves • Interschool & cross-school moderation of IMPACT on student learning • Collective efficacy through celebration • Improving learning design to include precision and deeper pedagogical decision-making and enactment **Evidenced by:** • Changed teacher practice • Improvement in LOA achievement for all students • Improvement in literacy outcomes for all students • Alignment of school plans and resources • Whole school professional learning plan	**Begins with:** • Linking AIP, whole school approach to pedagogy & school planning to system priorities (14 Parameters, Deep Learning, Literacy, State School Improvement measures) • Creating structures for & prioritising collegial engagement • Involvement in Principal LCs **Becomes:** • LWT across schools embedding feedback & sharing trends & patterns with colleagues to explore next best learning moves • Shared Responsibility & Accountability across schools • Authorship • Embedding collegial engagement opportunities focused on pedagogy **Evidenced by:** • Ongoing Collaborative inquiry informing planning • Active collegial engagement frameworks • School contributions for journal & Learning Fair & Expo • Sharing & learning across schools • Peer & Self-Assessment (school, staff and students) • Answers to the five questions for leaders • Innovative mechanisms involving caregivers in asking the five questions for students in parent teacher interviews (for example)
INVESTMENT	DESIGN	IMPACT	SCALABILITY

Aligning SERs approach to: CLARITY, L. Sharratt, 2019, Corwin Press; Deep Learning, M. Fullan et al., 2017. SAGE Publications Inc US; Measuring Human Return J. McEachen & M. Kane, 2018. SAGE Publications Inc US; State School Improvement Strategy, Department of Education, 2021. https://education.qld.gov.au/curriculums/Documents/state-schools-strategy.pdf

Narrative From the Field

I worked with a class teacher who was making some negative comments about new approaches and workload. I went into her class to demonstrate cooperative learning techniques—she was very skeptical, but after some discussion, we set up cooperative learning groups and began a program to develop social skills within the class. During the first lesson, she sat at the back of the class and marked some other work. I persevered and did weekly sessions with her class. By Week 3, she was participating in the lessons, talking to the children. We evaluated each lesson: what went well, what could be improved, and our next steps. At Week 6, she was giving me ideas about our lessons and what she wanted the children to learn. After eight weeks, she asked me when she could go to a cooperative learning academy so that she could learn how do it by herself. *Festina lente:* Make haste slowly!

—Linda Forsyth, Deputy Head Teacher,
Perth and Kinross Council, Scotland

To explore an additional example in which system and school leaders plan how they will put FACES on their data and make a difference for the students in their ten schools in most challenging circumstances, click on QR Code 2.1 to read about the Community Schools Case Study.

QR Code 2.1:
Community
Schools Case
Study

Deliberate Pause

- What data sets are most helpful to you in humanizing the FACES in your class, school, and system?

- How does knowing the data have an impact on what students learn?

- How do you ensure that each FACE counts and is accounted for?

- How do teachers know what data sets matter?

(Continued)

(Continued)

- Do teachers know what data sets look like for the whole school and system—beyond their class and school? In other words, do they get to see the big picture, and how they contribute to it?

Narrative From the Field

Kevin is a boy who came to me after being suspended from another school. He had experienced many in- and out-of-school suspensions while at our school due to at-risk behaviors and previous attitudes he had developed toward school. He rarely, if ever, completed any tasks or assignments given to him by his teachers. I worked with him to support his math and literacy skills from Grades 7 to 9. At the end of his Grade 9 year, he admitted that he learned a lot from the help I had given him. He moved on to high school, and I often wondered about how he was doing.

The Friday he was graduating from secondary school, he came back to the elementary school to find me and tell me he was graduating and to make sure I was attending the ceremony. Unfortunately, I wasn't working at that school anymore, so I didn't meet up with him as he had planned.

That night however, I attended the graduation ceremonies without him knowing that I was coming. Before the ceremonies began, he saw me and ran over to give me a big hug and tell me that he had tried to find me. He said he was so glad to see me. He thanked me for "believing in him" and told me that I was the one teacher who made him believe in himself. We took pictures of us together, and when he walked across the stage to receive his diploma, I had tears in my eyes—I knew all along, he could succeed . . . he just needed someone to "push" him in the right direction and show him that somebody cared!

—Deb Hodges, Intervention Teacher, I. V. Macklin Public School, Grande Prairie Public School District, Alberta, Canada

It is time to pull out our four big improvement drivers: Assessment, Instruction, Leadership, and Ownership. When these four forces synergize on a wide scale, you know that you have made every FACE count. We recommend starting with assessment.

CHAPTER 3

Making It Work in Practice—Assessment Literacy

Assessment has been the Achilles heel of educational reform. In the United States, especially since the 2001 No Child Left Behind legislation imposed standardized tests, the system has diverted practitioners away from school and system improvement as a process of capacity building and corresponding improvement. Instead, in the intervening twenty years, test scores have become the end in themselves—the be all and the end all. It is similarly true of other global jurisdictions such as NAPLAN, the national assessment in Australia.

The main problems with standardized assessments are: The tests and results are detached from the improvement process; new more fundamental goals such as those related to deep learning competencies like Critical Thinking (as in Parameters #3 and #13 and NPDL) are being neglected; and new questions are being raised about the narrowness of academic goals, and the corresponding boredom or lack of commitment on the part of increasing numbers of students. We cannot have standardized tests driving assessment and instruction in schools and classrooms; instead, we need large-scale assessments that give us authentic trends and patterns over time and teacher-developed assessments that inform instruction the very next minute. Authors' Note: We believe our 5 Questions (see Glossary) for students, teachers, and leaders at every level can do this.

On the limitations of standardized tests, our colleague, Andy Hargreaves (2019), has provided a sweeping analysis of the problem of large-scale assessments. Hargreaves makes the case that standardized tests on narrow subject matter has the effect of neglecting certain more basic matters such as deeper learning and well-being. Hargreaves also argues that a focus on *basics* without moving to higher-order thinking can inadvertently or otherwise distort learning. In this chapter we show how using the 14 Parameters can address many of Hargreaves' arguments such as "tests as a diversion" by developing literate graduates who can think critically. Then we show that it is possible to "have your cake and eat it, too," by designing teacher co-developed assessments that can address both the essentials and deeper learning goals. Let's start with an *assessment that informs instruction* example where the lessons are many, and we think highly convincing.

ASSESSMENT LITERACY

Beginning with the end in mind is good assessment practice that makes instruction more timely, relevant, and direction-setting. We model that approach here by beginning with a case study from Australia that demonstrates brilliantly our belief in the centrality of assessment literacy as the heart of system and school improvement—focused on quality teaching in EVERY classroom. You have to start where the student is—and put FACES on the data.

Assessment Case Study

Ballarat Clarendon College (BCC) is an independent regional school in Victoria, Australia, with 110 teachers and 1,200 students from 3 to 18 years old. The school's approach to improvement is progressive. The school leaders, David Shepherd and Jan McClure, appointed two teachers as primary-level mathematics specialists who co-teach (see Chapter 4) and open their classrooms to demonstrate to other staff how to assess in an ongoing way and integrate their data immediately into instruction. The teachers, Lani Sharp and Colin Esdale, share a strong belief

in the importance of developmental learning, so our work focuses on ways to effectively differentiate instruction using assessment data. Hence, we need current, high-quality, clear, unambiguous information on student learning that will allow us to make informed decisions about how to use our time most efficiently at the class, group, and individual levels in order to maximize learning. We know that this, in turn, relies on well-designed, accurate, and objective assessment instruments.

Assessment forms an integral part of the teaching and learning process at both formal and informal levels. By informal (diagnostic and formative assessments), we mean the information that teachers gather during lessons, to adjust the pitch, pace, and direction of current and successive lessons. Formal assessment (summative assessment) refers to information that is collected to provide an objective and detailed picture of what students do or do not understand at a point in time. Both informal and formal assessment practices have been a major focus at BCC, providing the staff with the powerful data their decision-making demands.

As they began their assessment journey, the BCC staff had to overcome three major hurdles:

- How to create assessments required to support many achievement levels and that allowed for several years' worth of student variation to provide a valid representation of each student's understanding

- How to ensure consistency from year to year so that data could be compared by teacher teams and between teacher teams when the program was replicated or became an across-grade program

- How to ensure their data scrutiny was accurate and could provide detailed information on which to base future teaching (assessment items for each level needed to be numerous, fine grained, and easily tracked)

Initial endeavors to solve these problems resulted in "tests" that became increasingly lengthy, as students worked through items either inappropriately easy or difficult, wasting their time and motivation, while Lani and Colin sought more detailed data.

The solution was to significantly expand the number of assessments available for each unit of mathematics to cover all students' developmental paths. Common assessment tasks were developed and organized into sections so that, although the instrument itself was very long, students

(Continued)

(Continued)

would see only instructional levels appropriate to themselves at the moment, not the levels the teacher knew the student could already achieve, or the levels well beyond students' current understanding.

The data from each assessment were recorded on a spreadsheet spanning Level 1 to Level 9, approximately the first seven years of mathematics learning. Figure 3.1 is an excerpt from one such spreadsheet.

The developmental nature of their approach has made pretesting unnecessary, because data are always available to show how previous cohorts of similar students achieved in this unit previously, whether during the last term or last year. What they have found useful is a mid-unit assessment allowing for mid-course adjustments to instruction. This allows them to keep their data current and to check that informal observations (ongoing Diagnostic and Formative Assessments) are accurate as recorded.

The structure of the BCC mathematics co-teaching approach rests heavily on the belief that assessments should be formative—that is, assessment *for* and *as* learning (see Glossary). The purpose of assessment is to guide the student's learning and to inform the teacher's instruction, as we say, "Data today is instruction tomorrow." Going even further, assessment, even at the conclusion of the year is not an endpoint, but rather, for teacher and student, it is evidence of progress made and a map of where and how each can proceed.

A. Guiding Student Learning

At BCC, teachers work hard to develop a focused learning culture in which students are aware of what they know and still need to learn, and they can use this information to take responsibility for their own learning. Lani and Colin realize that students' self-monitoring enables them to become lifelong learners, elements of which are part of the deeper learning concept. Scores on tests are not provided. Instead, students are encouraged to take a deeper look at their assessment and analyze their responses to each question. To facilitate self-monitoring, students highlight their mathematical achievements on *success criteria* cards (see Glossary). These are Success Criteria documents from their *developmental learner profile* (see Glossary) that make explicit what they need to be able to demonstrate to master each level. Students, who are learning developmentally and are given the resources to identify their strengths and weaknesses, become self-competitive and savvy at *self-assessment* (see Glossary), always striving for new personal bests. They have learned at BCC that not only do

Figure 3.1 Putting FACES on Mathematics Data at BCC

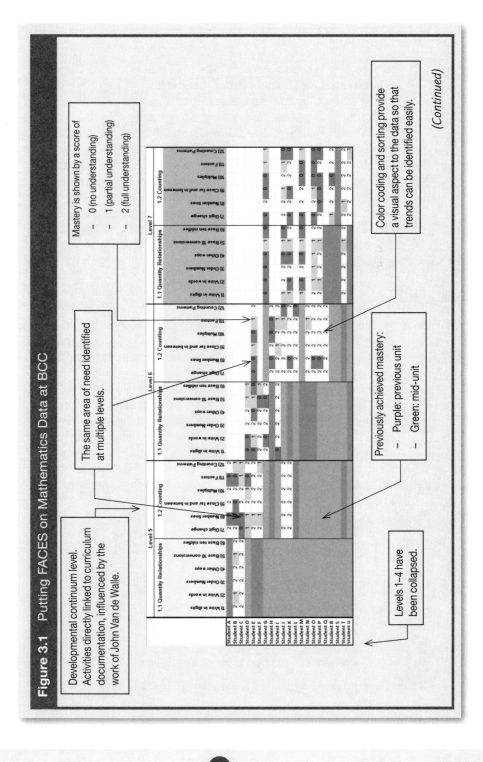

Developmental continuum level.
Activities directly linked to curriculum documentation, influenced by the work of John Van de Walle.

The same area of need identified at multiple levels.

Mastery is shown by a score of
- 0 (no understanding)
- 1 (partial understanding)
- 2 (full understanding)

Color coding and sorting provide a visual aspect to the data so that trends can be identified easily.

Previously achieved mastery:
- Purple: previous unit
- Green: mid-unit

Levels 1–4 have been collapsed.

(Continued)

(Continued)

teachers need to be able to see the individual FACES in the data, but also **it is essential for students to see themselves.**

As students become more aware of their learning needs and can track their progress and as tasks are pitched more accurately using the modeled–shared–guided–independent–application approach, the gradual-release-of-responsibility (GRR) model (see Sharratt & Fullan, 2009, pp. 22–62), behavior management issues are minimized and motivation is heightened. Although it is challenging to plan for and manage multiple tasks with student choice of learning arrangements, from Lani's and Colin's experiences, it is worth the effort because it creates a culture of entrusted responsibility and is based on factual, current, and shared data.

B. Informing Teacher Planning

The Common Assessment Task spreadsheets, shown in Figure 3.1, have become an essential resource always used to plan at the lesson level. Without this critical information, decisions made regarding activity selection, pitch level, lesson structure, or student groupings would be blind guesses.

The data can be used at whole-class, small-group, and individual planning levels. Generally, classes have a data range of three to four continuum levels (minimized because they regroup for instruction within same year-level classes). Knowledge of the group spread or clustering is valuable for defining instructional starting points and identifying general needs and misconceptions that can be addressed in a whole-group situation. Although lessons tend to begin and end with a whole-group session, the structure during a lesson does not follow a formula. The most efficient and effective method of differentiated delivery is dictated by the shape, nature, and spread of the data. Class structures include

- Whole class instruction, with differentiation at the task level for groups or individuals

- Focus group or "pullout group" teaching within the classroom

- Flexible, like-needs groupings (*not* fixed-ability groups)

- Mixed-ability groups

- Open-ended tasks that allow for varying levels of sophistication

- Peer instruction and peer and self-assessment approaches

Choices regarding methods of grouping and delivery, task selection, and task modification are made based on data that show the learning needs of the students, as a group and as individuals.

The effectiveness of this approach is due largely to the fact that their curriculum documentation and assessment tools have been created collaboratively. The mathematics team has developed a common language and understanding that enables team members to align practice and to maximize their ability to move all students' learning forward. Assessment co-construction also provides opportunities for collaborative reflection on the effectiveness of the team's practice. This reflection is a crucial part of ongoing teacher *collaborative inquiry* (Parameter #11; see Glossary and Chapter 4). The journey is by no means complete; however, the mathematics team members believe they are moving ever closer to teaching, learning, and assessing in a developmental way—a true co-planning, co-teaching, co-debriefing, and co-reflecting approach (see Chapter 4).

—Jan McClure, deputy principal, and Lani Sharp and Colin Esdale, co-teachers, Ballarat Clarendon College, Ballarat, Victoria, Australia

It is no surprise that BBC continues to stay the course: precision-in-practice across the year levels, K–12 and has been recognized as the non-governmental Australian Secondary School of the Year in 2019 and 2020. This timeless case study defines in practice what many assessment books and articles have focused on in theory: how to capture the impact that we all believe intentional assessment practices have on student learning. Dylan Wiliam (2011) defines what Lani and Colin are achieving when he writes:

An assessment functions to the extent that evidence about student achievement is elicited, interpreted, and used by teachers, learners, or their peers to make decisions about the next steps in instruction that are likely to be better or better founded, than the decisions they would have made in the absence of that evidence. (p. 43)

The Ontario Ministry of Education (2010a) underscores the importance of Wiliam's stance and the co-teachers' practice at BCC, noting that assessment, evaluation, and reporting practices and procedures must be *fair, transparent,* and *equitable* for **all** students.

What Have We Learned About Assessment Literacy From This Case Study?

First, Assessment Literacy here means one's capacity to determine students' (and student's) level of functioning within the curriculum unit of study using various informal and formal practices. This case study from BCC is a strong example of powerful assessment-literate practice. Lani and Colin, as co-teachers, care passionately about improving the learning for all their students; they begin and end their work every day by putting FACES on the data during their sacred collaborative conferencing time. They are Assessment Literate. We've used what we have learned from this case study as an advanced organizer for the assessment discussion that follows.

Through this case study, we have learned to

1. Begin by knowing the learners

2. Co-plan using student diagnostic data

3. Make Learning Intentions (from the curriculum expectations) and Success Criteria visible

4. Use continuous informal assessment during teaching

5. Deliver ongoing formative assessment and reflect on midcourse corrections through appropriately leveled formal assessment

6. Provide students with oral and written descriptive feedback

7. Create opportunities for peer- and self-assessment

8. Ensure that summative assessment informs next steps for students and parents

9. Use the Data Wall process to see the big picture and the detail—the FACES—so that teachers self-assess and reflect on their teaching. Data Walls as **Prevention** must proceed to Case Management Meetings as **Intervention**. When combined, Data Walls and Case Management Meetings create the Case Management Approach (Parameter #6).

10. Share learning with whole-school Collaborative Assessment of Student Work (CASW)

In the sections that follow, we elaborate on each of these ten components of high-impact assessment practice.

1. Knowing the Learner

Donald Graves asked audiences to draw three columns on a piece of paper. In the first column, they were to record the names of all the students in their classes. Graves scolded them for forgetting even one name and said that the one (or more) they forgot were not being acknowledged as humans, and he asked audiences to consider what that lack of acknowledgment might do to their students' self-esteem. In the middle column, they were to write ten things that they knew about each student in their class; he said that if they couldn't do this, they were failing their students. Finally, in the last column, they were to put a check mark beside the name of each student who knew that the teachers knew those ten things about them. His point was that if the teachers could not perform these tasks, they should get busy knowing their learners inside and beyond the walls of the classroom. No one in those audiences could forget the impact of those exercise questions—even after many years. In our terms now, Graves was asking then if the teachers knew the whole child to put a FACE to the learning data—could they humanize them fully and be reminded by doing so that they were talking about real kids with real hopes and dreams.

Good teachers spend time getting to know their learners—academically and social-emotionally. According to Cornelius-White (2007),

> [T]he power of positive teacher-student relationships is critical for learning to occur. This relationship involves showing students that the teacher cares for their learning as students, can see their perspective, and communicate it back to them so they have valuable feedback to self-assess, feel safe, and learn to understand others and the content with the same interest and concern. (p. 123).

In the BCC case study, the teachers and leaders modeled for us that they knew their students well—what they could do, what they couldn't do, and what they would be able to do with their continuing explicit instruction. They developed a developmental learner profile for each student, including the student's individual data, samples of current student work, their completed Success Criteria cards, and their anecdotal notes and written observations. They also developed an at-a-glance class profile that they brought to each of their daily planning meetings.

2. Co-Plan Using Student Diagnostic Data

When starting a new year with a new class or launching a new major topic, a teacher can review previous assessments and carry out any *diagnostic assessments* (see Glossary) needed to further clarify what students already know, to determine instructional starting points if uncertain, and to group students with like needs. Simply, the concept is to avoid having students sitting through classes where the instruction is about what they already know. How often does that happen? As Dufour and Marzano (2011) point out,

> The longstanding practice in American education has been for individual teachers to use assessment to provide a student with the opportunity to demonstrate his or her learning at the appointed time. The standard pattern has been, 'Teach, test, *hope for the best*, assign a grade and move on to the next unit.' Assessment has been used as a tool for sorting students into 'our A Students, our B students,' and so on. (p. 139)

Teachers at BCC know that *hope is not a strategy* when assessing students' understanding. They discuss that their assessments are ongoing and continue to be developmental and formative, doing away with the need to test what they already know about their students, which is a waste of instructional time. This is precision-in-practice instruction when co-planning moves to co-teaching, co-debriefing, and co-reflecting. A deeper discussion of the power of the co-planning, co-teaching, co-debriefing, and co-reflecting model is found in Chapter 4.

3. Make Learning Intentions and Success Criteria Visible

If *Learning Intentions* (LI) (see Glossary) deconstructed from state standards or curriculum expectations of what is to be taught, and teacher and student co-constructed Success Criteria (SC) are clear, visible in classrooms, and easily understood by students, students are more likely to be successful and hence engaged more readily. Success breeds success. When teachers incorporate evidence-proven teaching practices, such as visible LI and co-constructed SC, all students' achievement will improve. Thus, teachers are able to enjoy their professional practice more as specificity breeds success for teachers, too—that is, teacher and student engagement that moves to empowerment or ownership of learning.

For example, here is an LI from the Ontario Language Arts Curriculum (Ontario Ministry of Education, 2010b). The WHY has been added as students need to know the relevance of their learning:

[A]ll students will be able to develop questions and answers that reflect higher order thinking skills so that they become critical consumers of information. (See Appendix F.)

During their learning together about Higher Order Thinking Skills, teachers and students at Waterloo, Ontario's Park Manor Senior Public School (see discussion of Data Walls, later in this chapter) co-constructed and displayed the following *anchor charts* (see Glossary) in their classroom. These anchor charts help students be clear about the content, task, and the expectations to complete it. This reflects moving from state standards or curriculum expectations to transparency for students in what they will learn and what they need to be able to do to be successful. An important addition to the 5 Key Questions (Figure 3.6) that we have made is: Why are we learning this? This added question ensures that teachers and students make real-world connections to their units of study.

Figure 3.2 shows three sample anchor charts that detail what students are expected to know and to do in using "thick" answers in their work—that is, higher order answers that demonstrate the use of Critical Thinking skills and *big ideas* (see Glossary). The anchor charts support students at work; students and teachers review and revise them often. The most impactful anchor charts are those that are co-constructed with students and visible in classrooms to scaffold students' learning. This is about creating The Third Teacher—school and classroom walls that scaffold students' learning.

Prior to writing *FACES*, we moved away from developing rubrics (using scales ranging, for example, from "unacceptable" to "outstanding") to focusing on co-constructed SC in all classrooms. This shift occurred to us when one of us (Sharratt), who teaches, discovered that students said that they only wanted to know how to achieve outstanding work—and "What did that work look like?" We were determined then to be very clear about what SC looked like by providing anonymous strong and weak examples of real students' work and co-constructing the resulting SC. Students told us then and continue to tell us that this is the specificity they need to excel, to think through their own work toward a "personal best."

Feldman (2018) sums up our findings about the importance of specific SC to give students' accurate Descriptive Feedback (DF) and fair Summative Assessments. He explains that every teacher has his/her own beliefs and practices about assessment that ultimately influence teachers' pedagogical practice and grading system, making students' grades reflective of the teacher's grading expectations rather than on the student's academic performance. Due to this, there is an issue with variability in grading causing inequitable and biased grading practices that affect students' motivation and success. For us, this solidifies our case for assessments based on co-constructed, visible, transparent SC that every student understands! All assessment criteria are captured in the co-developed SC—there are **no** hidden assessment items. There should be **no** surprises if teachers and students are assessment-capable.

Figure 3.2 Sample Classroom Anchor Charts for "Thick" Thinking

"Thick" Answers Use G.W.A.

Givens

- What I know

Working it out

- Show attempted solutions (try different strategies)
- Use symbols, numbers, words, pictures, tables

Answer

- Explanation of solution
- Written summary

Students and teachers then co-developed success criteria for thick questions and thick answers, shown below. These anchor charts were displayed in the classroom for students' easy reference while completing their work.

SUCCESS CRITERIA for THICK QUESTIONS

Students can

- Have more than one answer
- Invite different opinions
- Encourage rich discussion (higher-order thinking)
- Encourage speculation, prediction, connection, and inference about an issue or idea

SUCCESS CRITERIA for THICK ANSWERS

Students can answer

- Using interesting, attention-grabbing, thought-provoking ideas
- Beginning with a clear statement
- Organizing in a clear, concise way
- Using evidence (proof) from the text, self, or world
- Restating opinion using similar words at the end of answer

Deconstructing LIs and co-constructing SC are only the beginning steps of the assessment literacy journey as Figure 3.3 shows. All other aspects of the Assessment Waterfall Chart in Figure 3.3—Descriptive Feedback, Peer- and Self-Assessment, and Individual Goal-Setting—depend on getting the SC right because these constructs must always refer back to the SC.

4. Use Continuous Informal Formative Assessment *During* Teaching

Throughout the teaching-learning cycle (see Appendix D), teachers use formative assessment—currently well-known in the research literature as assessment *for* and *as* learning. Formative assessment enables the teacher to position learners for individual attention or for group strategies within the content and concepts being taught. BCC teachers informally reflected on the level of pitch, pace, and

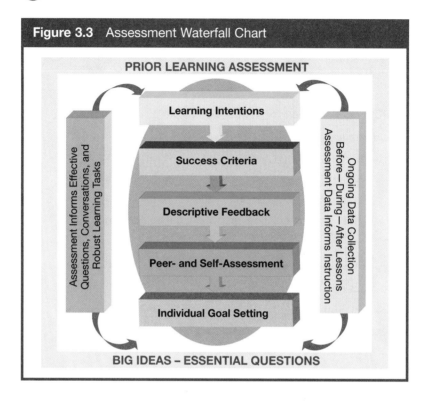

Figure 3.3 Assessment Waterfall Chart

PRIOR LEARNING ASSESSMENT

Learning Intentions

Success Criteria

Descriptive Feedback

Peer- and Self-Assessment

Individual Goal Setting

Assessment Informs Effective Questions, Conversations, and Robust Learning Tasks

Ongoing Data Collection Before—During—After Lessons Assessment Data Informs Instruction

BIG IDEAS – ESSENTIAL QUESTIONS

direction of the lesson *throughout* their teaching and referred to this as the informal, diagnostic assessment they did on an ongoing basis—keeping the FACES of their student foremost in their minds. To simplify, we think of Diagnostic Assessment as occurring **before** the unit begins (Prior Learning Assessment), Formative Assessment as occurring **during** teaching, and Summative Assessment as occurring **after** the unit of study is completed. Whatever it is called, we say that *assessment in real time is necessary* to know how the lesson is going. Real time assessment enables the teacher to determine how it's going and to decide to abandon the original lesson plan if it is not working in favor of a more relevant approach. The phrase "one size does not fit all" could never be more apt or important; assessment literate teachers know what to look for in the students' FACES because they are the immediate gauges of learning in getting them to a conceptual understanding of what is being taught. With practice, assessing the impact of a lesson by listening, asking clarifying questions, and observing classroom activity feed into teachers' judgment, which becomes action. In short, teachers must be flexible and adaptable to changing direction and revising approaches if students are not getting it.

5. Deliver Ongoing Formative Assessment During Teaching and Reflect on Formative Assessments as Part of Midcourse Corrections

We intentionally embed assessment into our description of best teaching practice. Since writing *Putting FACES on the Data* in 2012, we have become even more explicit by weaving together each component of Assessment Literacy as demonstrated in the Assessment Waterfall Chart as shown in Figure 3.3.

For us, deliberate assessment that informs differentiated instruction looks like leaders and teachers who:

- Understand that pieces of student work are data *so that* they use student work as evidence to move each student forward
- Develop ongoing formative assessments collaboratively *so that* these assessments are used daily in classrooms to inform instruction
- Develop a repertoire of assessment and instructional strategies *so that* they can access them immediately, matching strategies to students' needs identified by the formative data
- Develop a common language *so that* teachers and students use the same appropriate language and are assessment-capable
- Develop a deep understanding of curriculum expectations, develop student-friendly LI, post them in the classroom for all to see and discuss, and then co-construct SC with the students *so that* students develop an understanding of what is expected of them and how they will achieve success—no secrets!
- Develop an understanding of curriculum standards and how to construct rich, robust tasks based on them *so that* students receive meaningful, timely Descriptive Feedback (DF) (see next section) and can articulate clearly what they need to do to improve
- Develop and effectively use common forms of assessments to collaboratively assess student work (see Lesson 10 in this chapter) to reach consensus on quality student work *so that* there is an opportunity to change classroom practice needed

to ensure consistency of practice across the same grade levels within and across schools, as well as to assist in determining common forms of DF to the students

QR Code 3.1:
Guided and
Interdependent
Assessment
Literacy
Indicators

- Encourage students to self-assess and to set their own learning goals from explicit DF received *so that* students' voices are heard in classrooms as they begin to own their successes as well as own their unique personal needs and improvement strategies by being able to answer the 5 Questions (Figure 3.6).

- Using the GRR model, these are guided assessment practices that lead to teachers' and students' interdependent practices and ownership or application of impactful teaching and learning. See QR Code 3.1 for explicit guided and interdependent indicators that detail Assessment Literacy practices. QR Code 3.2 contains the original Grande Prairie Case Study.

QR Code 3.2:
Grande Prairie
Case Study

Deliberate Pause

- How am I impacting the learning for all students and teachers?
- How do I know?
- Do I start with knowledge of the learners?
- How do I select what is to be taught?
- How do I make the LIs easily understood for all students?
- Do teachers co-construct SC with the students? Evidence?
- Are all students and teachers improving?
- How do I know my students' work is at the same high level as that of other teachers of the same grades in my school(s)
- If not, why not?
- Do I give DF that is factual (against the SC), and do I give examples of how to improve?
- Where can I go for help?

6. Provide Students With Descriptive Feedback

At Armadale Public School (see final Case Study in this chapter), teachers' Professional Learning (PL) was focused on giving clear DF against the SC. Figure 3.4 shows their staffroom "learning board,"

Figure 3.4 Armadale Public School Staffroom Learning Bulletin Board

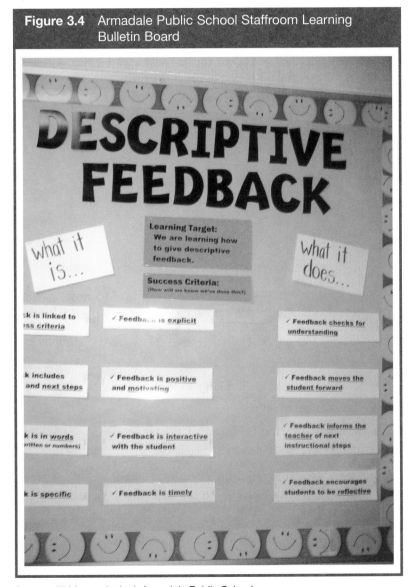

Source: Jill Maar, principal, Armadale Public School.

which is focused on what they have discovered about the critical importance of giving students and each other Descriptive Feedback, as well as bravely and routinely asking students for feedback on their teaching.

Beyond the positive value of very clear LI, classroom anchor charts, and SC, we know that students' understanding is furthered when they engage in *accountable talk* (see Glossary) in K–12 classrooms. This often occurs when they give or receive DF—a critical component of formative assessment. Teachers and students can learn to give specific DF against the SC that initiates the next level of learning. Descriptive Feedback provides students with practical, direct, and useful insights that outline how they can use the SC to achieve the intended LI. Such feedback comes from the classroom teacher or a student peer (once the SC are co-constructed), and it has an impact when it

- Focuses on the intended LI and the SC

- Is timely

- Identifies specific strengths

- Points to areas needing improvement and gives examples

- Suggests a pathway that students can take to close the gap between where they are now and where they need to be

- Chunks the amount of corrective feedback the student can handle at one time

- Models the kind of thinking in which students will engage when they self-assess

- Allows teachers to take immediate action in their daily effort to improve student work

- Offers students information about their work, product, or performance relative to simply stated LI and co-constructed SC

- Avoids marks, grades, or comments that judge the level of achievement

Deliberate Pause

Do students

- Engage in peer- and self-assessment giving accurate DF against the SC?

- Set their own individual learning goals and monitor progress toward achieving them?

- Seek clarification or assistance when needed? Know where to go for help, beyond the teacher?

- Assess and reflect critically on their own strengths, needs, and interests?

- Identify learning opportunities, choices, and strategies to meet personal needs and set and achieve goals?

- Persevere and make an effort when responding to challenges?

Descriptive Feedback can be oral, written, demonstrative, or collective (Sharratt, 2019). Most importantly, DF must be tracked by teachers so that they know what students are working on. Once students show that they can apply a skill (from their DF), teachers must have tracked the feedback well enough so that they do not accept any further work in which that skill is lacking. Tracking the DF is a critical part of the teaching-learning cycle (see Appendix D).

Explicit DF with examples is the key element in assessment that improves instruction and is best used by students when they articulate what next steps they will take to improve their learning prior to a summative point in their learning. Formative DF is only impactful when it precedes Summative Assessment.

To reinforce what is expected, teachers at Armadale Public School also post strong and weak anonymous student work samples so that students are surrounded with specific visual support for their learning. Figure 3.5 is an excellent example of a teacher's explicit teaching—showing the LI, co-constructed SC, a strong example of a retell (co-constructed by students and teacher), and a yes/no classroom anchor chart constructed cooperatively to further reinforce what the teacher is looking for (and not looking for) in students' work.

Figure 3.5 Sample Learning Intention, Success Criteria, and Anchor Charts at Armadale Public School

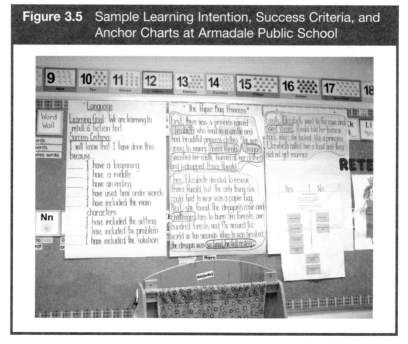

Source: Jill Maar, principal, Armadale Public School.

7. Create Opportunities for Peer- and Self-Assessments

Recall now a key point from the BCC case study "not only do teachers need to be able to see the individual FACES in the data, but also it is essential for students to see themselves." The ability to peer- and self-assess is the ultimate goal in teaching. Teachers must ask, "Can the student apply what has been learned to new situations?" This capability is developed only when teachers use the GRR model in instruction and students reread their work on their own volition to improve or when they use the teacher's DF to self-assess and improve their work, thereby becoming self-regulating learners—taking ownership of their learning, applying it to the next situation. When formal, summative evaluation takes place (discussed in the next lesson), students are part of the process, there are no surprises because they have been involved in ongoing discussions of how they have done. Peers can influence learning by helping, tutoring, providing friendship (that builds confidence in making changes), giving feedback, and making class and school a place students want to come to each day (Wilkinson et al., 2002, p. 61, as cited in Hattie, 2012). Self-directed and peer-directed learning (albeit facilitated by the teacher) is pedagogy at its powerful best. Dufour and Marzano (2011, p. 131) concur, suggesting that student-generated assessments are probably the most powerful and revolutionary form of assessments made available by performance scales. Here students approach the teacher and propose what they will do to demonstrate they have achieved a particular status on a proficiency scale. As Greenan (2011a) writes,

> By recognizing the relationship between understanding the curriculum expectations [state standards]; communicating what is expected to students; constructing Success Criteria with students (in language that they understand) and connecting it to their work; creating relevant and rich tasks; and using student-based assessment in the classroom that allows all student work to be honored and viable learning targets to be established by peers and self, all students will forge successfully into the next Century. (p. 13)

A "test" of how we are doing is whether students in every classroom can answer the five questions shown in Figure 3.6. We ask students these questions when we purposefully engage in Learning Walks and Talks in classrooms (see Chapter 5). They serve as evidence of students' deep conceptual understanding (or not) and ownership of their learning and next steps.

Figure 3.6 5 Key Questions for Students

1. What are you learning? WHY?
2. How are you doing?
3. How do you know?
4. How can you improve?
5. Where do you go for help?

The answers are revealing. When students can answer the 5 Questions confidently and accurately, then we know that self-assessment has taken place—because teachers have been explicit in making their expectations for successful learning transparent to their students. Hattie (2012) agrees with our laser-like focus, saying,

"If the learning intentions and success criteria are transparent, then there is a higher likelihood that students will become engaged in reducing the gap between where they started and where we would like them to finish." Hattie and Timperley (2007) both agree that

[W]hen students have the metacognitive skills of self-assessment, they can evaluate their levels of understanding, their effort and strategies used on tasks, their attributions and opinions of others about their performance, and their improvement in relation to their goals and expectations. They can also assess their performance relative to others' goals and the global aspects of their performance. As students become more experienced at self-assessment, multiple dimensions of performance can be assessed. (p. 94)

Most important, students know how and when to seek and receive feedback from others. The following story illustrates how one teacher has captured the essence of peer-assessment at the high school level.

Narrative From the Field

This short story is about "students helping students achieve," or an individualized approach to progress monitoring through peer mentoring. Year 3 secondary school students have weekly meetings with trained Year 6 secondary students to discuss their progress in school. After each meeting, next steps are agreed upon by both parties involved—and these are reviewed at the beginning of next week's meeting. The focused discussions form an artifact of progress and cover a wide range of areas (subject specific or not) as determined by the Year 3 secondary student. A teacher gets an overview of the meetings and can offer suggestions, but the agenda is always student-driven. The meetings offer a chance to look at particular subject problems or more general issues. They provide a chance to celebrate success and for each student to "be heard." The careful planning and arranging is well worth the effort as both Year 3 and Year 6 students are becoming more confident learners and very articulate problem-solvers.

—Gordon Livingstone, pupil support teacher, Renfrew High School, Renfrewshire Council, Scotland

8. Ensure That Summative Assessment Informs Next Steps for Students and Parents

Hattie (2012) distinguishes between formative and summative assessments by referring to the time at which a "test" is administered and, more important, by the nature of the interpretations made from the test. If the interpretations from the test are used to modify instruction while it is ongoing, then the assessment is formative. If the interpretations are used to sum up the learning at the end of the teaching, then it is summative. Thus, summative evaluation (what have students learned?)—a judgment made regarding how well a student has learned the materials, concepts, and content—concludes the teaching-learning cycle (see Appendix D). Clearly, too, at this point, teachers such as Lani and Colin at BCC reflect on the outcomes for the class and for individual students, adapting new insights into teacher planning for the next time a concept is taught or for the next topic with the student and the class. Thus, the summative assessment becomes diagnostic assessment for the next unit of work. Steve Stake (cited in Hattie, 2012) uses an apt analogy: "[W]hen the cook tastes the soup it is formative and when the guests taste the soup it is summative." We add that when the cook scraps the soup recipe (or modifies it), the summative assessment has become diagnostic. Whereas summative assessment has traditionally been an examination, it now often includes creative opportunities to demonstrate student learning, such as a skit, a poem, a learning fair or symposia presentation, a congress, and many other processes through which students can select to showcase their learning.

A summative assessment opportunity that significantly increases student and family ownership of the learning is the student-led conference, during which parents can play an important role in student's learning. Student-led conferencing (Millar-Grant et al., 1995) is a summative assessment process that validates the important role that families play in putting FACES on the data. When children present a significant piece of work and take control of a planned meeting to report on what they have learned and to review their progress during the term, magic happens!

Students are in charge of the meeting offering to parents and/or caregivers the students' own assessment of their learning. Self-reflection is the key to the success of student-led conferencing. It begins to occur when students select pieces of work to be presented, continues with rehearsing for the meeting with their parents, and ends with students conducting the presentations or meetings. Teachers are in the background as guides, when needed. When students can clearly articulate their own learning (a culminating event, but also a goal in any classroom), they have taken ownership of their learning.

The benefits of student-led conferencing are many:

- Leadership is evident.

- Confidence is strengthened.

- Students' voices are heard.

- Parents discuss student work and better understand expectations and student performance.

- Students' communication and thinking skills are increased.

- Parents are partners—as is evidenced in the stories below.

The following two snippets illustrate the power of students directing their own learning as they interact with their parents:

Student-led conferencing provides parents with an opportunity to become active participants in their child's education. Parents have an opportunity to see what their child has accomplished and what they want to achieve. Parents are involved in reviewing the work with their child, and through their comments, suggestions, and classroom visits, they are able to promote their child's learning. Portfolios offer tangible evidence of a student's work and, as such, provide an excellent basis for discussing student achievement during conferences. Parents are prompted to make encouraging comments, help their child set realistic goals, and make a plan to reach those goals.

—Shannon McDougald, principal,
St. Peter Catholic School, Cornwall, Canada

We believe that students will achieve more consistently when students, parents, and teachers set specific and individual learning targets together and focus harmoniously on meeting them. Parents and their children discussed and celebrated samples of their work in their "browsing boxes" and then set goals for the next term. Teachers were encouraged and at times surprised at how engaged and focused parents were while working with their children. Every teacher can confidently say that the student-led conference evening was an overwhelming success and paved the way for future learning on the part of both the student and the parent.

—Donna Nielsen, principal, Immaculate Conception
Catholic School, Cornwall, Canada

These are clear examples of how parents are critical learning partners (Parameter #12) through conversation with students and often much needed powerful influencers in the teaching-learning cycle (see Appendix D).

9. Create Data Walls and Case Management Meetings for Teachers' Self-Assessment and Reflection to See the "Big Picture" and the FACES!

The Case Management Approach, Parameter #6, is two-pronged: Data Walls and Case Management Meetings.

1. Data Walls

Data Walls are visual representations of some or many aspects of all students' progress. Sometimes referred to as *questioning walls* or *wondering walls*, they provide a forum for rich conversation among teachers so that every FACE is known. In that way they are a **prevention** tool. Finding a **confidential, private** place to display the data is as important as finding time to stand and discuss those FACES on the Data Wall. The process of finding a common assessment tool on which to evaluate and level students' work is a high-impact first step (see the discussion of collaborative assessment of student work in the next lesson). Once a common assessment task is agreed on and the levels of achievement determined, the next step is to place those FACES on sticky notes or tags to be reused as the students progress through the grade levels. Each student's name, photo, and assessment level are placed on the Data Wall in the order decided on by all staff. When students are leveled on the wall—as being below, within, or beyond their grade level—teachers can see who is lagging, who is stuck, who is succeeding, or who needs extending. Teachers discuss with each other what is needed to move all—each and every student—forward. Assessment drives instruction. The focused conversation becomes how can *we* move all our students forward? How can *we* extend the thinking of these high-achieving students? Once all students are placed in their levels on the Data Wall, and the overlaps of plummeting, staying still, and soaring students are noted, teachers stop saying '*I*' because it becomes a '*we*' challenge— teachers own all the FACES, even those they do not teach. When we have done this in our own work globally, leaders have noted that a sharing of ideas, strategies, and concepts starts almost immediately when they stand together with their teachers in front of the completed Data Wall. Every staff meeting, PL session and Learning Walk and Talk starts at the Data Wall. Leaders and teachers together make emotional connections to each FACE and also capture cognitive insights about each and every student regarding what instructional actions to take.

Figure 3.7 is an example of a Data Wall that puts student FACES on the wall. The Data Wall, at Park Manor Senior Public School in Waterloo, Canada, has all 280 students from Grades 6–8 on it, including the nine students in the special needs class. Blue sticky notes identify boys and pink notes identify girls. The school staff members are concerned about performance differences between girls and boys, and they want to be able to monitor the variance in an obvious manner. Each student's sticky note also carries a photograph (see an example in Figure 3.8).

But this Data Wall carries a lot of decision-making information. The principal, James Bond, writes about the key points that help his staff individualize their support for all students:

> Our Data Wall is in a confidential location we call the Staff Learning Center. It's a small room that we set up in order to come together to discuss issues like how to increase all students' achievement. Our learning goal for this year, arising from our data and connected to the Ontario Curriculum expectations, has been to improve the written communication for all students, paying particular attention to boys.

Figure 3.7 A Data Wall That Does More Than Just Put the FACES on the Data

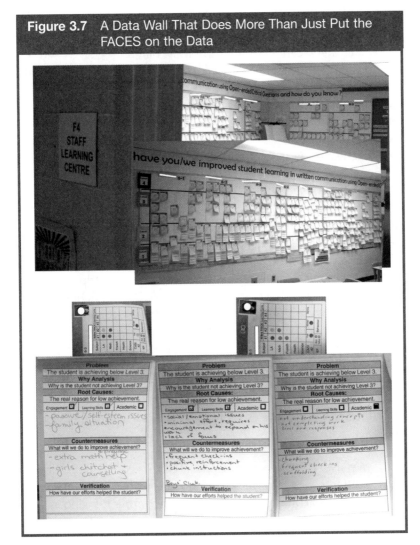

Source: James Bond, principal, Park Manor PS.

Bond writes, "For our teachers, the Success Criteria have been the teaching tool to make their expectations explicit. This year we are focusing on open-ended Critical Thinking questions, which we called 'thick' questions—most of my teachers are teaching at least four Thick Learning Cycles (TLCs)—each based on fewer than three clustered curriculum expectations. Once the teachers have completed their TLC, they place colored dots, based on their common assessment of thick questions and answers, on each student's sticky. Teachers can choose from four different colors—red for Level 1 (well below standard), yellow for Level 2 (below standard), blue for Level 3 (at standard), and green for Level 4 (above standard), corresponding to EQAO expectations [see Figure 3.8]. Therefore, a student could have 'dots' for math, language arts, science, French, and health, each taught by a different teacher. We do this to help teachers understand how well students are achieving across all subject areas.

"Based on a student's lowest, most recent 'thick' achievement, he or she is placed at the appropriate level on the Data Wall. This allows teachers to focus on the specific subject area in which a student struggled. If a student is achieving below Level 3, teachers complete a yellow sticky to determine the 'root causes' and develop 'countermeasures' [intervention strategies]. The pink strips along the bottom of the Data Wall are support for teachers [anchor charts], reminding them of the high-impact instructional strategies they are working on to get higher-order responses from students."

Figure 3.8 shows in close-up detail how a student has done in each subject area when the expectation for all students is that they can create open-ended questions and answers that demand higher-order thinking.

Principal Bond wrote the following explanation of this work to his staff:

- We use Thick Learning Cycle (TLC) scores to help identify students who are not achieving the expected Level 3 with respect to communicating their higher-order thinking in writing, to clarify why they aren't achieving, and to provide a focus for our discussions to help them get there. The TLC scores on the wall will track our progress toward our school's SMART (specific, measurable, attainable, results-oriented, time-bound) goals in our School Improvement Plan.

- I will help you post your dots, but I need you to use your collaboration periods to get all the current information on your students, so we can then place the FACES in the correct level.

- Once you place a dot, move the student's sticky to the appropriate level. There should be some interesting discussions when the level isn't clear, and I'm looking forward to it.

- Once we have identified who is achieving at Levels 1 and 2 (below standard), as in Figure 3.9, we can then add the yellow problem-solving sticky notes (Figure 3.10). These sticky notes should be the springboard for all our discussions during our collaboration time, staff meetings, and teacher release days.

Figure 3.8 Close-Up of a Blue Data Wall Sticky for a Boy

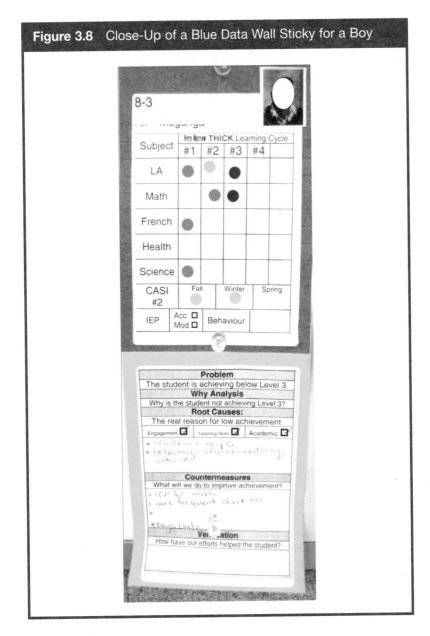

Figure 3.9 Example of Dots on Data Wall to "See" All Students' Achievement

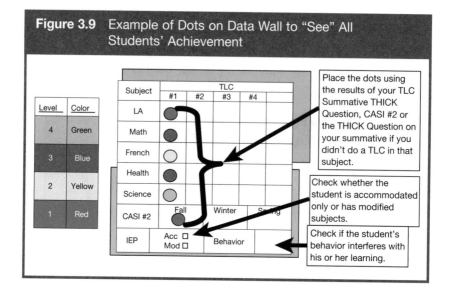

Principal Bond surveyed his staff regarding the value-added learning from developing the data wall and their comments follow:

- We were able to see student growth with respect to open-ended critical thinking (thick) responses over the year.

- It was very clear to see the FACES of who was struggling and whom to focus on.

- We were able to see the subjects in which students were successful and the subjects in which the same students struggled—which posed lots of questions for us.

- The yellow stickies highlighted initial variances in assessment practices between teachers and led to greater collaboration.

- Co-constructed Success Criteria offered subsequently greater consistency in assessing higher-order responses.

- The use of the stickies led to a student survey and a focus on more caring connections for specific students with certain teachers—resulting in teachers making emotional connections to and gaining cognitive insights about all students.

- The yellow stickies allowed us to narrow our focus and to pin-point the root causes of poor student achievement—and to take action immediately.

- By adding **Caring Connections** (shown in Figure 3.11) to each student's tag, teachers had to reflect on and sign their initials to indicate they had reached out to support a student. They developed Success Criteria about what a **Caring Connection** looked like and considered if they had personalized their work with students, by making a *well-being connection* with them. Then teachers and leaders were able to see at-a-glance which teachers had reached out to which students to make **Caring Connections** beyond their academic focus, and where students had no one. This action brought to light which students needed more support and personalization from teachers. Sharratt suggested that teachers and leaders might want to add their names, not just Xs, for the next iteration of the **Caring Connections** on their Data Wall.

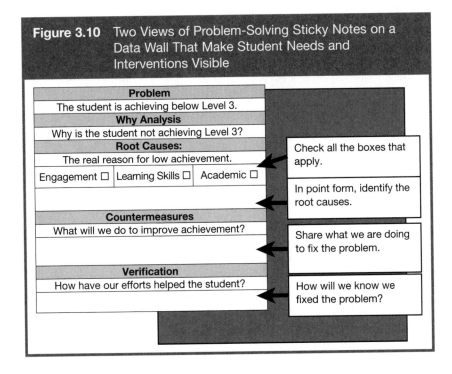

Figure 3.10 Two Views of Problem-Solving Sticky Notes on a Data Wall That Make Student Needs and Interventions Visible

Figure 3.11 Caring Connections on the Data Wall

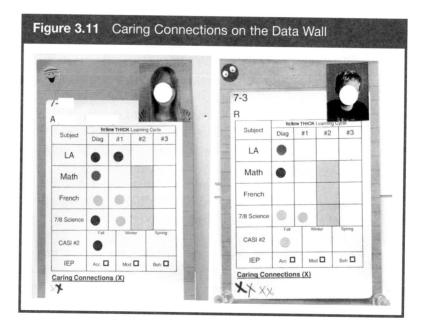

Principal Bond concluded that the Data Wall enabled teachers to see their efficacy with respect to students using open-ended, higher-order, critical thinking questions and answers. The Data Wall was visible to all teachers (**not** to students, parents, or community), so it made teachers aware and accountable to each other for the success of all students. By analyzing the root causes of poor achievement, Bond and his staff were able to narrow their focus to the key areas for effective countermeasures, or instructional interventions, and then to verify all students' improvement through the data. Data Wall discussions lead to identifying students who needed to come to Case Management Meetings—the other prong of Parameter #6.

2. Case Management Meetings

Putting FACES on the Data is not complete unless the Data Wall (assessment as **Prevention**) discussions lead to Case Management Meetings as discussed in Chapter 4. The Case Management Meeting is a forum for intervention in which we build the capacity of all teachers to be able to teach all students (instruction as **Intervention**).

Manor Park School's approach as described by James Bond is an outstanding example of the use of Data Walls as **prevention** followed by Case Management Meetings as **intervention** showing how all students' performance were on view and highlighting the interventions needed and acted on. The Data Wall helped Bond and his teachers determine which students they needed to bring forward for Case Management Meetings (see Chapter 4) to evaluate the best instructional strategies for those students—and for whom they individually had no answers for improvement. Engagement abounded—all teachers were engaged in these worthwhile growth-promoting processes: making students' growth and achievement visible by putting FACES on the data and supporting other teachers in seeing where alternative instructional strategies were needed. We think that this Data Wall and Case Management approach is alive—with precision-in-practice and endless possibilities!

10. Use Collaborative Assessment of Student Work as Critical Data

For BCC teachers, student work is housed in developmental learner and class profiles, which are brought to all planning and improvement team meetings—since evidence of student work as data must be at the forefront of all meetings at the school. For example, weekly after-school meetings, by division or department, may focus on growth and achievement of individual students by using common assessment tools and exemplars so that same-grade or same-course teachers can reach common understandings of the expected standards of students' work. This collaborative scrutiny of anonymous students' work samples, by leaders and teachers, promotes consistency and reflection on practice, ideally across classes within schools and across schools in a district. This will ultimately eliminate pedagogical variation between classrooms, which is a very real problem for so many parents. The goal with Collaborative Assessment of Student Work (CASW) is the whole-school implementation of consistent, high-quality assessment and instructional practices.

Reeves (2011, p. 116) cites Gerald Bracey (2005), Mike Schmoker (2005, 2006), William Sanders (1998), and Linda Darling-Hammond and Gary Sykes (1999), confirming our observation that the most significant variation is often not between one school system and another or even from one school to another, but *rather between one classroom and another.* Meetings in which teachers come together to develop a common assessment, discuss exemplars, and give feedback to the teacher and students provide places where teachers can learn and share new assessment and instructional approaches and, importantly, where they can develop a common, consistent language of practice. Collaborative Assessment of Student Work is a powerful process. Reeves (2011, p. 51) concurs that perhaps one of the best and most practical ways to improve accuracy is the collaborative discussion of student work. This is also a superb PL experience, allowing teachers to improve the quality, consistency, and timeliness of their feedback to students. Sometimes collaborative assessing occurs informally (e.g., when a teacher asks a colleague for help: "I'm on the fence about this particular project, how would you evaluate it?"). In more formalized CASW (*not teacher moderation, which is designed to assign a grade or mark*) teachers and leaders come together at a regularly scheduled time, set out operating norms and protocols for the process (Sharratt, 2019) to examine common work samples from *anonymous* students and, by sharing understandings of the LI and SC, to reach consensus about the levels the students have achieved, why a certain level is appropriate, and what are the next steps for this teacher and student. CASW is even more powerful when the reflections on the student work include these two questions:

1. What information does this work sample give us, as teachers, regarding changing our instructional practice?

2. What feedback will this teacher give this student?

As Harlen (2006) concludes:

Using the terms "formative assessment" and "summative assessment" can give the impression that these are different kinds of assessment or are linked to different methods of gathering evidence. This is not the case; *what matters is how the information is used [Interpretation is key!].* It is for this reason that the terms "assessment for learning" and "assessment of learning" are sometimes preferred. The essential distinction is that assessment "for" and "as" learning is used in making decisions that affect teaching and learning in the short term and future, whereas assessment of learning is used to record and report what has been learned in the past. (p. 104; emphasis added)

A quote from the Ontario Ministry of Education (2010a) *Growing Success* document, puts our urgent work in perspective: "Fairness in assessment and evaluation is grounded in the belief that all students should be able to demonstrate their learning regardless of their socio-economic status, ethnicity, gender, geographic location, learning style, and/or need for special services" (p. 34, citing Volante). This is an equity issue for us. Our FACES work is about ALL students, ALL teachers, ALL community members—and we really mean ALL!

As Reeves (2011, p. 28) says, the best coaches give direction in a way that will influence the action at precisely the right time. As well as being change agents, we believe that teachers and leaders are coaches who act as *Knowledgeable Others* for each other on the field and in the classroom (Sharratt et al., 2010).

As referenced in Figure 3.6, the 5 Questions for students are directly aligned to the 10 Assessments Lessons drawn from the BCC Case Study, and each question links to a construct in the Assessment Waterfall Chart (Figure 3.3). When asking the 5 Questions of students, we are determining how well students understand the intent of their units of study, how to be successful, how to improve, and where they can access help. It should be noted that although these questions are for students, they clearly can be used by teachers and leaders to measure their own precision-in-practice and evaluate their impact. The following chart, Figure 3.12, describes how these 5 Questions relate to assessment literacy to support teacher and leader self-assessment.

When leaders are reflective, focused and provide PL time to examine ALL students' learning, teachers and leaders together can produce amazing results, as is evidenced by the impact seen in the Armadale Case Study that follows.

Figure 3.12 Linking the 5 Questions for Students to the Assessment Waterfall Chart (Figure 3.3)

5 Questions for Students	Teachers Do . . .	Students Say . . .	Leaders Observe . . .
1. What are you learning? **WHY?**	• Deconstruct curriculum expectations to develop Learning Intentions (LI). • Work with students to develop LIs in student-friendly language. • Ensure students know why they are learning what they are learning. • Post LI's in classrooms for students' reference. • **Discuss and record the big ideas and essential questions (Chapter 4) for a unit of study.**	• "I am learning to discuss and use more descriptive words in my narrative writing." • "I am adding more descriptive words to my writing so the reader knows what I am thinking as an author." • **"I am learning about _____ because I will need to use it when I _____."** • **"Learning _____ will help me understand how to _____ in the future."**	• Purposeful talk among students in classrooms. • More student than teacher talk. • Whole group/small group—individual work in classrooms. • Students clearly articulate LIs and why they are learning them. Leaders identify that Learning Intentions are grade level appropriate, directly from the Curriculum Expectations • No students are saying "I don't know." • The five questions are posted and have obvious signs of being discussed and worked on in all classrooms to serve as a reminder of intentional teaching. • **Displayed anchor charts of big ideas and essential questions are annotated by students and teacher to unpack the vocabulary necessary to understand and articulate the concepts being studied.**

5 Questions for Students	Teachers Do . . .	Students Say . . .	Leaders Observe . . .
2. How are you doing?	• Co-construct with students how to be successful. Anchor charts are displayed in classrooms to make the learning evident. • Ensure that students use Success Criteria (SC) language and they understand what they look like. • Develop SC that are not checklists. • Add to SC as lessons progress.	• "I am able to do the first SC at a Level 4." • "I am working on the second and third SC." • "Here's my work that shows how I can do the first SC."	• Anchor charts/prompts/scaffolds are clearly visible in classrooms. • These charts are marked up (not laminated) indicating frequent use by students—who can answer "How are you doing?"
3. How do you know?	• Give timely, relevant feedback based on LIs and SC. • Work with students to identify success in student work and to fix up work that is not quite successful. • Teach students how to peer and self-assess accurately based on LIs and SC.	• "My teacher and I have talked about my writing, and we decided . . ." • "I got feedback on my narrative from my friends, and they said . . ."	• Written comments on students' work are explicit and do not include "well done" or "good work" or other such platitudes. • Teachers are giving explicit oral feedback and recording it for follow-up. • Documenting evidence of learning through pictures, work samples, postings, anchor charts, use of strong and weak examples in the classroom.

(Continued)

(Continued)

5 Questions for Students	Teachers Do . . .	Students Say . . .	Leaders Observe . . .
4. How can you improve?	• Model to students how to use Success Criteria to fix up work • Make anecdotal notes of written and oral feedback to give ongoing feedback. • Track and monitor feedback given to know students' progress and plan next steps.	• "I am working on being better at . . ." • "The teacher gave me this writing feedback sheet to put in my binder as my goals for this work."	• Students can clearly articulate their next steps to improvement of their work using the strong and weak exemplars or writing continuum posted in the room to discuss where student needs to go next.
5. Where do you go for help?	• Work with students on becoming independent, self-regulatory learners by teaching them where they can go for help beyond the teacher.	• "I go to [name of classmate] as s/he is very good at . . ." • "I look at the chart we made in class to remember where I can go for help." • "I go to our class website to look again at the lesson." • "I go to my parents or to a homework help online site when I'm stuck."	• Scaffolds in classrooms show discussions of where supports are for students' learning. • Students can articulate several places where they can go for help in addition to the teacher.

Source: Adapted from Sharratt and Harild (2015).

Armadale Case Study: "Attention to Detail" Works!

Jill Maar is the Principal of Armadale Public School, the district's largest elementary school, serving a highly diverse and multilingual community. Using the 14 Parameter Self-Assessment Tool (see Appendix A), Jill and her school leadership team developed and implemented a plan of action based on the following nine components:

1. **Improve the learning conditions:** attending to a clean, organized, bright, well-lit plant; regular maintenance and urgent repairs were needed in some areas because structure guides school behavior (Parameter #4).

2. **Give access to current and inclusive resources:** removing all school-based resources from classrooms (some had been well stocked with resources dating back to the 1970s, while others had very few resources); through centralization across the school creating a literacy room, math room, science room, including text resources, technology software, and math manipulatives; ensure that the resources used are reflective of the students' FACES in every classroom (Parameters #9 and #10).

3. **Centralize and streamline budget decisions:** developing a clear and transparent process to address essential needs and teacher accountability with "just right, just-in-time" resources (Parameter #10).

4. **Examine data and identify trends:** reshaping teachers' thinking about the importance of data when making instructional decisions (e.g., at-risk identification, Case Management Approach; Parameters #1, #6, and #14).

5. **Engage district curriculum consultant "experts":** facilitating PL based on teacher need and ensuring consistency of practice within and across grades, for example, these Knowledgeable Others assist in visioning and co-developing strategic plans, in co-constructing Data Walls, in implementing the First 20 Days (Fountas & Pinnell, 2001), in conducting Learning Walks and Talks in every classroom alongside leaders and teachers looking for evidence of students' thinking on the walls (see Glossary: the Third Teacher), in developing targeted long-range and unit plans, in demonstrating precision-in-practice alongside teacher colleagues, and in co-creating student inquiries (Parameters #1, #2, #3, #11, and #13).

(Continued)

(Continued)

6. **Strategically build a leadership team:** inviting *all* staff who are interested in being part of the leadership team; hearing student voices at meetings to get feedback regularly; sharing in building and implementing a school plan with SMART goal language (specific, measurable, attainable/aspirational, results-based, time-bound; Parameters #2, #4, #7, and #11).

7. **Renew focus on parent and family engagement:** extending library hours; holding parent and/or family town hall sessions, street festivals, and heritage and English language classes in the school (Parameter #12).

8. **Attend to early and ongoing interventions:** co-constructing Data Walls and regularly scheduling Case Management Meetings (CMMs); focusing Kindergarten and Grade 1 teaching on oral language as the foundation; using the Observation Survey as a valuable assessment tool to guide instruction (Parameter #5 and #6); building knowledge of how to teach every student by implementing successful practices uncovered at CMMs.

9. **Stay the course and hold our nerve:** protecting instructional time; honoring the uninterrupted literacy block; and designating specific time to meet to discuss program needs and students' increased growth and achievement (Parameters #3, #8, #13, and #14).

Jill is a dedicated instructional leader who as lead-learner—with will and perseverance—is a living example of how the 14 Parameters can bring support and focus to every leader and teacher in every school. Jill demonstrates modeled, shared, guided practice and the ability to apply the learning, not lock-step but in concert, matching the Parameters at the right time with the varied needs of her staff and students. Jill is an interdependent leader who understands how to bring all the Parameters to life in a school with 890 students and 67 staff members. The answer lies in the 14th Parameter—shared responsibility and accountability—and Jill's narrative below demonstrates how to reflect and integrate the Parameters to increase growth and achievement for each student.

Accountability and Responsibility at Armadale Public School: An Example of the 14th Parameter

Our sense of urgency to improve growth and achievement for all students while closing the achievement gap for at-risk students crystalized after analyzing a variety of data sources. As a team, we needed to firmly establish our shared beliefs and understandings to ensure that *all* teachers could support *all* students in reaching *high* expectations in *all* subject areas (Hill & Crévola, 1999). Initial student gains have been achieved, as evidenced in the latest data collected both qualitatively and quantitatively.

Jill reports that her team has collaboratively set high expectations for the learning growth of both teachers and students. In taking responsibility for implementing the Parameters, they have achieved the following:

- Job-embedded PL, based on student needs, has increased the consistency of practice within and among classrooms. Teachers are beginning to model lessons in one another's classrooms on a monthly basis, thereby building capacity and understanding.

- PL is active in each division/key learning stage. The identified focus is assessment-based instruction with all teachers' participating in Collaborative Assessment of Student Work (CASW).

- Teachers are using a variety of assessment tools and instructional approaches to meet the learning styles, interests, and needs of every student.

- Teachers are building class and student profiles and attending Case Management Meetings to identify high-impact approaches.

- Teachers and students can clearly articulate what the LIs are and what SC are needed to achieve them, as evidenced through daily Learning Walks and Talks.

- Two teams (of five teachers each) are engaged in Collaborative Inquiry and meet bimonthly to review their data, research, and follow-up actions.

- Ninety-eight percent of the staff have volunteered to participate in a biweekly professional book club and bring supporting student evidence to their discussions.

- An increase in the usage and frequency of centralized resources has been acknowledged through not only centralized tracking systems but also the observations and comments of teachers and students who are accessing them.

- Student needs are at the forefront when making budget decisions with year level/divisional teams.

- Attendance at family and/or community school events has increased by 200 percent (School Council sessions have grown from 8 members to 67; Early Years parent sessions on average have 48 to 50 parents attending now on a regular basis).

The quantitative data also confirm that by continuing to improve learning conditions, celebrating collaborative practices, and sustaining a culture of trust, transparency and learning, students are beginning to show performance gains (see Figure 3.13).

Figure 3.13 shows significant reduction in the number of students at risk in Kindergarten through Grade 5—especially those at Level 1 (below expectation)—in one year of intense, focused precision-in-practice. While the at-risk numbers still need to be improved further, Jill considers the skill sets used in Kindergarten–Grade 5 interventions to be necessary in Grades 6 to 8, and she will provide PL sessions for these staff to provide for that increased instructional capacity. What is impressive is that Jill knows every student and has her finger on the performance pulse at Armadale. She is able to provide up-to-the-minute assessment results for each student on the whole-school Data Wall. She and her teachers can name the at-risk students individually and clearly articulate what they are doing for each one. We believe that this is the essence of the 14th Parameter. In implementing all the Parameters, Jill has daily conversations with teachers and works alongside them to co-plan, co-teach, co-debrief, and co-reflect (Chapter 4). She is truly an evidence-based, knowledgeable, and passionate leader: *consistent, persistent, and insistent* on quality assessment that informs instruction in every classroom.

Figure 3.13 Summary of Armadale Students Identified as At Risk in Reading*

Grade	October Planning Process				February Planning Process			
	Enrolment Numbers	Number of Students At Risk			Enrolment Numbers	Number of Students At Risk		
		Level 1 or Below	Level 2	Total At Risk		Level 1 or Below	Level 2	Total At Risk
Kindergarten	75	68	0	68	77	11	35	46
1	92	42	13	55	83	29	17	46
2	94	23	28	51	87	11	23	34
3	82	26	14	40	78	8	21	29
4	70	7	15	22	70	6	12	18
5	83	14	26	40	83	7	26	33
6	106	11	24	35	107	5	29	34
7	87	14	19	33	86	14	17	31
8	109	18	16	34	108	17	20	37
Total	798	223	155	378 (47%)	779	108	202	233 (30%)

"At risk" defined as Level 2 or below on a 4-point scale.

Even if a system has established a vision and an infrastructure of support (e.g., through PL sessions about the 14 Parameters offered by the district and aligned and restated in learning networks), the presence of responsible and accountable leaders demonstrates that strong leaders can accelerate the pace of progress.

Narrative From the Field

What if you knew precisely how your students were performing on an exercise or assignment in real time? Or what if you could track each student's Internet search movements during assigned class tasks at the end of class so that you could adapt your questions or change your direction the next day? What if you could track the entire class against their own "personal best" working patterns and know their levels of engagement and what factors motivated them during any given part of the lesson?

"That's fanciful! You're dreaming," you may say. But these capabilities have either arrived or may not be so far off in the future.

The Australians, who have more international sports success per person than most populations, are not only focused on winning at competitions, their coaches are intentional about winning *and* to do so by getting the best possible performances from their athletes in training sessions. Like instructional coaches and teachers everywhere, they know that competitive performance bests come only after periods of high-performance training with intense DF that the athletes can use to adjust their tempo and their body movements.

Sound familiar? Sound like the teachers and leaders in the BCC or Armadale Case Studies?

A good teacher knows that assignments that begin at the students' current capability and stretch them forward—combined with DF against the SC—provide students with the opportunities to develop optimally to perform best on those assignments and in future assessment situations, depending on the foundational skill being taught or practiced. Descriptive Feedback from instantly available data is the basis of ongoing formative assessment interpreted by a teacher who has put FACES on the data, and who will therefore know how to offer precisely the unique messaging a student needs (at their own performance level, using motivational and instructional phrases that will work for them).

Unbelievable? Next century, maybe? No, NOW!

GPSports in Australia offers GPS equipment that enables coaches to determine what players are doing in training sessions and during games. Real-time heart rate monitoring tells coaches how hard players are working, enabling the coaches to know when to let athletes rest or when to encourage further intensity. Accelerometer technology measures all accelerations and decelerations, reporting g-forces the athlete's body has endured, important information because too many g-forces above a certain level lead to excessive muscle damage, resulting in delayed recovery time. Via digital medical technologies, immediate blood oxygen levels can demonstrate that on-field training or play has been at peak, or less. Postgame analysis of the GPSports on-field tracking can show if athletes have been in the correct on-field playing positions relative to the ball and team mates.

In education, new online and digital media learning tools offer such immediate tracking and progress reporting and capture formative assessments of content learned. After-class analysis of these data can inform the teacher of next steps—and, in many cases, during-the-lesson analysis by the student can lead to immediate feedback, leading to better learning. As the BCC math teachers showed in their case study, they can be more effective teachers for a range of students in a class, because of the various real-time assessments *for* and *as* learning that they provided even though they are not high tech assessment technologies.

"Not for me," you say?

Who uses this system to improve sport performance? Only the "who's who" of high-performance premier league teams in soccer—Manchester United, Real Madrid, AC Milan; in NRL Australian Rules Football—St. George, Manly Sea Eagles; and many more. But dozens of second-tier teams (e.g., the North Ballarat Roosters), several sports research centers, and many university and school teams do as well.

The question that should be asked is, who in field sports *doesn't* use it? Only the reality of domed stadium retractable roof structures that preclude GPS functioning, stops U.S. National Football League teams from using this technology during games and practices.

Who uses more recently developed combination of exercise and digital communications technologies to support and evaluate their personal training? In the ten years since first writing *FACES*, millions have purchased products such as Peloton and less expensive reporting technologies such as FitBit for their personal use; tens of thousands

(Continued)

(Continued)

of gyms worldwide have made very real businesses from large classes and individual users employing varying levels of technology. Long-distance assessment of effort; "descriptive" feedback of the users' bio-performance measures; collegiality of instructor and/or coach and peer support combine to make every workout a more motivated and more engaging workout.

Who uses real-time measurement in the classroom or during homework sessions? Teachers like Colin and Lani use ongoing real-time tools that can summarize and show individual student performance. Teachers during the COVID 19-forced remote learning sessions found many ways to assess their students' engagement and immediate understanding of content by using ZOOM or TEAMs or Google Classroom.

Whatever our positions within education, there are tools that permit ongoing performance assessment—we can know and must know what we are looking for in good performance, in great performance, and in unacceptably low performance—and we must know how to follow "seeing it" by offering feedback that optimizes the performance immediately. Not for us, as leaders and teachers, but for the benefit of the FACES—our students.

Source: J. Coutts, with reference to GPSports, www.gpsports.com, Adrian Faccioni, president.

Just as we must be precise in our assessment strategies that inform instruction daily in classrooms, we need to be precise in selecting the differentiated PL opportunities afforded to teachers and leaders. The online, web-based CLARITY Learning Suite (CLS), Sharratt et al. (2020), is one way of doing just that. The CLS is scaffolded PL that focuses on the research conducted initially by Sharratt and Fullan (2012) in *Putting FACES on the Data* and uses the evidence-proven 14 Parameters as the conceptual framework. CLS is made up of 12 online Modules that reflect the system and school improvement work for leaders and teachers at every level, based on Sharratt's (2019) *CLARITY: What Matters MOST in Learning, Teaching and Leading.* Participants join an online community of learners that is set up virtually through the Membership Directory. A reflection on leadership to do this improvement work, considering knowing the learners, assessment, instruction, leadership, and ownership, is woven throughout each session in the CLS modules. CLS is an accredited Master's of Education Course at the University of Southern Queensland and the University of South Australia. For more information, see www.clarity learningsuite.com

Assessment as a Culture of Accountability

In *Nuance* Fullan (2019) uses a threefold framework to explain successful change examples: joint determination, adaptability, and a culture of accountability. The first 13 Parameters encompass joint determination and adaptability. As we said at the beginning of this chapter, accountability has been the bugbear of system change. If you make it a driver it fails; if you omit it the system drifts. Elmore (2004) put it this way: No amount of external accountability will be effective in the absence of internal accountability. Where a culture of purposeful interaction becomes part of an organization's internal culture, where they accept Parameter #14—shared responsibility and accountability—that becomes the critical capstone. Yes, summative assessment is essential. But only if it is part and parcel of an organization's comprehensive internal culture that incorporates shared responsibility along with a natural propensity for that organization to satisfy itself that it is getting results, and that interacting with the outside in that respect is both a responsible thing to do *and* benefits both the organization and its sponsors. Many "ifs," but as acceptance of shared responsibility and accountability matures, organizations become more willing to externally share their results.

All the assessment information we have covered in this chapter (not to mention the next three "improvement driver" chapters) sounds like a lot of work. Well, it is and it isn't. First, when lots of people are collaborating and coordinated in doing the work together or in teams, it is in fact less work for each of them. Second, if you get assessment literacy right from the beginning, it saves considerable time later, so follow the processes in each of the above 10 Lessons. Third, student labor, so to speak, becomes a free and very willing resource as students engage in peer- and self-assessment and are empowered to set their own goals for learning.

We turn now to Chapter 4, where we discuss how assessment in practice is accomplished with will, perseverance, and galvanizing forces around our second powerful driver, Instruction.

CHAPTER 4

Making It Work in Practice—Instructional Intelligence

Many jurisdictions have worked hard to move schooling from a one-size-fits-all mentality to placing the goals, aspirations, and context for each individual student's learning at the heart of the matter—ensuring that every student matters! While these jurisdictions are making progress, the challenge for leaders is how to make this shift occur in the large numbers of systems, schools, and classrooms. Assessment that drives instruction is complex, even though we strive for what we call credible *simplexity*. The simple part is that you need to focus on just a small number of things, the complex part is how to make these jell; the leadership chemistry underlying this change is a precise, finely tuned craft. As professionals, leaders and teachers must develop increasing intentionality and finite precision in their practice to make it happen. In this chapter we continue the journey into Instruction, also making note of integrating our most recent work on New Pedagogies for Deep Learning (NPDL) into the 14 Parameters of FACES.

As we show in Chapter 3, analyses of student achievement data provide system and school leaders and classroom teachers with rich sources of information. However, these data alone often do not tell a complete story until several other available data sources are scrutinized more carefully. That process is putting FACES on the information.

For us, there are three tiers of instruction (Figure 4.1)—each of which is informed by student data and each of which provides further student data:

Tier 1—Good First Teaching and Classroom Practice— an expectation in every classroom—is the use of specific, intentional assessment practices (discussed in Chapter 3) to design instructional approaches, which include strategies that reflect the many differing student needs in every classroom.

Tier 2—Case Management Approach (CMA)—is a systematic, two-pronged process comprised of co-constructing Data Walls and conducting Case Management Meetings (CMMs). A CMM is an internal support mechanism <u>for teachers focused on instruction</u>—a place in which to plan the implementation of alternative or new strategies to respond to a teacher's self-identified need for assistance with specific teaching of learners identified on the Data Wall. The real benefit of a CMM is that it is a forum to build leader and teacher capacity to teach ALL students.

Tier 3—Ongoing Intervention—is escalation for support of students with the use of intensive instruction that directly serves the most struggling learners—when everything else has been tried.

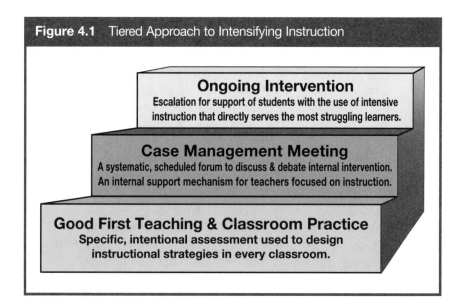

Figure 4.1 Tiered Approach to Intensifying Instruction

Ongoing Intervention
Escalation for support of students with the use of intensive instruction that directly serves the most struggling learners.

Case Management Meeting
A systematic, scheduled forum to discuss & debate internal intervention.
An internal support mechanism for teachers focused on instruction.

Good First Teaching & Classroom Practice
Specific, intentional assessment used to design instructional strategies in every classroom.

Tier 1–Good First Teaching and Classroom Practice

There are so many good texts. Indeed, libraries are full of texts and resource banks on what comprises good teaching and impactful classroom practice. Our intent here is not to repeat but rather, within a brief summary, explain how assessment data—when interpreted correctly—more fully engages, indeed empowers every student and positively impacts instruction, enabling teachers to teach optimally. In Chapter 3 we discuss Assessment Literacy, including knowing the learner, understanding the value of using assessment to drive differentiated classroom instruction, and having high expectations for ALL students.

As Hattie (2009) says, "[I]t is teachers using particular teaching methods, teachers with high expectations for all students, and teachers who have created positive student-teacher relationships that are more likely to have above average effects on student achievement" (p. 129). The quality of instruction is the strongest predictor of student achievement. That is, poor instruction predicts poor student achievement (although some students excel in spite of their teachers), and strong instruction promotes high student achievement. However, any chapter on effective instruction must begin with a caveat. No single instructional strategy or purchased program is guaranteed to result in high levels of student learning. *Instructional intelligence* (see Glossary) occurs when teachers combine high-impact strategies that consider every learner's needs (Bennett et al., 2001). Curriculum (content + assessment + instruction) must be personalized. Learning happens in the minds and souls of individuals—not in the databases of multiple-choice tests (Robinson, 2009, p. 248). Putting FACES on the data happens easily and naturally when assessment and instructional approaches are aligned—following one after the other every day in a never-ending cycle of perfecting practice for each FACE. Starting with that end in mind, we discuss what our vision is for all graduating students—the literate graduate.

The Literate Graduate

According to the United Nations Educational, Scientific and Cultural Organization (UNESCO, 2006),

The United Nations Literacy Decade (2003–2012) was launched because "literacy for all is at the heart of basic education for all . . . [and] creating literate environments and societies is essential for achieving the goals of eradicating poverty, reducing child mortality, curbing population growth, achieving gender equality and ensuring sustainable development, peace and democracy."

A good literacy program for critical literacy learners continues to comprise three components: making meaning, language study, and *inquiry-based learning* (see Glossary; Harste, 2003). Literacy instruction is our theory of action, not only in the international K–12 reform agenda, but also here—to narrow our focus on evidence-proven instructional approaches that benefit all students. As many others, we believe that **literacy is freedom.**

Assessment reminds us to begin with the end in mind (see Chapter 3), and we did just that. We asked what literacy skills our high school graduates need so that they can be contributing world citizens, We found that literate graduates embrace multiple forms of *multi-literacies* (see Glossary)—often simultaneously—and therefore must be able to do the following:

- Write with purpose and clarity

- Communicate effectively using a variety of text forms

- Read for purpose and pleasure

- Think critically

- Locate and access information from a variety of sources

- Use oral communication appropriate to purpose and audience

- "Read" and interpret multiple text forms

- Articulate a point of view

- Question and respond using higher-order thinking skills (see Appendix F)

- Problem solve

(Adapted from York Region District School Board, 2004)

After identifying the all-encompassing skills that a literate graduate needs, it is easy to chunk our discussion of instruction into manageable pieces. We begin with literacy in Kindergarten; continue with support for strong classroom instruction, including an effective literacy approach and cross-curricular literacy; and conclude with Collaborative Inquiry. Clearly, these skills represent basic foundational skills required to work and learn with ever-evolving new technologies. We also show toward the end of the chapter how Collaborative Inquiry has been incorporated in the NPDL and FACES work.

The Literate Graduate Begins in Kindergarten

Children do learn to read and write in Kindergarten. Don't let anyone tell you that they can't or that they aren't ready developmentally. What happens in Kindergarten predicts high school graduation rates (Hanson & Farrell, 1995). If children don't begin to learn to read, write, do math, and think critically in an engaging Kindergarten learning environment, high school graduation rates will reflect the poor and late start.

QR Code 4.1:

Temple et al. (1998) report, in their study of the Chicago Child Parent Center (CPC) program in preschool through third grade, that

> prohibit regressions indicate that family and student characteristics measured in the early school years predict high school dropouts. Simple regressions from that large urban sample indicate that variation in the probability of school dropout can be explained in the participation in the CPC program . . . evidence of this kind is rare. (p. 21)

It is virtually impossible for Grade 1 teachers to get students to read at the expected levels by year-end, if they enter unprepared, below expectation. We continue to work diligently with Kindergarten teachers, as well as child care providers, to provide the Professional Learning (PL) needed so that the teachers know how to use flexible whole-group, small-group, and independent approaches as part of the Gradual Release/Acceptance of Responsibility (GR/AR) teaching model. This approach will ensure that teaching teams can scaffold and support learning in responsive ways.

QR Code 4.2:

Time for focused talk and opportunities to be exposed to print in meaningful ways need to occur. The 100-minute literacy block in Kindergarten provides a deliberate structure (that is joyful and meaningful) so that the teacher can scaffold the learning intentionally as well throughout the rest of the day (Parameters #3 and #13). Again, assessment for learning (Chapter 3) begins in Kindergarten to determine instructional starting points for each child. As we have said, high school graduation depends on a strong literacy focus in Kindergarten and beyond.

As Schleicher (2011) demonstrates, 2009 Programme for International Student Assessment (*PISA;* see Glossary) results show that, in general, students who attended preprimary education (Kindergarten) performed better in reading at the age of 15 than students who did not. In 32 Organisation for Economic Co-operation and Development (OECD) countries, students who attended preprimary education for more than one year outperformed students who had not done so—in many countries by the equivalent of well over 1 school year. This finding held in most countries, even after accounting for students' socioeconomic backgrounds. However, across countries, considerable variation existed in the impact of attendance in preprimary education and reading performance at age 15 years.

Among OECD countries, in Israel, Belgium, Italy, and France, students who attended preprimary education for more than 1 year performed at least 64 score points higher in reading than those who did not, which corresponds to the equivalent of roughly 1.5 school years. Again and notably, this was the case even after accounting for students' socioeconomic backgrounds. These results underline the importance of preprimary education.

On the other hand, in Estonia, Finland, the United States, and Korea, no marked difference in reading scores was found between those who attended preprimary school for more than 1 year and those who did not attend at all, after accounting for students' socioeconomic backgrounds. In his presentation, Schleicher (2011) notes, as we do, that the one factor that might explain the variations in the impact of preprimary education on later school performance is the quality of the preprimary education.

This hypothesis is supported by the fact that the impact tends to be greater in education systems in which preprimary education is of longer duration, has smaller pupil-to-teacher ratios, or benefits from higher public expenditure per pupil. When this impact is compared according to socioeconomic background, in most OECD countries, there is no significant difference in the impact between students from socioeconomically disadvantaged and advantaged backgrounds. Students benefit equally from attending preprimary school in 31 OECD countries, including Japan and 25 partner countries and economies. The United States is the only OECD country for which PISA results show most significantly that disadvantaged students benefit more from preprimary education than do other students—an equity and excellence issue for us.

We also believe that the rigor of schooling (starting in preschool) must be examined with an expectation that high-impact literacy practices are givens—always in a joyful learning environment. Figure 4.2 demonstrates what is possible in a Kindergarten classroom. Shared and interactive writing is a focus in a Kindergarten classroom at Armadale Public School, Canada (see Chapter 3), where literacy is taught in an engaging, purposeful, and joyful way. Careful consideration has been given here to setting up the classroom learning environment, the Third Teacher (Sharratt, 2019, pp. 9–10), using materials and resources wisely, displaying anchor charts (see Glossary) to scaffold students' learning, developing the common language of instruction and supporting teachers in identifying students' instructional starting points.

Deliberate Pause

- Are your expectations for all students high enough?

- Is there planned and purposeful literacy learning in Kindergarten?

- How is *oral language* (see Glossary) the foundation of all Early Years programming?

- How do teachers model, share, and guide reading and writing beginning in Kindergarten?

The bottom line is that Kindergarten students can learn to read and write regardless of their starting points relative to socioeconomic status in the classroom. Accept no less.

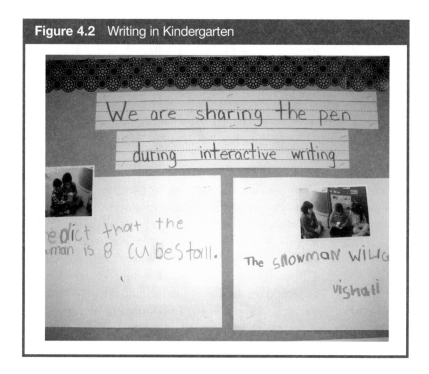

Figure 4.2 Writing in Kindergarten

Components of an Effective Literacy Program

The literate graduates' credentials begin to be formed in Kindergarten, and literacy learning continues throughout students' school experiences. Successful instruction comes from using the GR/AR model discussed here (modeled in Appendix A) as a modeled, shared, guided, independent, and application approach (**five steps**) to teaching the flexible, responsive literacy strategies that must be intentionally planned and visible over the course of a day or week in all classrooms:

- Modeled (teacher does; student watches)
- Shared (teacher does; student shares)
- Guided (student does; teacher guides)

- Independent (student does; teacher observes)

- Application (students can apply their learning to other texts, genres, subject areas)

The ten essential components of a flexible literacy approach are: modeled reading/think aloud; shared reading; guided reading; independent reading; applying reading skills; modeled writing, shared/interactive writing; guided writing; independent writing; and applying writing skills to all subject areas. These components are coupled with Word Study, Phonics Instruction, and Vocabulary Building— teaching what each student needs to become a literate learner. These components are powerfully connected when teachers use the GRR model in their teaching. This approach to teaching results in the "gradual release AND **acceptance of responsibility**" (GR/AR) by all students for their own learning—**our ultimate goal** for all our FACES.

Oral Language is the Foundation

Strong literacy instruction begins with reading and writing, surrounded by a rich oral language program. Oral language in K–12 classrooms is the foundation of all good teaching and learning. Oral language beyond the early years morphs into *Accountable Talk* (see Glossary). Accountable Talk takes many forms, both for students and teachers. Practitioners need to be aware of classroom talk—who is talking, how they are talking, and to whom and about what they are talking. International consultant Carmel Crévola (personal communication) believes there is core pedagogy for all teachers, of all year levels, and across all subject areas, in the area of oral language development. Her work centers on the connections between the language development of every student in the class (student talk) and the link to the teacher' instructional language (teacher talk).

Oral language should permeate the environment at every grade level as talk supports the thinking processes and talk develops the reader and writer before beginning each of those learning processes. As eight-year-old Elizabeth said in *Book Talk* (Chambers, 1985), "I don't know what I think about a book until I've talked to someone about it!" (p. 138). The same is true for writing. Oral rehearsal in writing is a necessary prerequisite for thoughtful writing pieces. Thus, the critical part of literacy block planning is the intentional integration of teaching of oral language skills that weave reading and writing skills together. Just as reading and writing are taught intentionally, so must speaking and listening skills be taught. Lucy McCormick Calkins (2001) puts it this way, "In schools, talk is sometimes valued and sometimes avoided, but . . . and this is surprising—talk is rarely taught. . . . Yet talk, like reading and writing, is a major motor—I could even say the major motor—of intellectual development" (p. 226). Talk must be taught! Accountable Talk is discussed on page 137 in this chapter.

The Literacy Block

During the uninterrupted literacy block, the time begins with a teacher-directed whole-group mini-lesson. The teacher then circulates among the working groups to guide and support students' learning—taking one or two guided reading groups, as appropriate—while students are working on relevant literacy activities or reading or writing independently. Finally, the teacher concludes by facilitating a sharing time that we call a *congress*, which involves reflecting on and consolidating learning with the whole group, for example, a time (not to be missed) when teachers and students refer to and reflect on the deconstructed Learning Intentions and co-constructed Success Criteria, described in Chapter 3. An example of a detailed weekly literacy block planner is found in Appendix E (M. Sharratt, 2011).

Common core principles of a responsive, flexible literacy program (K–8) include the following:

- Reading, writing, viewing, representing, phonics, phonological awareness, media, and oral language

- Modeled, shared, guided, independent instruction, student application, and practice

- Flexible groupings (homogeneous, heterogeneous, large group, small group, and one-to-one)

- Intentional, powerful texts using a variety of leveled media that reflect students' FACES in the class

- Nonfiction and fiction writing

- High-impact, differentiated instructional strategies

- Daily and varied assessment strategies
- Higher-order-thinking questions and answers

A comprehensive resource for teaching each of these core literacy components is found in *A Guide to Effective Instruction in Reading: Kindergarten to Grade 3* (Ontario Ministry of Education, 2003). A similar guide to instruction is available for Grades 4–6.

Deliberate Pause

There are 5 Questions teachers must ask as they plan for relevant, targeted instruction for all students:

1. What am I teaching?

2. Why am I teaching it?

3. How will I teach it?

4. How will I know when all students have learned it or not?

5. What then? Where can I go for any help needed?

Differentiated Instruction

The above five focusing questions must be at the top of all teachers' minds when they are planning for instruction. When teachers begin their planning for instruction, they keep the end in mind— what do the state standards or curriculum expectations say that I am teaching? Which can be clustered together? How can ongoing diagnostic and formative assessments (see Chapter 3) help me group together students with similar needs? Differentiating the instruction throughout the teaching-learning cycle (see Appendix D) becomes critically connected to improving learning. Differentiated Instruction provides for the diverse needs in each classroom. Students are more engaged when the instruction is differentiated and when they are in flexible groupings that meet their individual needs at that moment. Instructional strategies, such as the GR/AR model (model used in

Appendix A), collaborative group work, and *graphic organizers* (see Glossary), become powerful enforcers and enhancers of democratic, differentiated learning environments where students' voices are heard often. Differentiated Instructional takes careful, co-constructed planning with year-level partners who engage in co-planning, co-teaching, co-debriefing, and co-reflecting.

Hattie (2012) reminds us that teachers must have a clear reason for differentiation of instruction, relating what they do differently to where the student is located on the progression from novice to capable, relative to the Learning Intentions and Success Criteria (see Chapter 3). Hattie warns, however, that even though students might be structured in groups or pairs, most activity is still individual or whole-class instruction. Continuous observation of this during many Learning Walks and Talks should provide a reason for focused whole-staff PL and to speaking constructively with noted teachers as the practice must cease.

We believe that differentiation of instruction is more than flexible groupings. We add the importance of the GR/AR model when teachers scaffold the level of learning for each student through modeling, questioning, clarifying, chunking, sharing, rehearsing, guiding, and making their thinking visible through words, pictures, and symbols—all to make meaning of their world.

In differentiating instruction, teachers use ongoing assessment practices to create instructional processes at the students' level to bring each of them to the next level of instruction—"one size doesn't fit all." In this *intentional* teaching, teachers must know what comes before and after the skills being taught, how long to teach a skill and in what depth—definitely an art and a science! Co-planning is key for teachers at various stages in their careers (see 4 Cs at end of this chapter)! In short, teachers and leaders need to put FACES onto their instructional tactics, skills, and strategies selected.

Rich Authentic Tasks

According to Bereiter (2002):

> Educating is more than teaching people to think—it is also about teaching people things that are worth learning and [teaching them] to be able to discern what is worth learning. Good teaching involves constructing explanations,

criticizing, drawing out inferences, finding applications . . . if the students are not doing enough thinking, something is seriously wrong with the instruction.

We often ask, "Who is doing the most talking and thinking in this classroom?" Research tells us that students become involved in *authentic learning* (see Glossary) when tasks enable them to answer their own questions and explore their own interests . . . teachers report that students "come alive when they realize they are writing to real people for real reasons or reading real-life texts for their own purposes" (Duke & Duke, 2006). Willms et al. (2009) report that effective teaching is characterized by the thoughtful design of learning tasks that do the following:

- Require and instill deep thinking
- Immerse the student in disciplinary inquiry
- Are connected to the world outside the classroom
- Have intellectual rigor
- Involve substantive conversation

These characteristics can often be captured in collaborative, well-thought-out group work situations—group situations that differ incredibly from just putting students into groups without structure, roles and responsibilities, and thoughtful intent. We call this **instructional intelligence** (Bennett et al., 2001), which enhances the learning of both the individual and the group. Instructional intelligence includes five elements: positive interdependence, face-to-face interactions, individual accountability, some structured activity and social skills, team-building and group processing skills (Bennett & Rolheiser, 2001). All the elements are woven carefully into rich, meaningful learning tasks for students and teams. For example, refer to Figure 3.2, regarding open-ended thick questions and answers. Such questions could be: In your opinion, is homework a good or bad idea? or Do you think biking is a sport? Why or why not? Ultimately, we are striving to develop students who can capture the *big ideas* (see Glossary) in texts, novels, or curriculum units and in their own writing to raise their level of thinking and to be able to articulate a critical stance (Greenan, 2011b).

City et al. (2009) state that the instructional task is the actual work students are asked to do in the process of instruction—not what teachers think they are asking students to do, or what the curriculum says that students are asked to do, but *what they are actually asked to do.*

> A rich authentic task requires higher-order thinking, involves student inquiry as a way of constructing knowledge, relates to the broad categories of achievement and expectations outlined in the curriculum, makes connections across subject areas, and relates classroom learning to the world beyond the classroom. (Ontario Ministry of Education, 2004)

Deliberate Pause

- How are students required to use old and new ways to think about and solve problems?

- How are tasks designed to be relevant to and authentic for students?

- Do disciplines come together, and can they be explored in the tasks?

- How does the task prompt thinking and creativity and stimulate curiosity?

- Do students need to confer, consult, and communicate with others?

- How is students' thinking visible?

- When are students required to write down and reflect on their thoughts?

- If we were to watch you teach over a 2-month period, what would we see that would increase the learning and life chances of your students?

Questions and Student Inquiry

Teachers must continually ask reflective questions about their own practice to promote higher-order thinking (see Appendix F) on behalf of all their students. Questions are also good for students' reflection, as in the example shown in Figure 4.3, which is a classroom co-constructed *anchor chart* of how students think they should ask and answer questions.

Figure 4.3 demonstrates how teachers involve students in thinking through the success criteria needed and in making their thinking visible.

At all levels, in all classrooms, higher-order questions beget higher-order thinking and answers—when married with teachers' skilled competence (instructional intelligence) in providing wait time, checks for understanding, Descriptive Feedback (see Chapter 3), and scaffolded learning so that students can make new meaning. Moss and Brookhart (2009, p. 122) write that engaging students in generating effective questions helps them perceive themselves as autonomous and independent learners, producers of knowledge, and generators of important lines of inquiry.

Figure 4.3 Co-Constructed Anchor Chart of Higher-Order Questions at Armadale Public School

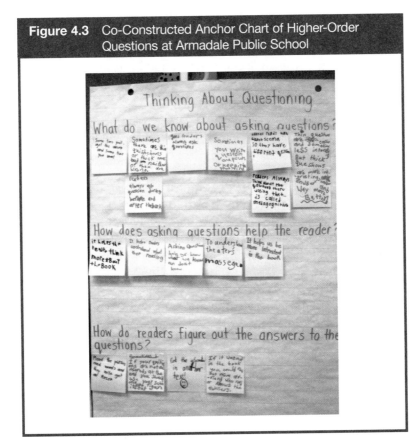

The Power of Writing

In *Realization* (Sharratt & Fullan, 2009, pp. 38–40), we said that at the classroom level, successful elementary and secondary teachers use the progression of modeled, shared, guided independent practice and application in all their teaching approaches to ensure that students experience scaffolded learning through which *they gradually accept responsibility to become independent learners—and owners of their learning.* This is particularly true in using writing to increase students' literacy achievement in every discipline. From our experience, an increased emphasis on writing, in many forms for all kinds of purposes, is a critical key to improving student learning. Internationally recognized literacy expert Margaret Meek (1991) did not mince her words about the power and magic of writing:

> Literacy begins with writing. A mark, a scratch even, a picture or a sign made by one person which is interpreted and understood by others may be regarded as a form of writing. The idea is simple enough. Once we have grasped it, even the hieroglyphics of the Egyptians seem, if not familiar, then at least part of the same world as our word processors. To me, writing seems to be a perpetual and recurrent miracle. (p. 18)

Meek again used a broader view to reinforce the importance of writing, stating:

> Those who study the history of writing are convinced that it is one of the most momentous of all human inventions. It makes possible the use of language beyond speech. It makes us conscious of language itself in ways that affect both our public and private lives. It creates what is to read, and, therefore, readers. (p. 23)

We watched the literacy coach from one of our highly successful Ontario schools guide practice by *demonstrating nonfiction writing techniques for staff members.* Like many, she and her principal believe that when students are engaged in authentic writing tasks, requiring higher-order and critical thinking, significant improvement is evidenced in both reading and writing criterion-based assessments. We know we can bring all students successfully to reading through individually crafted, authentic, nonfiction writing tasks.

Allen (2003) concurred:

> As a nation we can barely begin to imagine how powerful K–12 education might be if writing were put in its proper focus. Facility with writing opens students up to the pleasure of exercising their minds in ways that grinding on facts, details, and information never will. More than a way of knowing, writing is an act of discovery. (p.1)

Now we are saying it again. As writers ourselves, we know the higher-order and metacognitive skills involved in writing that we are trying to express above in rich authentic tasks, in connecting cross-curricular content, and in emphasizing higher-order thinking skills that students must have to become critical thinkers, problem solvers, and successful in adapting to the changes that will be necessary as we progress through this next industrial revolution. At every turn, we model the moral imperative of establishing writing as the hallmark of not only a literate graduate but of a literate society. Reeves (2010) strengthens our thinking by saying,

> Consider the case of nonfiction writing, a powerful cross-disciplinary strategy that has consistently been linked to improved student achievement in reading comprehension, mathematics, science, and social studies. . . . It is an established fact that a majority of students in the United States need improved writing skills and that our failure to respond to this evidence causes employers, and colleges to spend billions of dollars to address writing deficiencies. Where has that overwhelming quantitative case led? Kiuhara, Graham, and Hawken (2009) conducted a national study on the teaching of writing to high school students and found that evidenced-based teaching practices to support writing were insufficiently used with any degree of frequency and depth. The teachers in the study claimed that they had not been sufficiently trained to teach writing, with the high percentage of teachers believing that they were ill prepared in this subject directly related to their failure to apply writing strategies in the classroom. In other words, teachers do not do what they do not know. (pp. 73–74)

This leads us to reflect on the very serious shortfall in teacher preparation programs if we expect them to prepare the next generation of learning-leaders for an unknown world beyond the rapid development of technologies, ever more complex engineering demands, ever more options for potential careers due to that explosion in digital capability, not to mention responding to the social stresses of evolving pandemic-producing viruses.

Student Inquiry and Higher-Order Thinking

We believe that rich authentic tasks, such as nonfiction writing, lead to higher-order thinking needed by all children and youth forging ahead into the work force and society as they change so breathtakingly rapidly. Innovative Teaching and Learning (ITL) Research project director Maria Langworthy (personal communication, June 2011) concurs and writes that

> the evidence is converging on a simple truth: expanding and deepening student learning is directly related to the *content and quality of teaching.* Technology can and often does support high quality teaching. However, to strongly impact student learning, technology must be integrated with learning goals and combined with fundamental pedagogical capacity-building. In parallel, teachers and school leaders must be empowered to use this capacity through the modernization and alignment of learning objectives [intentions] and assessments across all system levels. (personal communication)

Some educators continue to wax eloquently about the need for new outcomes for 21st-century learners in a digital world. We both agree that the term *21st-century learning* is "over-used and irrelevant." Beyond the majority of students gaining proficiency, we feel that we should be aiming for the vast majority of students being able to engage in higher-order thinking. **Advanced proficiency is the new norm.** Learners must have the skills to demonstrate the appropriate application of higher-order thinking skills to a wide range of learning and life tasks.

We argue that the same successful pedagogy thesis—assessment that informs instruction—is valid today and will be valid tomorrow. We believe that if sufficiently high performances or achievement standards are expected of learners and if sufficiently high-quality training is available and demanded of teachers, then all learners will excel beyond our expectations.

The essential skill for successful teaching from the first step has always been to teach in a manner that appeals to the learner. This takes us back to the basic questions, "What do I know about the learner that can get her interested beyond just playing back to me what she memorized, wrote, or determined from the internet?", and "How can I deeply understand the FACE of that learner from the assessments and information I have?"

Educators at any level cannot permit themselves to have any excuses about using technology in teaching. Sure, some background understanding of the technologies is necessary. More important than knowing how to *run them* is knowing how to determine answers to the same questions about what the student is learning based on the way those FACES learn and what they have already learned. Experiences in remote learning during the pandemic have under-lined the need to know whether the student has access to technol-ogy at home and at what level the student is using it or permitted to use it. Again technology is an enabler and a disabler; therefore the key questions beyond technology in use remain, "Can students move beyond simple comprehension to in-depth inquiry?" (see Appendix F), and "Can teachers use emotional connections and cog-nitive insights to put FACES on results and immediately change their pedagogical course with the students' progress (or lack thereof) to improve the results?"

Our most important gift to students is to teach them how to continually learn and think critically as they progress through the predicted five to eight different careers they will have. Since the late 1990s, the Galileo Project, sponsored by TELUS in Alberta, Canada, has conducted research on learning with technologies. Their *Evidence of Learning in the 21st Century Classroom* (Galileo Educational Network, 2008) was created to guide leadership for learning with technology. This continuum identifies the low to high ranges of the following elements: tasks, assessments, learning environments con-ducive to learning when learning is engaging, self-direction, rela-tionships in a learning community, role of the teacher from guide to learning designer, teacher strengths, and teacher as learner. The lan-guage is strong, purposeful, and very much the language of inten-tional instruction and focused self-assessment that must be reflected in current leader and teacher PL. For further information, see www.galileo.org/research.html.

So learning *is* different for our students today! At its best it is both entertaining and deeply empowering. It is about well-defined high standards, assessment, and instruction and may be more professionally demanding and commensurately more rewarding, too, because higher-order thinking is central (Fullan & Watson, 2011).

The role of technology in society is incredibly complex, given that it is both sophisticated and dangerous. Technology is essential to achieving success on both the micro and macro levels. One of us examined the whole technology phenomenon in *Stratosphere: Integrating Technology, Pedagogy, and Change Knowledge* (Fullan, 2013).

Cross-Curricular Literacy Connections

As a basic skill, higher-order thinking engages students in inquiry, rich authentic tasks, and an exploration of the big ideas. It is achieved when teachers cluster state standards or curriculum expectations across the disciplines, assess students' strengths and needs, and plan to embed literacy competencies in instruction in ALL subject areas (Parameter #13). For example, for students to make sense of their world, teachers can make cross-curricular connections in the following ways:

- Modeling reading from the current history theme (using the *think aloud* strategy to model what good readers are thinking as they read)

- Writing different genres in science (teaching procedural writing)

- Making thinking visible in a mathematical problem-solving lesson (using pictures, words, and symbols to explain the thinking)

- Using a graphic organizer in a geography lesson (locating the main idea)

- Building a word wall in health and nutrition (strengthening understanding of the subject area language)

It is critical for teachers (especially in middle and high schools) to find time to discuss with and to demonstrate to each other what cross-curricular literacy instruction looks like and then to implement teaching the language of the disciplines and the literacy skills in the content areas across ALL grades and subject areas. Because the integration of literacy in all subject areas is central, cross-curricular connections must be valued and utilized in support of literacy instruction at all grade levels. Authentic

QR Code 4.3

assessment and instructional practices begin by students seeing themselves as real practitioners as displayed in Figure 4.4. The article by Lent is here in QR Code 4.3.

According to PISA statistics (Schleicher, 2011), although 15-year-olds who read fiction are more likely to achieve high scores, it is students who read a wide variety of materials who perform particularly well in reading. To consolidate understanding and embrace metacognition, students need multiple opportunities to share their understanding using many of the different types of communication shown below. We know, for example, that weakness in reading or writing skills provides barriers to success in mathematical problem solving. Thus, teachers must explicitly embed at least one literacy instructional strategy in every subject area lesson. To do that, all teachers need to know and be able to use strategies to develop vocabulary and comprehension skills—strategies that good readers do naturally.

While struggling readers need explicit strategies to help them negotiate texts, to consolidate understanding and embrace metacognition, students need multiple opportunities to share and extend their understanding. Some concrete mechanisms for doing so that we have seen on our Learning Walks and Talks and at celebratory Learning Fairs (see Chapter 5) include the following:

- Word walls to build the vocabulary of the discipline

- Making text-to-text, text-to-self, and text-to-world connections using sticky notes or using highlighters to mark the main ideas

- Putting concepts in students' own words while reading the text

- Reading comprehension strategies explicitly taught at all levels using the subject text to model think alouds, inferring, predicting, visualizing, and finding the main idea

- Graphic organizers to organize the essential ideas in a text

Figure 4.4 Real-World Cross-Curricular Literacy Connections

What are Literacies within the Disciplines? The following lists for each of the major content areas, while not comprehensive, can act as starting points through which communities of teachers can begin to think in terms of disciplinary literacy (Lent, 2016).

	Read	Write	Think
Science	*When scientists read, they* • Ask "Why?" more than "What?" • Interpret data, charts, illustrations • Seek to understand concepts and words • Determine validity of sources and quality of evidence • Pay attention to details	*When scientists write, they* • Use precise vocabulary • Compose in phrases, bullets, graphs, or sketches • Use passive voice • Favor exactness over craft or elaboration • Communicate in a systematic form	*When scientists think, they* • Tap into curiosity to create questions • Rely on prior knowledge or research • Consider new hypotheses or evidence • Propose explanations • Create solutions
History	*When historians read, they* • Interpret primary and secondary sources • Identify bias • Think sequentially • Compare and contrast events, accounts, documents and visuals • Determine meaning of words within context	*When historians write, they* • Create timelines with accompanying narratives • Synthesize info/evidence from multiple sources • Emphasize coherent organization of ideas • Grapple with multiple ideas and large quantities of information • Create essays based on argumentative principles	*When historians think, they* • Create narratives • Rely on valid primary and secondary sources to guide their thinking • Compare and contrast or ponder causes and effects • Consider big ideas or inquiries across long periods of time • Recognize bias

	Read	Write	Think
Math	**When mathematicians read, they**	**When mathematicians write, they**	**When mathematicians think, they**
	• Use information to piece together a solution	• Explain, justify, describe, estimate or analyze	• Consider patterns
	• Look for patterns and relationships	• Favor calculations over words	• Utilize previous understandings
	• Decipher symbols and abstract ideas	• Use precise vocabulary	• Find connections
	• Ask questions	• Include reasons and examples	• Estimate, generalize, and find exceptions
	• Apply mathematical reasoning	• Utilize real-word situations	• Employ mathematical principles
English Language Arts	**When students of English (authors) read, they**	**When students of English write, they**	**When students of English think, they**
	• Understand how figurative language works	• Engage in a process that includes drafting, revising, and editing	• Reflect on multiple texts
	• Find underlying messages that evolve as theme	• Use mentor texts to aid their writing craft	• Ask questions of the author
	• Assume a skeptical stance	• Pay attention to organization, details, elaboration and voice	• Consider research or other ideas
	• Pay attention to new vocabulary or words used in new ways	• Rely on the feedback of others	• Discuss ideas and themes
	• Summarize and synthesize	• Avoid formulaic writing	• Argue both sides of a point

Source: Lent, R. (2017). *Disciplinary Literacy: A Shift That Makes Sense.* https://www.ascd.org/el/articles/disciplinary-literacy-a-shift-that-makes-sense

- Strategies to read and navigate the variety of formats used in electronic or printed texts, which can be dense or confusingly busy

- Supplementary sources with easier or simplified content if students can't read the level of the materials used (raising the key question of whether teachers are able to determine the appropriate readability of the printed or electronic resources that they use)

- Bump-It-Up Walls (see Glossary) to make Success Criteria visual and use incremental scaffolding for students

For additional cross-curricular literacy strategies, ideas, and support, see www.curriculum.org/thinkliteracy/library.html. Additionally, Appendix G is an impressive handout that displays explicit cross-curricular literacy indicators for successful teaching of literacy in all content areas at the middle and high school levels. Repeating for understanding here: literacy is not just "literature"; it is the capacity to understand expressions of content in various curricula and to thoughtfully replay those using one's own words or other forms of communication, expressly being able to do so alone or in collaborative groups, which in itself demands another higher form of literacy.

Education across Canada may not be perfect; however, the provinces have done their research and attempted to implement the findings with some applaudable rigor. With solid gains and even more growth in precision-in-practice at every year-level, it is easy to understand Canada's accomplishments in PISA, 2018:

- In Reading, 15-year-olds in Canada score 520 points compared to an average of 487 points in OECD countries.

- 15-year-olds in Canada score 512 points in Mathematics compared to an average of 489 points in OECD countries.

- In Canada, 15-year-olds score 518 points in Science, compared to an average of 489 points in OECD countries.

- Fourteen percent of disadvantaged students in Canada are academically resilient (OECD average: 11 percent).

Source: Education GPS - Canada - Student performance (PISA 2018) (oecd.org) accessed April 28 2022.

Self-Assessment Leads to Higher-Order Thinking

We are zeroing in on the connections made between the FACES seen in assessment and the FACES known in instruction. The connector is the strong desire to have all students able to use higher-order thinking—***now a basic skill***—evident in areas such as nonfiction writing, robust authentic tasks, and cross-curricular content. Non-negotiable work has started in many jurisdictions to first assess students' ability to attain higher-order thinking skills and then translate the assessments into classroom instruction. Students' ability to self-assess and own their improvement involves high-order thinking as seen in the K–12 use of Bump-It-Up Walls (BIUWs).

Bump-It-Up Walls (BIUWs)

BIUWs bring together Assessment Literacy and Instructional Intelligence as they provide students with a visual scaffold of expected practices when they are co-constructed. BIUWs allow students to improve their work by comparing it to anonymous exemplars and by following explicit next steps to achieve it (Sharratt, 2019, pp. 139–142). Bump-It-Up or Performance Walls are visual displays of rich performance tasks that explicitly show what low-level (Levels 1 and 2) work might look like compared to Level 3 (expected), and Level 4 (the highest level) work looks like (Sharratt, 2019, p. 139).

BIUWs help teachers communicate clear expectations and help students develop the thinking skills required to become evaluators of their own work. They are classroom Data Walls and provide students with a visual reminder (and visual Descriptive Feedback) of what the Success Criteria look like and how to get there. BIUWs provide guidance for students to use in self-assessment and goal setting. They anchor the learning and ensure a common vision of the Learning Intentions and Success Criteria. When what it takes to get to the next level is shown on the BIUW and discussed often in class, students and teachers can deconstruct what is required to move the piece of work from a low to high level.

Embedded Instructional Coaches

Assessment that drives instruction through the lens of literacy and fueled by seamless technology use is easier for teachers who have the support of a coach (Parameter #2). Coaches work alongside classroom teachers, the principal, and vice-principal during the school day, demonstrating proven assessment and instructional practices in classrooms and at staff meetings. Instructional coaches are co-leaders and co-learners alongside their principals and vice-principals. These evidence-proven teaching experts with cross-grade experience, continuously demonstrate their credentials by also teaching in their own classrooms part of the day and respectfully inviting other teachers into their classrooms to watch them teach.

Instructional coaches are not "named" on their seniority or other unwritten criteria. It is critical that instructional coaches be selected wisely on the basis of being exemplary teachers who are respected by their peers as knowledgeable, approachable, supportive, and ongoing learners (Sharratt, 1996, p. 100). This position is the key element in making job-embedded learning viable and visible. We insist on saying that these part-time Knowledgeable Others (Sharratt et al., 2010), often known as *instructional coaches*, are critical because our research tells us that PL, delivered by credible colleagues, must be embedded as close as possible to the area of improvement—the classroom and the teacher. Successful instructional coaches are time-tabled in, during the school day, to work with principals, focused on instructional leadership (see Chapter 5), and alongside classroom teachers to co-plan, co-teach, co-debrief, and ultimately co-reflect (Sharratt & Fullan, 2009, pp. 51–56). The singular purpose of this process is to ensure that everyone becomes better at the craft of teaching—an outcome often realized when principals and teachers become co-learners in the never-ending process of improvement (M. Sharratt, 2004).

The operative word here is *embedded*. One of us, along with Jim Knight, argued that coaches are useless unless their role is part and parcel of an integrated strategy to achieve whole-system reform (Fullan & Knight, 2011) as accomplished in the Wollongong Case Study in Chapter One.

Co-Teaching–Co-Planning–Co-Debriefing–Co-Reflecting

Instructional coaches and classroom teachers or any two teachers may partner to collect and interpret class data and then use the data to determine a focus and action. They co-plan a lesson (or lessons) with a very specific purpose(s) that is (are) engaging for the students. They focus on the standards or curriculum expectations, use various data sources, and use co-planning as the process. ***They each must identify an area that they are working on to improve in their assessment and/or instructional practices for the process to be authentic.*** Partners usually take at least an hour or more to co-plan a lesson, plan to video it, and then co-teach the lesson. The data sources that they take from the lesson are: (1) How engaged were the students?; (2) Was the content understood?; and (3) Was higher-order thinking visible? The co-teachers have several check-in points throughout the lesson to determine if all students understood the content.

After the co-teaching is completed, they meet to co-debrief, reviewing the video recorded as the lesson was being taught. They discuss what went well, what they could tweak, and what are the next steps in thinking about all the FACES in the class. This model allows teachers to think about whether they

- Give immediate oral or written Descriptive Feedback and make note of it

- Develop explicit Learning Intentions and co-constructed Success Criteria—in student-friendly language

- Organize groups collaboratively and hear if all students are engaged in Accountable Talk

- Engage in higher-order questioning and thus hear higher-order answers (see Appendix F)

- Achieve robust authentic tasks that make students' thinking visible

- Reach the needs of *all* students—clearly seeing all FACES

The PL goals really begin from this point. Not all teachers or leaders would feel comfortable being recorded and having their teaching analyzed the first time they try co-teaching; however, after a trust in the co-teaching experience is reached, co-teaching partners begin to feel sufficiently comfortable to digitally record their lessons. This is an opportunity to listen for student responses to the teaching and for carefully worded analysis, discussion, and co-reflection on each teacher's personal goals for learning and improving practice.

Following agreed on norms of interpersonal interaction when watching the recorded lesson together allows for honest feedback and goal setting for the next co-teaching cycle. At that point, the partners trust each other to be regularly engaged in candid, open dialogue that questions their assumptions and reaches deeply into what it means to teach and learn with the needs and competencies of all students in mind. *A reminder regarding digital recording of lessons—the objective is to determine the lesson's impact on students' thinking, so the process of reviewing the recording is to watch the students' behavior and listen for their responses to the lesson being taught compared to what was planned.*

The co-teaching cycle shown in Figure 4.5 is the most powerful way to improve teaching practice and to implement the changes in assessment and instruction that we've studied, observed, and discussed in this book.

It pushes professionals to make their practices transparent and public for them to become increasingly more skilled, reflective, and thoughtful. Some of our co-teaching partners are now meeting with students at the end of every term to have them reflect on what worked or what was challenging for them, and what changes in teachers' classroom practices they, as students, would make to better meet ALL students' needs. These "data" sources have allowed teachers to be aware of the critical importance of hearing students' voices and considering their viewpoints—clearly hearing from ALL the FACES. Prior to setting out on the reflective practice process, which may appear to be intimidating due to having to "expose" one's teaching practice, it is important to establish strong norms and protocols (Sharratt & Planche, 2016). They provide for absolute respect for honest transparency in discussions such that reflective practice becomes a foundational and simultaneously supportive PL tool for teachers and leaders in systems and schools.

Crucial to the success of having Instructional Coaches and using the 4 Cs cycle is that time must be scheduled into the school day. This is not simply "time together" for teachers, *Reflective practice* (see Glossary) as a process moves beyond ordinary PL to become a *state of thinking that occurs when teachers comfortably explore and perfect their high-impact assessment and instructional approaches that improve their teaching performance.* As Hattie (2012) says, "Teachers are change agents—their role is to change students from what they are to what we want them to be, what we want them to know and

Figure 4.5 The Co-Teaching Cycle—Deep and Deliberate Reflections on and Change in Practice With a Teaching Partner

Step 1: Co-Plan

- Find protected time with a trusted colleague or KO to plan, teach with video, debrief, and reflect
- Discuss what you each want to improve about your practice to give each other Descriptive Feedback during the process (your Collaborative Inquiry focus)
- Begin with the curriculum expectations, then plan the assessment to deconstruct the Learning Intentions, co-construct the Success Criteria, and provide a cognitively demanding performance task for students to be able to demonstrate their learning (Chapters 4 and 5)
- Plan the before, during, and after the lesson (Chapter 4), thinking about flow, timing, and pace
- Plan to use research-proven, high-impact instructional strategies differentiated based on student need (Chapter 5)

Step 2: Co-Teach

- Set up a digital recording device, like the swivel camera if possible, to follow the voice and images of the moving teachers
- Work side-by-side in a classroom
- Co-facilitate classroom Accountable Talk, hearing every student's voice
- Observe during teaching, "Who is doing the most talking and the most thinking in the classroom?"
- Monitor students' self-assessment by asking them, "What are you learning? Why? How are you doing? How do you know? How can you improve? Where do you go for help when stuck?" (See Chapters 2 and 9.)
- Change pace and flow if necessary
- Give ongoing Descriptive Feedback to students against the Success Criteria
- Check for students' understanding and learning against the Success Criteria

THE CO-TEACHING CYCLE

Step 3: Co-Debrief

- Examine the video clip to look/listen for: more students' voices than teacher voice; higher-order questions and responses; creative critical thinking; students' use of the Success Criteria; students self-assessing and self-correcting
- Discuss teaching practices and prompts used
- Assess if the taught, learned, and assessed curriculum-based Learning Intentions were aligned using student work samples as evidence
- Give each other Descriptive Feedback about the Collaborative Inquiry question that each wanted to improve about his or her practice, looking closely at the video clip as a personal data source
- Use work samples to assess students' understanding and learning growth against the co-constructed Success Criteria. Ask, "Were they the correct Learning Intention and Success Criteria?"
- Decide what needs revision

Step 4: Co-Reflect

- Discuss the co-teaching process: What worked? What didn't work? What would we do differently next time?
- Engage with partner in an open, honest dialogue about improving practice
- Identify and understand what changes in practice and beliefs need revision for you each to become consciously and competently skilled
- Plan next steps for students' and teachers' learning in this cycle of inquiry

Source: Adapted from Sharratt and Harild (2015).

understand—and this, of course, highlights the moral purposes of education." *Reflective practice makes teachers change agents of their own practice.*

Tier 2–Case Management Approach– Instructional Intervention

If Tier 1 instruction is strong classroom teaching, then most of our students will be well served by very skilled teachers who continually use a variety of assessment tools to keep abreast of learners' progress and to prepare for purposeful instruction. Yet there will still be students for whom teachers may find it difficult to develop just the right instructional approaches to move their learning ahead. We call the next level Tier 2—a case management approach—focusing on classroom instruction, *not dwelling on behavior.*

The case management approach is used to put a spotlight on how all students are progressing with the specific intention that not one FACE will slip through the data cracks. This approach (Parameter #6) begins with the co-construction of Data Walls as **prevention** (Chapter 3). Data Wall discussions form a consensus about which students they want to know more about, that is, why these students aren't achieving, why they are stuck or not being extended. This need to know and to change students' growth and achievement leads to timetabled Case Management Meetings (CMMs) as **intervention** that occur during the school day. These CMMs are **not** to be confused with multidisciplinary special education meetings, often with outside personnel attending, that focus on behavior, discipline, psychosocial assessments, family backgrounds, and the like. It is critically important that CMMs **not** be perceived as or ever become opportunities for punitively dressing-down a teacher for "failing" to achieve. The CMM may be a teacher requested or teacher encouraged forum for the discussion of a specific student's work as data, for those students who are plummeting, staying still, not being extended or presenting as instructional challenges for their teachers. The focus is instruction. The CMM is an opportunity to build teacher and leader capacity to teach ALL students.

Case-by-Case

There isn't a single teacher or leader who hasn't had at least one student whose learning performance they just can't seem to change. The wisest among us have gone to colleagues and honestly bared ourselves with request for ideas we could use. At the school or grade level, the CMM provides teachers with such support for working with these students by focusing on next steps in instruction. To provide the greatest support and input, CMM membership always includes the principal, the presenting classroom teacher, and the instructional coach or Knowledgeable Other. Optionally, it may include other teachers, if available (e.g., the special education teacher or the teacher-librarian or Specialist Teachers, whose time may be freed up by teachers not in class, vice principals, or by creative timetabling). The meeting, led by the instructional coach or principal, as chair, follows a template (see Appendix C).

Because CMMs are quick (lasting 15–20 minutes max), teachers must come prepared with the student's work in the area in which instructional help is requested. The template guides the process for the teacher to present the student's work, describe strengths and areas of need, and for the attendees to recommend one or two instructional strategies from which the teacher can select (that hasn't already been tried) for 3 weeks. After that time, the forum is reconvened so that the teacher can report back on the progress and the assembled group can offer new suggestions if the first recommendations are not working. In the meeting, participants provide feedback and support to the classroom teacher, and between the initial and report-back meetings, they will often "walk and talk" in the classroom to see how suggested strategies are progressing and to offer encouragement and support to the teacher.

This approach not only ensures that all teachers in the school have a collective responsibility to own all students' achievement, but also that teachers win with every meeting they request. At worst, the teacher's repertoire of strategies has grown, and if the strategies did not work as intended for the target student, very often the instructional strategies prove to be good for the whole class—"necessary for some, good for all!" In fact, this is a proven strategy that strengthens the instructional capacity of every teacher and leader participating in CMMs to teach every student.

Specific Steps to Success

The following provides a step-by-step process used by ourselves and so many others that readers can make their own, according to their contexts:

1. Time for Case Management Meetings (15–20 minutes, max) is scheduled into the timetable with classroom coverage flexibility that permits each teacher to bring students forward.

2. The chair is either the principal (who always attends) or the instructional coach.

3. Attendance at the Case Management Meeting is confirmed.

4. Time on task is critical. A template (see Appendix C) is followed to lend reassurance to the factual and objective nature of the ensuing conversation.

5. The classroom teacher presents student work as data and evidence of the help being sought.

6. The teacher discusses what they have already tried; all voices around the table are heard.

7. A clear and specific instruction strategy recommendation is made and recorded. The classroom teacher agrees to practice—deliberately practice—the chosen strategy in their classroom for at least 3 weeks and with continued support of colleagues present on a "reach out/go to" basis until the next meeting.

8. The next meeting of the same group is scheduled before the initial meeting ends.

9. The classroom teacher reports back on the success or failure of the recommendation, with the student's new work as evidence. A Follow-up Template is used for this meeting (see Appendix C also).

10. Another cycle begins. All successful strategies are collected (e.g., held in a shared space like Google Drive or in a QR code on the Data Wall). This feedback to all staff on how improvement was achieved builds capacity across the staff to teach all students.

Love et al. (2008) write that, when a teacher brings a student forward to these group meetings, we must guard against the group's natural inclination to identify the problem as student-related: "It is easier to put the burden on students rather than examine our own practices more closely" (p. 351). In research that Love conducted,

> their verification process [similar to the above case management process] proved to be a valuable learning experience, as it demonstrated the need for ensuring that a problem really did exist before throwing money and time at it in order to make it better. (p. 351)

Practitioners from the field who have experienced the very positive outcomes generated by CMM send us anecdotes, like the following, that highlight the power of the case management approach in putting FACES on the data.

Narrative From the Field

Chloe, a Grade 4 student at our school, started off her school year reading at a Fountas and Pinnell level L. When looking at this in terms of grade level, Chloe was reading at a mid–Grade 2 level (almost two grades below expectation). As a result of our school's strategic plan to address literacy instruction and student learning over the past 2 years, combined with the individual teacher's commitment to supporting his students, the teacher brought Chloe, who was a worry for him and for the leadership team, to one of our regularly scheduled case management meetings. It is exciting to share that Chloe is now reading independently at level Q (mid–Grade 4) and is at an instructional level R (end–Grade 4) as a result of our laser-like commitment to literacy and our recommended instructional strategies to improve her learning level. Chloe improved two grade levels in 9 months!

We attribute this success to the following literacy commitments we have all made as a team:

- A case management approach in which Chloe's needs were identified, appropriate instructional strategies and supports were selected, and regular follow-up was maintained by the Principal/coach leading the case management team

(Continued)

(Continued)

- Uninterrupted literacy blocks

- Daily small-group instruction and one-on-one conferring at the student's level

- Access to quality reading material for all students regardless of reading ability

- Teachers' commitment to using the same instructional vocabulary with students

- Use of teacher anecdotal notes to support next steps for instruction for each student

- Embedded time to meet as grade-level teams to discuss student assessment, instructional practices, and necessary interventions

- Quality professional development tied directly to supporting our literacy goals

- Our staff approach that all students are our students

Given the intense focus on building a common commitment to our vision of literacy instruction, and rigorous analysis of teacher practice and student skill development, we have seen unprecedented growth in our students' reading abilities. Chloe's success, in leaping two grades forward to catch up to her peers, is but one of many individual stories of the data telling us that what we are doing is making a difference for all our students.

—Joanne Pitman, principal, Aspen Grove Public
School, Grande Prairie, Alberta, Canada

Tier 3–Early Intervention

During the teaching-learning cycle (see Appendix D), teachers use ongoing assessment data to determine intervention strategies needed. All teachers thus become capable intervention teachers and teach all students in their classes in our Tier 1 and Tier 2 model. Every teacher can put FACES on the data—using the information gathered through diagnostic and formative assessment and using instructional interventions that meet a wide range of learning needs. This often takes the form of reteaching using varied instructional approaches and different materials, and providing more time for students to learn new concepts and to see things more clearly. Students revise and practice based on the Descriptive Feedback they receive, and ultimately they own their learning by setting their own individual learning goals (see Chapter 3).

After good first teaching including classroom intervention (Tier 1) supported by a parallel case management approach (Data Walls and Case Management Meetings) and teacher-supported interventions (Tier 2), if students are still not learning, then the next level of intervention is what we call *early intervention* (Tier 3). We don't discuss intervention at every grade level, other than early intervention here, because the literature is clear that students who don't achieve standard by Grade 3 will most likely never achieve standard and their life opportunity windows narrow drastically. For this reason, we believe our moral imperative is to catch children early before it's too late!

We know that teachers who consider themselves *intervention teachers* at every level know the instructional starting points of each FACE, and how to progress their work beyond what was ever thought possible.

As a guideline for jurisdictions to consider, we believe there are 5 Markers of an impactful intervention. All Educational Interventions Must Be:

Early—begin in The Early Years

Evidence Proven—reflect increased, authentic results year after year

Sustainable—ensure all teachers become intervention teachers

Customized—match the intervention selected to each student's needs

Timely—set and achieve targets, with high expectations, in a reasonable time frame

When these 5 Markers are in place, teachers see gains in student work as shown in Figures 4.6 and 4.7. We must remember that the best indicator of all students' growth and achievement is student work–used as data. Ethin has shown incredible improvement within the first 4 months of school. Do all your teachers know how to teach "the Ethins"?

All students **must** achieve—some against seemingly insurmountable odds. Educators can provide for students only when they are with them—that time being often defined as "between the bells." There are many examples in the assessment and instruction chapter of how to accomplish amazing things, between the bells and within the resources most schools and systems can provide, through precision-in-practice using co-constructed Data Walls as prevention and CMMs as intervention. Teachers and leaders need to use the information shared in Data Wall conversations and at CMMs to create inquiry questions (discussed in the next section) to deepen understanding of effective, expected practices that will empower each learner. This leads us to think about the importance of leaders and teachers who do the work described in this text, day in and day out, and the commitment they make to ALL students' learning, growing and achieving by committing to:

- learning what trends the data in my system/school are showing me and taking action;

- creating a process of building a system/school Data Wall and taking underperforming student FACES from the wall into CMMs and following up with leader and teacher support through triage strategies recommended;

- ensuring every teacher becomes an intervention teacher, knowing how to teach every student; and

- having a proven system intervention strategy in place, to ensure that every student can read fluently with comprehension, write, speak and listen with purpose by the end of Grade 1.

A focus on assessment and instruction drives professional collaborative inquiry.

Figure 4.6 Ethin's Writing at Week 1 of Grade 1

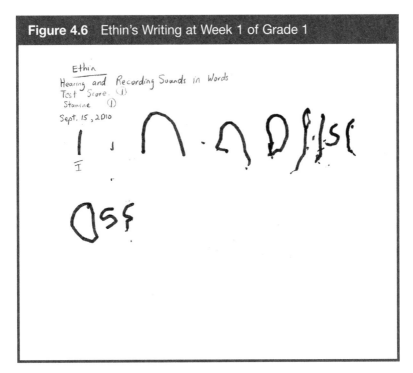

Used with permission.

Collaborative Inquiry

We can sum up two improvement drivers that we have discussed so far—assessment and instruction—in two words: Collaborative Inquiry. We have experienced Collaborative Inquiry in many guises in education: action research, reflective practice, Collaborative Inquiry, and now collaborative professionalism. There must be something to it, given that it keeps coming back—if only with new titles and slightly different nuances.

In fact, Kurt Lewin, the creator of the action research concept, clearly identified that action research carried out by teachers in schools should bear scientific characteristics (Ostinelli, 2008). Donald Schön (1983) developed a body of knowledge describing teachers as

Figure 4.7 Ethin's Writing at Week 17

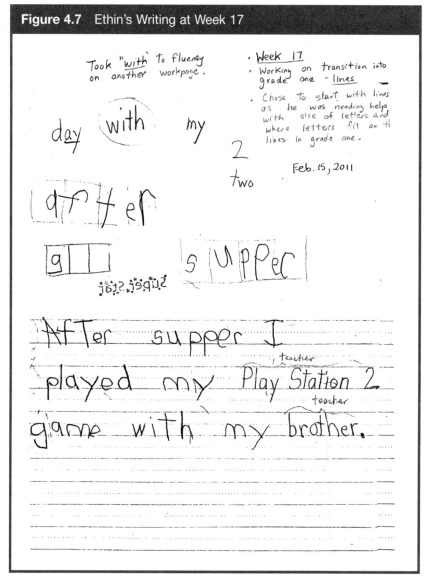

Used with permission.

reflective practitioners and making a huge impact in bringing research theory and practice together in a reflective way. At that point, educators began to write anecdotal notes and observations on what they were experiencing and thinking about in their teaching. Both the original action research theory and the later reflective practice were individualistic pursuits by teachers in classrooms without necessarily using data to inform their question of interest or connecting their learning to other colleagues or to whole-school improvement. Earl and Katz (2006) highlighted the use of data for informed decision making and insisted that data must be used to serve continuous inquiry as an aid to making wise decisions at every level of the organization, not just to answer the question of the day.

Today, we look to whole-school approaches to inquiry and to teachers at least in pairs, questioning their practice, scrutinizing their data, and reflecting on what's working, what's not working, and what could be "even better if . . ." in their classrooms.

Deliberate Pause

- Are system, school, and student growth and achievement data driving the inquiry process?

- Are multiple data sources driving the Collaborative Inquiry and instruction in classrooms? How do you know?

- Are Collaborative Assessment of Student Work, instructional coaching time, Case Management Meetings, early intervention processes, the 4 Cs and Collaborative Inquiry the operating norm in your school? How do you know? What evidence tells you that they are having an impact?

- Is the PL for teaching staff informed by data that differentiates learning options? Is the PL you are leading improving student learning? How do you know on a daily, weekly, and monthly basis?

For us, professional Collaborative Inquiry is at its best if it is a whole-school approach focusing on system, school, and student data and resulting in actions that are revised, updated, or improved via learning from a continuing cycle of deep, collective thought, conversations,

Figure 4.8 Collaborative Inquiry Cycle

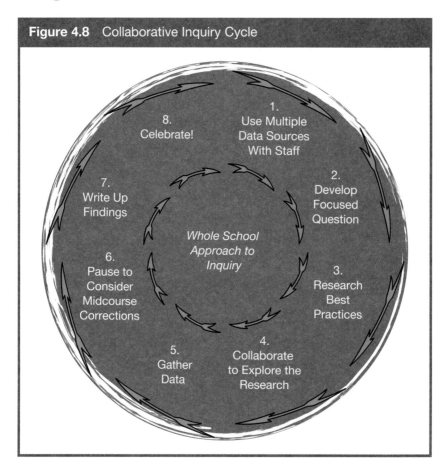

and data review sustained over a period of time. Figure 4.8 shows the Collaborative Inquiry cycle and its components graphically:

1. Using multiple data sources related to school and student improvement with the whole staff

2. Developing a focused question concerning school and classroom practice to increase students' growth and achievement

3. Scouring the research literature to understand current best practice pertaining to the inquiry question—teachers often conduct a book study of related research on their chosen topic

4. Finding time to collaboratively explore answers of practice aligned to the research

5. Gathering information and data from multiple sources, including district PL sessions, networking groups, book study, listening to experts on webcasts and at conferences, trialing new practice, observing each other's practice, and making decisions about what does and doesn't answer the initial inquiry question

6. Taking a deliberate pause to consider any midcourse corrections needed

7. Writing up findings to inform (a) PL sessions needed for school staff, (b) next steps in school improvement planning, and (c) annual reports of improvement

8. Celebrating the final report, which is the best part—often in a learning symposium format that mobilizes the new learning—an event that we call a 'Learning Fair' (see discussion below)

9. Beginning another inquiry—often related to the one just completed

After working together with the Catholic District School Board of Eastern Ontario, we attended their culminating event, a Learning Fair. There we saw the Collaborative Inquiry process presented by one school staff group whose members spoke to their journey to answer their Collaborative Inquiry question, which they created in response to student achievement data. Figure 4.9 reflects data related to students' scores in using the reading comprehension strategy of making connections. The data indicated that 52.13 percent of students were below standard (Levels 1 and 2) and only 9.40 percent were performing above the standard (Level 4), which was their target for all students.

After scrutinizing these data, the staff agreed that their whole-school Collaborative Inquiry question would be the following:

By using the gradual-release-of-responsibility model, how can we increase our students' ability to make connections between information and ideas in a reading selection, connections that use the reader's personal knowledge and experience?

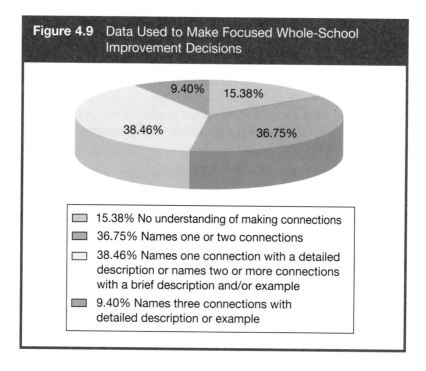

Figure 4.9 Data Used to Make Focused Whole-School Improvement Decisions

- 15.38% No understanding of making connections
- 36.75% Names one or two connections
- 38.46% Names one connection with a detailed description or names two or more connections with a brief description and/or example
- 9.40% Names three connections with detailed description or example

During their Learning Fair presentation, teachers and the principal then shared their Collaborative Inquiry journey of discovery. From start to finish, they

1. Focused on below-standard students

2. Established an action plan with timelines

3. Planned pre-, midcourse, and post-assessments

4. Held a book study to read recent research in evidence-proven reading strategies

5. Included modeled lessons by the literacy coach to demonstrate making connections

6. Developed classroom anchor charts, clear Learning Intentions (tied to the curriculum expectations and standards), and co-constructed Success Criteria in student-friendly language

7. Practiced explicit teaching in their classrooms (a) using guided questions and (b) modeling text-to-self, text-to-text, and text-to-world connections

8. Marked common assessments collaboratively (CASW)

9. Reported that in one of the classes the teacher had made a difference for 13 of the students, who improved from Level 2 (below level) to Level 3 (at standard)

In short, all students in the school improved in their ability to make connections between text to self, text to other texts, and text to the world. In their final Collaborative Inquiry report, published for the Learning Fair, the school team wrote:

> We used 3 data sources to help us determine our students' greatest need. After carefully looking at the data, we determined that students were having difficulty making meaningful connections related to personal experiences and outside materials. This also meant that students were having difficulty understanding and identifying their learning processes in reading.
>
> Through systematic and guided instruction, we created lessons that were centered around rich, fictional texts and the use of high-impact strategies. We used our first lesson as a diagnostic to help lead us in planning the lessons that followed.
>
> We know that we made a difference because students began to show evidence of their learning. They were able to understand the differences in the connections they had been making before to the more meaningful connections they were now able to make. Students were able to tell us how their connections helped them understand the text being read and how it helped them in their writing. Students were very receptive to the lessons and showed immediate transference of information (Application phase in GR/AR). They began almost immediately to use the language and strategies we had modeled in class. As well, teachers were willing to share, ask questions of each other, and be open to trying new instructional strategies.
>
> For us, this example of a yearlong Collaborative Inquiry cycle, in which the classroom instruction planned was specific to the data, underlines the importance of using data to inform instruction. It also demonstrates our shared beliefs and understandings in Parameter #1—that all leaders, teachers, and students can clearly articulate why they lead, teach, and learn the way they do to increase all learners' achievement.

In Chapters 3 and 4 we have developed a "language of assessment and instruction" that will promote rich discussion and a depth of understanding among professional educators—with the sole underlying purpose of putting the FACES on the data—to make every student's progress count. When we reflect on the key topics covered in this chapter, such as instructional coaching, co-teaching cycle, a case management approach, and Collaborative Inquiry, we agree resoundingly with Chappius (2007) that these approaches are exemplary models of PL that work well because they are on site, job-embedded, sustained over time, centered on active learning and student outcomes (Parameter #11).

Narrative From the Field

Several years ago, in June, Alistair arrived in my secondary Year 5 class to do higher maths. He started by telling me that he was no good at maths and his secondary Years 4 and 5 teachers had confirmed this by telling him that he would probably not stay in my class once he received his results in August. In August, he got a pass at the lowest grade for the credit, but it meant he could stay in my class. We got on well, and I noticed that he was good at seeking clarification on many points. He said he had always been told that if he didn't understand something straight off, then he probably would never "get it." The different approach in my class (of ask and discuss) made him feel more confident. Regular chats with me about his work settled him into a pattern of working hard and achieving. He passed (with a B), went on to do advanced higher math (got a C), then went on to university to do maths teaching. He keeps in touch with me and has now changed his path to a straightforward maths program to widen his options. I know my instructional approaches made a difference to Alistair. He might be a teacher yet!

—Pauline Ward, maths teacher, St. John's
Academy, Perth and Kinross Council, Scotland

We conclude this chapter by making connections between the use of data, Assessment Literacy, and Instructional Intelligence to answer the question, "How do you know that ALL students are progressing?" The Cleveland State High School Case Study provides us with an illustration of pulling these Big Ideas altogether.

Cleveland District State High School Case Study

Within South East Region (SER), many schools stand out as having achieved significant improvement in their Report Cards (A–E) results and on other important data points that can predict student success. This is a case study of one secondary school where staff have focused on "the work" necessary to improve all students' growth and achievement. Their stunning results serve as evidence that putting FACES on the Data and taking action really works—in elementary and secondary schools, in fact in ALL schools!

Cleveland District State High School (CDSHS), situated 30 km east of Brisbane in the Redlands area of Southeast Queensland, now has 2,200 students (12–18 years old) from Year 7 to Year 12. As the regional population has grown in the last 10 years, CDSHS has doubled in capacity.

Background—Why Improvement Needed?

Following a school review in 2020, CDSHS embarked on a new 4-year strategic plan that incorporated many of the recommendations from the review. While for many years, the school has delivered impressive educational outcomes to the community and has a strong reputation, which is evidenced by the number of out-of-catchment enrollment applications, it was clear that a more coordinated, more focused and precise improvement agenda could be implemented. English, Maths, and Science were target areas with Writing being the key general capability improvement area across all years.

Data—Before and After the Work

The following highlights several areas that have seen significant improvement in results that are grouped by student learning achievement and engagement. It's important to emphasize that this is not a cherry-picking exercise as a large number of school success indicators improved. The validity and reliability of report card or Levels of Achievement (LoA) data are paramount to staff values and the indicators selected were areas given priority in the school's improvement agenda.

Table 4.1 Student Learning Achievement at CDSHS

Key Performance Indicators	Before Work	After Work
Year 8 English A-C	2019 – 80% (Sem 1)	2021 – 96% (Sem 1)
Years 7, 8, 9 Maths A-C	2019 – 85.5% (Sem 1)	2021 – 90.8% (Sem 1)
Years 7, 8, 9 Maths A-B	2019 – 48.3% (Sem 1)	2021 – 50.9% (Sem 1)
Years 7, 8, 9 Science A-C	2019 – 82.3% (Sem 1)	2021 – 84.6% (Sem 1)
ATSI Year 8 English A-C	2019 – 63%, 2020	2021 – 96.7% (Sem 1)
ATSI Year 8 Maths A-C	2019 – 50%, 2020 (Sem 1)	2021 – 76.7% (Sem 1)
ATSI Year 9 Maths A-C	2019 – 48%, 2020 (Sem 1)	2021 – 72.7% (Sem 1)
NAPLAN Writing Year 9 (Writing is our key general capability improvement area)	2019 – 520.3 (Qld State schools – 521.8)	2021 – 537.8 (Qld State schools – 522.1)
Year 12 Queensland Certificate of Education	2018 – 91.8%, 2019 – 92.6%	2020 – 98.9%
Year 12 Graduate with a Graduation Qualification	2018 – 95.4%, 2019 – 94.5%	2020 – 100%

ATSI: Aboriginal and/or Torres Strait Islander

Table 4.2 Student Engagement at CDSHS

Key Performance Indicators	Before Work	After Work
All attendance <85%	2019 – 18.3% (Sem 1)	2020 – 13.9% (Sem 1)
ATSI attendance	2019 (Sem 1) – 78.4%	2021 (Sem 1) – 83.8%
Student Disciplinary Absences SDAs (Years 7–9)	2019 (Sem 1) – 90	2021 (Sem 1) – 70

Focus of Improvement

It was auspicious that as staff formed our new strategic plan, they had the opportunity to join the *Leading Learning Collaborative* (LCC) with Sharratt, using CLARITY (2019), as part of a South East Region's improvement agenda. Using data, all staff selected four Parameters of the work to focus on:

- Parameter #1: Shared Beliefs and Understandings
- Parameter #3: Quality Assessment Informs Instruction
- Parameter #6: Case Management Approach
- Parameter #14 Shared Responsibility and Accountability

These Parameters were chosen collaboratively by ALL staff agreeing that implementing them would be beneficial to addressing the recommendations of the school review. In addition, four pillars were designed by leadership and other stakeholders as the structural focus of the improvement agenda:

- participatory leadership model for the Executive Team;
- senior leadership strategic improvement cycle;
- broader leadership development process; and
- systematized Case Management Approach

These four pillars were implemented concurrently as the mechanism to leverage the selected Parameters toward success for CDSHS. Details of the four pillars follow.

Participatory Leadership Model for the Executive Team

The Executive Team (ET) moved to a functional model with specific leadership portfolios and accountabilities defined using the important goals and key performance indicators with lag and lead indicators, to guide performance in driving implementation of Parameters #1 and #14 while utilizing Sharratt's CLARITY as the key text for all staff.

Senior Leadership Team
Strategic Improvement Cycle

Staff at CDSHS employed a robust improvement cycle tailored to the needs of each Head of Department and faculty. This process employs the Queensland Department of Education's Cycle of Inquiry and moves from data analysis to data informed decision making on an explicit and focused improvement agenda that highlighted one or more of the four prioritized Parameters. An accountability line-of-sight was provided through the cycle with agreed on goals, processes, and milestones aligned to the school's Annual Improvement Plan and Strategic Plan, which were prioritized explicitly in the cycle. This created an improved focus and provided precision for the improvement work.

Leadership Development Program

Developing leadership capabilities that could deliver the goals of the Strategic Plan was critical for the success of the improvement agenda. The specific capabilities were carefully defined to align with the skills and abilities required to achieve the school's improvement agenda. These were tailored to three different identified leadership teams:

1. Senior Leadership Team (SLT), Exec Team, Heads of Departments, and School Deans.

   The SLT focused on capabilities to develop Parameters #1 and #14 through sharing of key sections of Clarity on leadership development days, involvement in LLC sessions, sharing of LLC resources, and involvement in the Strategic Improvement Cycle.

2. Tier III (Teachers who held a position of authority within the school as a coordinator and had aspirations to become future Heads of Departments).

3. Tier IV (Teachers who aspired to hold coordinator positions in the future).

   Tier III and Tier IV developed capabilities through a Professional Learning Community with *Putting Faces on the Data* (Sharratt & Fullan, 2012) as a shared text coupled with an action research project to apply learnings from the text through a Case Management Approach.

The final pillar of the focused work was the design and building of a systemized Case Management Approach aligned to Parameter #6. This model sought to provide a school-wide basis for incorporating Data Walls in conjunction with Case Management Meetings.

Several teams started using the CMM process and from this Collaborate and Manage (CaM) was developed as our systemized case management tool. CaM provides a method to allow teams to collaborate with efficacy incorporating Sharratt's protocols and norms. Additionally, a line-of-sight was developed incorporating explicit lead and lag goals for each team. As staff capabilities and confidence developed, CaM was scaled across teams and additional functionality was incorporated to allow for interoperability between teams so students could be referred between teams. Accountability was prioritized based on agreed key performance indicators that reinforced Parameters #1 and #14.

The Work and Processes in Achieving Staff Buy-In

Critical factors provided the means to achieve all staff buy-in, such as:

1. Providing and insisting upon a professional and moral purpose to our work through a Putting Faces on the Data approach.

2. Providing clear expectations, accountabilities, and a line-of-sight to ensure commitment to obligations and achievement of goals across the College.

3. Incorporating an organizational feedback model to permit resources to be re-deployed and new resources to be deployed in an agile and effective manner. The SLT Strategic Improvement Cycle is a good example of this organizational feedback; another example is the SLT Bridging meetings held twice a term, when the chair of each Case Management team presents on the goals, strategies, and progress of each student being case managed. Further, the Tier III and Tier IV

teams present their work to peers as part of their leadership program—when the best examples are chosen to present to SLT—has become a prized point of recognition.

4. Having all teams communicate their progress to all staff after each of the above meetings is a key protocol of the Case Management philosophy that CaM facilitates.

5. Designing strategies to incorporate intentional collaboration with precision was a key attribute to contribute to staff buy-in. A pivotal aspect of this was co-creating organizational processes with staff that optimized workflow. Further, an agile design philosophy was applied to encourage feedback, ideas, and suggestions to improve processes. Many staff contributed to these forums, and their contributions were recognized, which built in a cycle of positive reinforcement of school goals.

6. Capitalizing on great work to ensure student success by celebrating and acknowledging performance. This was achieved in several ways, including recognition in the Executive Principal's weekly email to staff on our strategic improvement progress, in one-to-one meetings between members of the Senior Leadership Team and staff, at staff meetings, and in individual emails. Leaders continuously evaluated what they could learn from the great work to scale effective processes to other teams and recognized specific staff member's role in this.

In this process, it became apparent, once again, that for professionals there is nothing more satisfying than seeing the great work expanded and utilized by other professionals to create success for ALL students.

IMPACT!

The results can be seen in three areas as shown in Tables 4.1 and 4.2:

- Students' academic achievement success and improved engagement; leading to empowerment of leaders, teachers, and students (Parameters #1 and #14).

- Systemic processes and tools that provide a solid foundation to ensure sustainability of the work and to continually mobilize resources including *staffing the improvement agenda* (Parameters #14 and #10).

- Increased capabilities of staff and broad sharing of innovative ideas to enable delivery of great outcomes for students and the whole community of stakeholders aligned to the school's strategic plan (Parameters #1, #4, #6, and #14).

Leadership Lessons Learned

The dimensions of leadership in FACES have been instrumental in shaping the improvement agenda of CDSHS. Leaders and aspiring leaders must be highly knowledgeable about the rationale, model, processes, protocols, tools, and evaluation of change before any meaningful and impactful instructional leadership can be achieved in a sustainable way. However, the *key lesson learned* is that leaders must *not only be knowledgeable but also have the intent to continue to learn and challenge themselves to create the conditions for excellence*. Central to this is deep leadership reflection.

Crucial to the success at CDSHS has been a commitment to the fidelity of the work to ensure staff have the ability to reproduce the agreed on strategies to produce effective and efficient outcomes. The use of systematized organizational workflow processes provided staff confidence in implementing best practice. Centered on a process of each team defining an intervention goal for each at-risk student at the start of the Case Management Meeting cycle then during each meeting defining a success measure was integral to students' and teachers' success in implementing the process with integrity.

The importance of fiduciary responsibilities among school leaders is important to provide a solid and broad-based accountability framework. A rich resource of shared data allowed school leaders to assess progress and make adjustments. Leaders and teachers at CDSHS learned that if they were serious about **ensuring student success,** then they were serious about their commitment to **every student succeeding**. Their work of CLARITY (2019) in shared tasks continues as they expand processes and systems to new teams to scale-up successful processes across all aspects of the College. (Mr. Leonard McKeown, Executive Principal, Cleveland District State High School, Queensland Department of Education, South East Region, Australia, personal communication, January 2022).

Deliberate Pause

The successes in the Cleveland District State High School case study occurred due to several factors. Think about:

- The simplexity of structural changes in the way leadership (SLT) worked—moving to a functional approach. Could that occur in your school?

- Does everyone see themselves in the work? Teacher buy-in is critical—so important to circle back to Parameters #1, #6, and #14—**often**.

- How could you introduce and implement the Case Management Approach in your elementary or secondary school and at the system level?

- There is a positive relationship between attendance improvement and improvement in classroom assessment that informs instruction. What does your attendance statistical analysis look like? How does it look within the various elements of cultural diversity in your system or school?

- How does dramatic school population growth change the culture of a school? What can be done to ensure the new culture is indeed a shared, learning-focused culture that works?

At St. Jude's I believe our thinking has shifted to many people taking responsibility for student growth rather than one teacher in their classroom for 1 year. Growth is an ongoing process. There are more open discussions now, and the analysis of data across cohorts and years happens across the school and is a shared responsibility to pinpoint needs and to work toward **all** students making growth from the time they begin at St. Jude's to the time they leave. All staff are now involved in the learning, from classroom teacher to learning support to school leaders and administration.

—Natalie, Learning Diversity Teacher, Eastern Region, Melbourne

Link to Deep Learning

This chapter on Instruction focuses primarily on a broad definition of literacy growth and achievement resulting in Critical Thinking in every classroom, in every subject area. We have also referred here and there to the new work that Fullan is part of that focuses on *deep-learning* that resulted in the NPDL model captured in Figure 4.10. The full NPDL model is presented here.

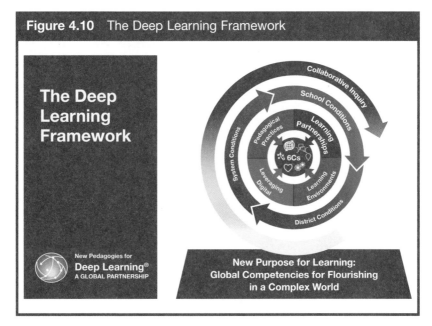

Figure 4.10 The Deep Learning Framework

Reproduced with permission of NPDL (2020, p. 222).

In NPDL the learning goal expands to what we call the 6Cs: character, citizenship, collaboration, communication, creativity, and critical thinking. Everything we have said in this chapter about instruction applies but is elaborated on to include other aspects of what we call the *learning design*. The latter is essentially what we call in this chapter *instruction*—and in NPDL this includes *pedagogical practices* as discussed here in Chapter 4, along with *learning partnerships*, *learning environments* (see Glossary: The Third Teacher), and *leveraging digital*. 'Collaborative Inquiry' the reader will notice is a *wraparound* phenomenon of NPDL, while in *FACES* it is integrated as Parameter #11. In effect, the models are entirely compatible, with NPDL expanding to include societal competencies, like citizenship.

Thus far we have shown that powerful impact is achieved by knowing the FACES behind the data and by zeroing in on assessment and instruction made precise by putting FACES on that data. Improvement has happened due to widespread, focused action in elementary and secondary schools alike. This applied energy was *unleashed* by confident and courageous leadership teams—the subject of Chapter 5.

CHAPTER 5

Leadership— Individualizing for Improvement

In previous chapters we detailed the skills and practices that underlie our improvement drivers 1 and 2—assessment and instruction. Here we look at improvement driver 3—leadership—as identified by our research respondents, beginning with the Kingsthorpe State School case study. For another related example click on QR Code 5.1 and read the St. Joseph's Catholic Primary School case study.

QR Code 5.1: St. Joseph's Catholic Primary School

A. School Context

Kingsthorpe State School is located in a fast growing community within the Darling Downs South-West Region of the Queensland Department of Education, Australia. The K–6 school's enrolment is 230 students and growing rapidly.

The student demographics rating for Kingsthorpe is 969, below the national average of 1,000 as identified through the national Index of Community Socio-Educational Advantage (ICSEA) scale. This rating means students have a lower-than-average educational advantage.

(Continued)

(Continued)

The geographical catchment area is a mixture of farming and rural residential properties. A high percentage of parents with students at this school travel to the nearby cities of Toowoomba and Brisbane City to work; and many of these parents utilize the Outside School Hours care program. The Parents and Citizens Association is an active and enthusiastic group who contribute to the overall school direction in a positive manner.

B. School Staffing

Kingsthorpe State School is permanently staffed by:

- 1 Principal

- 1 Head of Curriculum

- 1 Administration officer

- 16 Classroom teachers (12 full-time; 4 part-time)

- 8 Teacher aides (working various hours)

- 2 Cleaners

The following specialist/support staff also service the school on regular timetables:

- Special education teacher (5 days per week)

- Health and Physical Education (HPE)

- Music

- Language other than English (LOTE)—Japanese

- Instrumental music teacher (1 day per week)

- Guidance Officer (5 days per Term—approximately 10 weeks in duration)

- Visiting Speech Pathologist

1. School Improvement Journey

Kingsthorpe State School's collective commitment to providing a quality well-balanced individualized education for all students has been underpinned by a collaborative school culture and relational principal. Teacher leaders are empowered to utilize the key strategic attributes of visioning, collaboration, and differentiated staff support to know how students are evidencing learning to co-construct and refine their whole school improvement journey.

James Leach became principal at Kingsthorpe State School in 2016. Prior to this role he had been a deputy principal at a large school where they had engaged in Putting FACES on the Data using the 14 Parameters as a self-assessment tool (Sharratt & Fullan, 2012). In his first term at the school, Leach sought to understand the school context through the following lenses: community expectations, staff culture, teacher capability, and student learning needs. He accessed a wide variety of data including

1. **The 2015 School Review Report**

   This report indicated:

   a. Members of the school community interviewed believed that the school had the potential for continued improvement.

   b. The school was yet to develop a narrow and explicit improvement plan to impact significantly on classroom practice.

   c. The school had experienced significant leadership change over a lengthy period of time, which had directly impacted on relationships and the cohesiveness of the staff.

2. **Staff and Parent Opinion Survey**

Figure 5.1 data showed a decline in staff and parent satisfaction between 2013 and 2015. This data set is often utilized as a school community culture indicator.

(Continued)

Figure 5.1 Staff and Student Opinion Survey Data 2013–2015

1 Shared Beliefs and Understandings

1. All students can achieve high standards given the right time and the right support.

2. All teachers can teach to high standards given time and the right assistance.

3. High expectations and early and ongoing intervention are essential.

4. All leaders, teachers, and students can articulate what they do and why they lead, teach, and learn the way they do.

3. **Student Learning Data**

   NAPLAN is the Australian National Assessment Program for Literacy and Numeracy that is implemented each year for students in Years 3, 5, 7, and 9. The highlighted student data in Figure 5.2 shows the mean reading and writing **score** for students in Year 3 had consistently been below the national average. The Year 5 mean reading and writing score for students had inconsistent trends moving between below and similar to the national average mean student scores.

Utilizing this data source and a focus on improving student learning due to red results in Figure 5.2, Leach identified and documented that there was an immediate need to:

✓ Build the data literacy and teaching **capability** of staff

✓ Implement processes and practices to ensure there was **consistency of practice across the school** to evidence student learning and

✓ Utilize **intentional collaboration** processes so that there was a shared ownership of the school's improvement journey and shared accountability for all students' learning.

Driven by this strong sense of urgency, the principal identified the need to ensure there was shared ownership of the improvement journey, which resulted in the implementation of a distributive leadership model to co-construct and co-lead the first phase (Figure 5.3).

In 2016, Sharratt came to work with schools across the region on the FACES agenda, including intensive work to implement the 14 Parameters (Chapter 1). During pupil-free days at the beginning of 2017, Leach strategically forefronted clear expectations on how the school would collaboratively develop and reflect their collective beliefs (Parameter #1) and co-construct the meaning of shared responsibility and accountability (Parameter #14). His first priority was to establish a collaborative learning culture through the creation of a collective sense of urgency. As Leach said,

I presented the data to the staff and for many this was the first time they had seen it. I simply asked the staff... "So what is this data set telling us?" This question and subsequent activities identified

(Continued)

(Continued)

Figure 5.2 Years 3 and 5 NAPLAN Data Mean Student Scores 2008–2021

Year 3

	Reading	Writing	Spelling	G&P	Numeracy
2008	353.1	389.1	373.5	357.8	367.2
2009	375	404	368	395	424
2010	388	375	369	373	354
2011	364	365	373	389	367
2012	366	386	371	371	350
2013	380.8	406.0	393.4	411.3	359.6
2014	372.6	373.7	375.7	355.1	394.4
2015	362.7	376.5	355.1	376.2	355.5
2016	382.2	390.1	394.4	403.9	367.2
2017	403	404	398	426	382
2018	400	369	386	401	389
2019	436	432	417	434	406
2021	433.1	384.2	423	398.3	365.5

Year 5

	Reading	Writing	Spelling	G&P	Numeracy
2008	479.5	476.0	494.5	468.0	471.7
2009	464	487	469	478	474
2010	444	479	467	463	486
2011	451	425	453	473	457
2012	441	417	451	430	448
2013	475.9	469.8	500.0	487.0	465.6
2014	483.8	453.0	475.1	482.6	476.5
2015	450.5	446.3	447.3	450.7	443.1
2016	460.6	440.3	471.5	497.8	473.6
2017	515	447	487	484	491
2018	494	449	499	506	486
2019	487	462	487	492	480
2021	508.8	471.7	484.6	507.6	480

Legend:
- Below National Average
- Similar National Average
- Above National Average

Figure 5.3 Principal Summary of Key Focus Areas Emerging

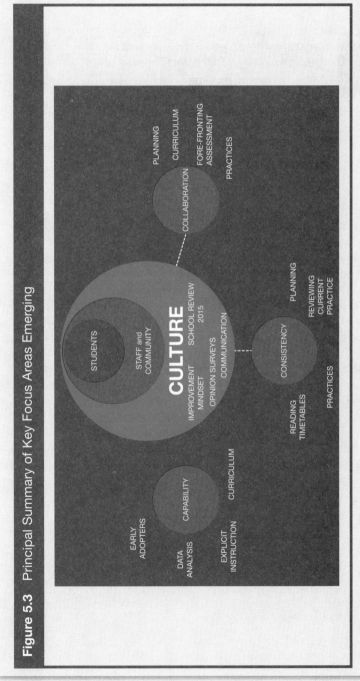

(Continued)

Source: Tania Leach, Kingsthrope State Primary School

(Continued)

> *that only 65% of students were reaching the national minimum standard in NAPLAN. This realisation provided the sudden sense of collective urgency and all staff agreed that we had to do something about it!*

Through the implementation of intentional collaborative processes (Parameter #11) and a focus on identifying solutions and opportunities, the staff developed their Explicit Improvement Agenda outlined in Figure 5.4.

1. Improving Reading Comprehension

As the school staff engaged in learning together, they also acknowledged the importance of valuing and deepening current practice. The agreed process began with teachers visiting in each other's classrooms during guided reading instructional time to observe and identify pedagogical practices (Parameter #3). Teachers were provided with additional release time to engage in this activity, with the principal and head of curriculum timetabling themselves into each teacher's classroom (Parameter #2).

During allocated staff meetings (Parameter #7), the existing pedagogical practices were synthesized, which identified the need for consistency of practice and language across all classrooms. Staff noted that due to the variety of practices and support resources within classrooms, students often had to "relearn what learning looked like" as they moved from class to class and from year to year.

Utilizing a working party structure, the staff developed their reading approach to reflect evidence-based practices. Incorporated within this (Figure 5.4) were quality teaching practices and pedagogies (Parameter #3) which included

- Goal Setting

- Targeted and Descriptive Feedback

- The Gradual Release of Responsibility

- The BIG 6 Reading Areas

- Explicit Instruction

Figure 5.4 Kingsthorpe's 2017 Improvement Agenda

Improving Reading Comprehension

- Implement the School Wide Pedagogical Framework featuring "*Explicit Instruction*" with a specific focus on the teaching of Reading Comprehension strategies and processes.
- Embed consistent teacher Data Analysis Skills to focus on precision and differentiation in teaching.

Enhancing Staff Capability & Collaboration

- Continue to embed Tier 2 PBL practices into our school culture.
- Develop "Coaching and Feedback" processes across the school.
- Enhance participation in Professional Learning Teams.

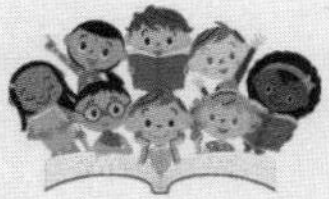

Every Student Succeeding

- Provide quality feedback to ensure student success.
- Deliver, successfully, "*Investing 4 Success*" programs and initiatives.

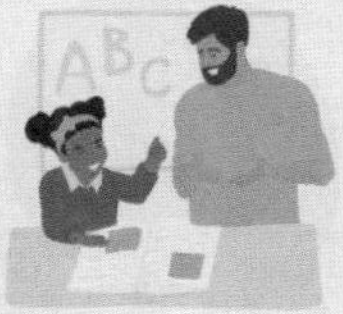

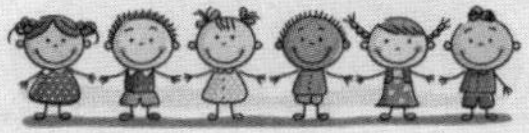

(Continued)

Source: children holding hands image by halepak/istock.com; teacher and student image by Visual Generation/istock.com; children reading image by habun/istock.com

Figure 5.5 Whole School Reading Placemat

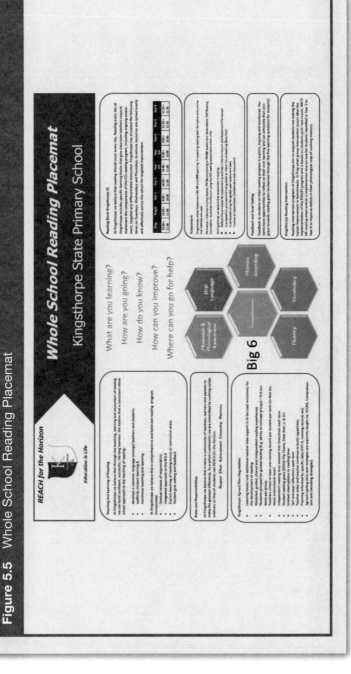

Source: Tania Leach, Kingsthrope State Primary School

2. Enhancing Staff Capability and Collaboration

Acknowledging the need to value and embrace the current expertise and perspectives of the staff, they were surveyed to identify their support preferences. As a result formal Professional Learning (PL) sessions with a focus on knowledge-building and consistent implementation were scheduled.

Source: Tania Leach, Kingsthrope State Primary School

These structures included in-school and after school PL (Parameter #8). Where the expertise sat within the school, staff facilitated the learning, which included the principal (Parameter #4). At other times, Knowledgeable Others (Parameter #2) connected with the school to build knowledge capabilities.

Utilizing research, staff co-constructed a set of posters to reflect the Big 6 Ideas of teaching reading. This process supported staff to unpack the critical aspects and connect them to their teaching practice and student learning (Parameters #3 and #13). These poster drawings were turned into professional posters (Figure 5.6) and are a resource utilized within each classroom to gain consistency of practice.

Instructional coaching (Parameter #7) and peer feedback processes (using the co-developed pedagogical look-fors) were optional for staff, with 100% of staff choosing to utilize these supports. Staff identified that these processes helped them explore the effectiveness of their teaching delivery resulting in a collaborative learning culture that empowered all staff to develop shared knowledge and practices in a trusted, safe, and supported environment (Parameters #8 and #11).

Supporting staff through targeted resource allocation (Parameter #9) ensured staff were valued as the improvement work was completed within school hours. Teachers were provided with additional noncontact time during each week to complete and analyze Running Records (see Glossary) and were allocated full planning days at the end of each term to utilize their data to inform their next teaching and learning cycle.

(Continued)

(Continued)

Figure 5.6 Kingsthorpe Staff Co-Constructed Reading Instruction Posters

Source: Tania Leach, Kingsthrope State Primary School

Another critical aspect of this learning journey was the presence of the leadership team led by the principal in classrooms each and every day (Parameter #4). With a focus on student learning, the leadership team would connect with students, join in activities, or simply ask, "What are you learning today?" This practice evolved into formal Learning Walks and Talks (Parameter #14) that utilized the 5 Questions for students (Sharratt & Fullan, 2012; Sharratt, 2019).

Literacy blocks and centralized resources (Parameters #3 and #9) were also formalized with a teacher aide assigned the task of managing the distribution and return of literacy materials. Literacy blocks were timetabled with two additional staff members (teacher aides and a leadership team member) allocated to each classroom for guided reading sessions (Parameter #2). Within the Kindergarten classrooms for 6 months of each school year, an external speech pathologist was employed on a part-time basis to support students' oral language development.

With the direction clear and continually participating in regional PL days with Sharratt, 2016–2019, putting FACES on the data through the Leading Learning Collaborative (LLC) approach became the springboard for the next phase of the school's improvement journey, which led to the next priority: building the data literacy of teachers.

Staff members identified that they had an abundance of assessment data but noted it was rarely used to inform their teaching (Chapter 3; Parameters #3 and #13). As a result of this, a review and reduction of the school's assessment schedule occurred to ensure assessment was purposeful, aligned to students' goals, and used to inform instruction. This process also identified the need to build staff's knowledge in how to conduct accurate Running Records (Parameter #5) and analyze them to inform flexible guided reading groups and student reading goals.

The staff utilized their established intentional collaboration processes (Parameter #11) to continue to refine their selection of teaching approaches though the supported data-driven process of co-constructing a Data Wall (Figure 5.7) that led to targeted Case Management Meetings (CMMs) (Parameter #6), specifically to identify and take action on behalf of students who needed support in demonstrating age-appropriate reading behaviors.

The unpacking of students' learning needs also supported teachers in providing targeted and Descriptive Feedback to students (Parameter #3). Through this process, teachers' assessment literacy was deepening and for the first time there were specific, clear, and consistent whole-school learning expectations in reading.

(Continued)

(Continued)

Figure 5.7 Kingsthorpe Data Wall With a Student Card and Case Management Meeting Notes

Source: Tania Leach, Kingsthrope State Primary School

Figure 5.8 demonstrates that the intentional teaching through the selection of evidence-based pedagogies was supported through the school's Case Management Meeting process (Parameter #6). When this process was initiated, the detailed templates in Figure 5.8 were utilized (see Appendix C). Teachers were encouraged to bring "tricky" students to discuss, and CMM notes from the templates used were recorded on the student Data Wall cards using QR Codes (Parameter #6). As the process

Figure 5.8 Case Management Meeting Template, Example, and Protocols

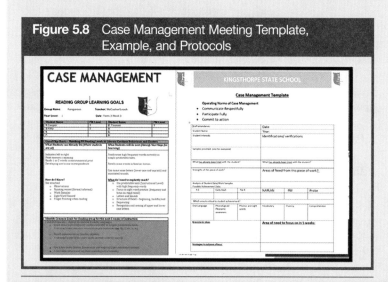

Source: Tania Leach, Kingsthrope State Primary School

developed, and Follow-Up CMMs were held, teachers began to value the reflective cycles and sharing of instructional approaches and strategies (Chapter 4), utilizing this process to celebrate significant student learning gains at the end of each term (Parameter #14). This notion reflected the valuing of the collective expertise developing within the school and highlighted the impact of intentional collaboration.

Growth in student learning was beginning to be evidenced by the end of 2017. Results were ascribed to: clarity and specificity around what the learning and teaching of Reading looked like through the implementation of CMMs, targeted student learning goals and Descriptive Feedback to teachers and students through collaborative data analysis (Parameter #8).

The observable improvements in student data, using triangulated diagnostic, formative, summative, and external assessments provided a celebration point as the learning improvement work continued to gain momentum (Parameter #14). A highlight for the school was being recognized nationally by the Australian Curriculum, Assessment and Reporting Authority (ACARA) for significant student growth (gain) in the 2017 NAPLAN assessments.

Over the next 4 years, Kingsthorpe staff and students continued to implement cycles of learning duplicating the established processes to identify targeted literacy goals. With NAPLAN and diagnostic data readily available in the form of *PM Benchmarks* (see Glossary) and *Probe levels* (see Glossary), teachers continued to refine the development of learning goals through the use of resources that explicitly triangulated students' reading behaviors evidenced across multiple data sets to the Department of Education's literacy continuum and the school's Data Wall. The Data Wall (Parameter #6) was regularly utilized and became a "business as usual" process that demonstrated how students' literacy data to inform their next steps in learning was becoming an embedded way of working at Kingsthorpe State School.

With continual student learning being evidenced, the school moved their focus to improving students' assessment literacy with the implementation of co-constructed Learning Walls (Sharratt, 2019, pp. 144–147) and Learning Walks and Talks (*FACES*, Chapter 6). Teachers' and students' clarity of learning expectations deepened to a point where they were now unpacking and discerning the differences between an A, B, and C Levels of Achievement standard within planning sessions (Parameter #8) and with students through the development of deconstructed Learning Intentions and co-constructed Success Criteria (Chapter 3). To support the ongoing reflection of how the improvement focus was impacting on student's ability to own and articulate their

(Continued)

(Continued)

learning journeys, Learning Walks and Talks and the 5 Questions for students (Figure 5.9) became a valued process.

Kingsthorpe shared their precision-in-practice learnings through cluster school co-planning (Parameter #7), Collaborative Assessment of Student Work (Parameter #8), and Learning Walks and Talks (Parameter #14). This sharing facilitated further refinement of teaching practices and confirmed the validity of teacher judgments. Leach acknowledged the importance in valuing the work as many teachers identified "that they had never shared outside of their classroom, let alone with other schools before this learning journey began."

Figure 5.9 Five Questions for Students Reflective Tool

Questions for Students	Students can answer these questions when:
1. **What are you learning? Why?**	• Teachers deconstruct the curriculum to develop Learning Intentions (LI) • Teachers co-construct with students Learning Intentions in student friendly language • Learning Intentions are on display in classrooms for students to refer to
2. **How are you going?**	• Teachers co-construct with students Success Criteria (SC) using age appropriate language • Success criteria are on display in classrooms for students to refer to
3. **How do you know?**	• Teachers give timely, relevant feedback based on Learning Intentions and Success Criteria • Teachers explicitly teach students how to peer and self-assess based on LI's & SC
4. **How can you improve?**	• Teachers provide ongoing feedback based on LI's and SC's and plan the next steps with students
5. **Where will you go for help?**	• Teachers teach students the attributes of independent learners and where they can access help beyond the teacher

Source: Sharratt (2018). *CLARITY*

3. Every Student Succeeding

Staff members' feelings about Kingsthorpe's achievement record was further validated in 2021 with an acknowledgment of their achievements by the Queensland Department of Education, who published a "bright spot" paper highlighting how the use of instructional leadership and intentional collaboration with Case Management Meetings and Learning Walks and Talks facilitated students' improvement at Kingsthorpe. In addition to this, the range of student learning data being collected continued to show student growth in the NAPLAN relative gain data between 2016 and 2021. Not only were students reaching the national minimum standard (Figure 5.10), but also *all* students were achieving at a significantly higher score (identified in bands) with significant growth in the mean student scores (Figure 5.11). Note: The *red* or below expectation has been eradicated in years 2018–2021! Bravo to principal James Leach and all staff at Kingsthorpe SS.

Another key indicator of success was the rate or gain of learning evidenced for each student or cohort. The gain at Kingsthorpe was above the national gain for students who were in Year 3 in 2016 and Year 5 in 2018 and Year 3 in 2017 and Year 5 in 2019 as outlined in Figure 5.12.

C. Evidence of Impact

In the following impressive data chart, note that *green* indicates above National Gain! One staff member summed it up, reflecting back on their learning journey, by stating:

> *When I think back on all we have achieved, I can see that it took a lot of time and practice to be confident in what we were implementing, but we were given voice (agency) and support in how we did this. We now have such clarity on what student learning should look like and what students' next steps are, and how to get them there—**that** is worth it!*

Kingsthorpe has come a long way since their first review in 2015. The 2019 school improvement review highlighted the impact this focused work has had on the school's culture, positively indicating:

- The school leadership team has established an evidence-proven improvement agenda (Parameters #4 and #14).

- The school priorities align to the school's vision and values. The school has a clearly articulated high expectations that "all

(Continued)

Figure 5.10 Percentage of Students Achieving the National Minimum Standard

Year 3

	Reading	Writing	Spelling	G&P	Numeracy
2008	86.4	100	100	95.5	95.2
2009	90.0	100.0	90.0	95.0	100.0
2010	90.0	100.0	90.0	95.0	100.0
2011	84.2	88.9	88.9	88.9	82.4
2012	85.7	100.0	96.4	92.9	88.9
2013	85.0	95.0	90.0	95.0	89.5
2014	78.3	91.3	93.5	78.3	91.3
2015	83.9	93.5	87.1	87.1	83.9
2016	96.6	96.7	96.7	83.3	93.3
2017	100.0	100.0	100.0	95.7	100.0
2018	93.0	97.0	93.0	97.0	100.0
2019	100.0	100.0	100.0	100.0	96.0
2021	100.0	100.0	100.0	100.0	100.0

Year 5

	Reading	Writing	Spelling	G&P	Numeracy
2008	80.3	81.7	87.5	84.7	87.3
2009	94.7	94.7	94.7	89.5	89.5
2010	94.7	94.7	94.7	89.5	89.5
2011	89.5	78.9	89.5	89.5	89.5
2012	70.6	75.0	75.0	75.0	87.5
2013	84.6	83.3	84.6	84.6	84.6
2014	89.3	88.9	92.6	81.5	85.7
2015	91.3	95.5	86.4	90.9	95.7
2016	65.2	78.3	87.0	87.0	78.3
2017	100.0	86.4	90.9	90.9	100.0
2018	96.0	96.0	100.0	100.0	96.0
2019	100.0	88.5	100.0	93.0	100.0
2021	100.0	88.0	96.0	96.0	100.0

Legend:
- Below National Average
- Similar National Average
- Above National Average

Figure 5.11 Student Cohort Mean Score

NAPLAN MEAN SCALE SCORES–Kingsthorpe SS

Legend: Below National Average / Similar National Average / Above National Average

Year 3

	Reading	Writing	Spelling	G&P	Numeracy
2008	353.1	389.1	373.5	357.8	367.2
2009	375	404	368	395	424
2010	388	375	369	373	354
2011	364	365	373	389	367
2012	366	386	371	371	350
2013	380.8	406.0	393.4	411.3	359.6
2014	372.6	373.7	375.7	355.1	394.4
2015	362.7	376.5	355.1	376.2	355.5
2016	382.2	390.1	394.4	403.9	367.2
2017	403	404	398	426	382
2018	400	369	386	401	389
2019	436	432	417	434	406
2021	433.1	384.2	423	398.3	365.5

Year 5

	Reading	Writing	Spelling	G&P	Numeracy
2008	479.5	476.0	494.5	468.0	471.7
2009	464	487	469	478	474
2010	444	479	467	463	486
2011	451	425	453	473	457
2012	441	417	451	430	448
2013	475.9	469.8	500.0	487.0	465.6
2014	483.8	453.0	475.1	482.6	476.5
2015	450.5	446.3	447.3	450.7	443.1
2016	460.6	440.3	471.5	497.8	473.6
2017	515	447	487	484	491
2018	494	449	499	506	486
2019	487	462	487	492	480
2021	508.8	471.7	484.6	507.6	480

(Continued)

(Continued)

	Figure 5.12 Student Cohort Learning Gain Between Year 3 and Year 5 NAPLAN Assessments			
	National Gain 2016–2018	**Kingsthorpe Average Gain 2016–2018**	**National Gain 2017–2019**	**Kingsthorpe Average Gain 2017–2019**
Reading	83	108	75	85
Writing	44	38.7	60	74
Spelling	83	101.8	85	103
Grammar & Punctuation	68	91.3	60	74
Numeracy	92	118.4	86	103
Aggregate Gain	370	458.2	366	439
Average Gain	74	91.64	73	88

students will have one year's growth for one year's schooling." All priorities have targets, timelines, and a responsible officer identified. Staff members are united in their commitment to the school priorities (Parameter #1).

- The sharp and narrow focus on the school priorities since the last school review has positively impacted on systemic data (Parameter #14).

- Staff members monitor student achievement data across the school (Parameters #3 and #6).

D. Leadership Lessons

When principal James Leach was asked why he thought the learning journey had evidenced a significant impact on school culture, staff capability, and student learning, he identified the following leadership takeaways:

- All decisions centered around what was **best for students**. This ensured they were focused on and collectively committed to the *right work* (Parameters #1 and #14).

- Placing a focus on the **school culture** through valuing staff expertise and focusing on collaborative inquiry established the platform for ongoing reflection and learning (Parameter #11).

- **Visible and present leaders** in classrooms on a daily basis demonstrated the leadership team members' commitment to co-learning and walking alongside teachers (Parameter #4).

- Identifying **teacher leaders** as integral to the leadership structure within the school to complement the formal leadership team. This in turn enabled the authentic implementation of a distributive leadership model that supported the shared ownership of the learning journey (Parameters #2 and #4).

- **Precision-in-practice** through the use of collaborative processes and clarity of expectations, roles, and accountabilities ensures there is line-of-sight alignment between what we say we do in classrooms and the subsequent impact on student learning (Parameters #3 and #13).

- **Staying the course** by ensuring staff are supported and accountable. Formalizing celebration points and having transparent conversations about how the leaders support each teacher to be successful. Teacher support is therefore not a one-size-fits-all but is differentiated to meet all teachers' unique needs and to build leadership capability (Parameter #14).

It was clear that the collaborative learning culture fostered and supported by Principal James Leach provided the foundation for their improvement journey (Parameter #4). With an unrelenting focus on student learning, every process and practice was selected and contextualized to provide clarity for and of learning (Parameter #1). (Dr. Tania Leach, Associate Dean, University of Southern Queensland, personal communication, January 2022)

Know-ability, Mobilize-ability, Sustain-ability

The Kingsthorpe State School journey to impressive school improvement results parallels our research findings. Recall that in our survey we asked educators, "What are the top three leadership skills needed to put FACES on the data?" In response, 45 percent said that, to lead with credibility, leaders must first model knowledge of classroom practice—assessment and instruction—what we call *know-ability.* Further, 33 percent said that the ability to inspire and mobilize others through clear communication of commitment was essential—what we call *mobilize-ability.* Finally, 21 percent said that knowing how to establish a lasting culture of shared responsibility and accountability was crucial—what we call *sustain-ability.* These are three factors that represent a specific focus by leaders to get results—exactly what James Leach modeled first and his staff continue to model for other schools in their cluster in the case study that opened this chapter. Next, we expand on each of these three areas to clarify what great leaders and teachers do—together—to put FACES on the data.

1. Know-ability

Principals need to have a strong and compelling message, but they also must "know their stuff." James Leach's first step was to analyze student achievement data to gain knowledge of all students, not only to make well-informed decisions but also to have a compelling message that made teachers and parents want to buy in to the hard work ahead. A nearly universal finding in school improvement efforts has been "the need for strong, academically-focused principal leadership (Calman, 2009, p. 17)." Principals must be knowledgeable about high-impact classroom practices if they are to "champion the importance of assessment for [and as] learning [and instruction, discussed in Chapters 3 and 4] by ensuring a consistent and continuous school-wide focus on student learning; and by using classroom, school, and system data to monitor progress" (Ontario Ministry of Education, 2010a).

How can principals use data to monitor progress so that they can lead in schools, such that putting FACES on the data becomes a daily occurrence? The Kingsthorpe Case Study is very instructive for us: Know-ability begins with prowess in teaching, learning, and leading. Andreas Schleicher (2011) further defines its impact by saying that the quality of an education system cannot exceed the quality of its teachers and principals.

Our intent is to uncover the "how" of being a knowledgeable leader and describe it clearly, using examples, as we delve into the complexities of the leadership skills needed to put the FACES on the data.

Know-ability: Knowledgeable Other

According to the respondents in our research, the key is principals' deep structured understanding of evidence-informed assessment and instructional practices in classrooms as defined by the term *The Third Teacher* (the learning environment). The principal must be the lead learner, modeling continuous learning, committing to being a co-leader and co-learner with teachers, and participating in tangible assessment and instructional practices as the "Knowledge-able Other" (Sharratt et al., 2010). As Knowledgeable Others, school leaders know what it looks like to use data to improve instruction in each class across the school. They are mindful to stay the course by maintaining, reviewing, and monitoring units of study, lesson plans, and school improvement plans, ensuring there is alignment between the vision in the plan on paper and classroom practices recorded in unit and lesson plans and seen during Learning Walks and Talks.

Data-driven instruction and the ubiquitous presence and use of assessment data are core themes for promoting and maintaining efforts to improve. Principals lead the Case Management Approach (Parameter #6), in which the Data Wall is used to identify (1) individual students to be tracked and corrective action to be taken on an ongoing basis (see Chapter 3), and (2) teachers who have the opportunity to use the Case Management Meeting as a collaborative forum to discuss students who present them with instructional conundrums (see Chapter 4).

Knowledgeable principals know how to improve the performance of teachers who are struggling and how to reward and support their best teachers. They provide risk-free environments in which teachers work together to frame good practice. That is where teachers and principals conduct field-based research (Collaborative Inquiry, Parameter #11; see Chapter 4) to confirm or disprove the approaches they develop and implement on behalf of students. This demands that high-quality school systems, in general, and school leaders, specifically, pay attention to how they select and train their staff (Schleicher, 2011).

Know-ability: High Expectations

"Challenging satisfactory teachers (and leaders) to be good and the good to be outstanding is a significant factor in creating high-performing schools" (Davies & Davies, 2011, p. 178). Leaders who are outstanding continually ask themselves:

✓ Are our expectations high enough?

✓ Are all students excelling—not just getting by—or going unnoticed?

✓ Am I leading by example?

Then they clearly articulate the expected use of data to drive instruction (see Chapters 3 and 4), provide differentiated PL opportunities for teachers to see and experience strong practice in action, monitor the implementation of data use and differentiated instruction by being in classrooms conducting Learning Walks and Talks (Sharratt, 2019), and by following up on these with teacher conversations after many times in their classrooms, being clear about the implementation of expected practices.

Teddlie et al. (2000) identified the following five high expectations of staff that principals need to address:

1. Expecting new teachers to have a good understanding of the school before they arrive

2. Expecting a high level of teacher participation in professional development activities

3. Expecting detailed monitoring by staff of student activities, including homework

4. Expecting staff to make the students' academic achievement their first priority

5. Expecting staff to manage their time effectively to ensure maximum student time on task

To this list we add

6. Expecting staff to use data to inform instruction for every student every day

Know-ability: Data Use

In a study conducted by Louis et al. (2010), principals and teachers reported increasing efforts to develop the capacity of teachers to engage collectively in data analysis for instructional decision making that were often associated with professional learning communities initiated and assisted by district training. **They found that princi-pals played a key leadership role in establishing the purposes and expectations for data use, in providing structured oppor-tunities (collegial groups and time) for data-use training and assistance, and in providing access to expertise and follow-up actions.** However, they said that they saw no evidence that teachers do this on their own . . . and if the district wasn't using the data to make educational decisions for educational improvement actions, it was unlikely to be happening at the school level.

Therefore, alignment of strategies such as data use is an issue that must be nonnegotiable (Parameter #6). If districts expect that schools are using data for instruction, then they had better be mod-eling how at the regional level and monitoring the implementation of data use at the school level. Know it and show they use it. As well, if principals expect teachers to be using data for instruction, then they must provide the primary leadership. What does this mean in real time in a big or small but always busy school? In response to this notion, the Ontario Ministry of Education (2010a) documents that principals must champion the importance of assessment for and as learning (see Chapter 3) by ensuring a consistent and continu-ous school-wide focus on student learning and by using classroom, school, and system data to monitor progress.

We describe here an exemplary model of how to use data for school and student improvement. Principal Jill Maar (see Armadale Case Study in Chapter 3) works diligently to improve all students' performance—one teacher and one student at a time. In short, Jill and her team know how to put the FACES on the data and make every student matter! Let's take a walk and talk with her.

Know-ability: Data Drives Instruction

At Armadale Public School (PS), learners' progress is monitored with rigor at 4- to 6-week intervals, when teachers bring their data, **using a Venn diagram format** (Figure 5.13), for frank discussions of where and how students are progressing in each class—rating them "below," "at," or "above" standard, using *Running Records* in Grades K–3 classrooms, and *higher-order thinking (HOT) skills* (see Glossary), for example, in junior and intermediate classrooms. Figure 5.13 shows where each student is in a mixed Grade 1 and 2 class. The focus of each teacher conference with Jill is to determine strengths, needs, and next steps for each and every individual learner. These courageous conversations put the spotlight on what teachers are doing (or not doing) for individual students in every class—Kindergarten to Grade 8. Teachers articulate why they are doing what they do and how it is going (Parameter #1). Red flags indicate where different intervention strategies are needed for struggling students, and discussions follow about what teachers will be teaching in the next 4 to 6 weeks and where the flagged students will be when the next check-in with Jill is planned. In that way, she has a pulse on the achievement of every FACE in her very large school. Figure 5.13 shows a powerful but simple visual that has made a difference to putting FACES on data so that students who need to be noticed and require interventions are indeed noticed at Case Management Meetings where interventions are indeed discussed and actioned.

Figures 5.14a and 5.14b illustrate a developmental learner profile that Jill and her leadership team developed to put FACES on every student. It shows a Kindergarten profile—note the specificity of the data collected. Teachers develop a learner profile for every student in every class at every year-level at Armadale PS and these profiles are examined regularly with Jill. These two powerful examples of data use by the Principal and teachers reflect Shulman's belief (2010, p. 2) that data represent "[t]he most common, profound and pervasive catalyst for improvement" that schools have identified. In Shulman's study, "[S]chool teams systematically identified strengths and challenges at the individual-student, grade and overall school levels. The information obtained was used to set goals and identify target areas for improvement; it often laid the foundation for the school [improvement] plan," as is the case at Armadale. We differentiate between a Data Wall that is a whole-school approach to owning all the FACES and class Venn diagrams that are part of developmental learner profiles. Both are critically important in knowing and owning all FACES. Armadale PS uses both data collection tools regularly.

All decisions about the focus of instructional practices, training needs, resource requirements, identity of support for student needs, and the placement of support staff are grounded in the outcomes of the data analyses. Our research suggests that principals must be committed to looking for living data by "walking" in classrooms both to observe and note successful practice, to confer and to share their no-name, nonevaluative observations and next steps with all staff members during staff meetings.

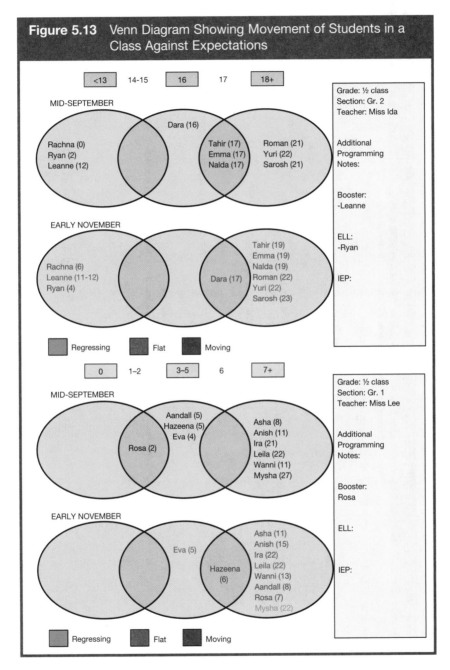

Figure 5.13 Venn Diagram Showing Movement of Students in a Class Against Expectations

Developed by Armadale PS Literacy Leadership Team

Figure 5.14a Developmental Learner Profile for a Pre-Primary/Kindergarten Class

Two-Year Developmental Learner Profile—Kindergarten

Junior Kindergarten (JK): 4-year-olds / Senior Kindergarten (SK): 5-year-olds

M F

Phonological Awareness

	Oct	Mar	Oct	Mar	Oct	Mar
1. Sentences to words						
2. Words to syllables						
3a. Hearing rhymes						
3b. Producing rhymes						

4. Sounds to words

5. Words to sounds

I = Independent   S = With support   N = Not yet

Letter ID and Sounds

O Can identify letter name ▨ Can identify letter name and sound

	A	K	I	T	D	O	W	C	L	M	V	F	S	Y	E	G	P	X	J	Q	H	B	R	Z	N	U
JK																										
SK																										

	c	k	l	t	d	o	w	c	l	m	v	f	s	y	e	g	p	x	j	q	h	b	r	z	n	u
JK																										
SK																										

Concepts of Written Materials When Reading (R) and Writing (W) (Check when concept is demonstrated)

	Front cover	Title	Text starting point for reading	Text is written from left to right	Return sweep (text is written from top to bottom)	Voice/ print match (1 to 1)	Leaves spaces between words	Identifies beginning and end of a sentence	Reads left page before right	Punctuation ? " " . , !	Identifies a letter	Identifies a word	Identifies Capital letter	Lower-case letter
JK R														
JK W														
SK R														
SK W														

Reading Text Level (Record date: M/D/Y)

0	1	2	3	4	5	6	7	8	9	10	11	12	13	14	15	16	17	18	19	20	21

Developed by Armadale PS Literacy Leadership Team

Figure 5.14b Developmental Learner Profile for a Pre-Primary/Kindergarten Class

Two-Year Developmental Learner Profile—Kindergarten

Junior Kindergarten (JK): 4-year-olds / Senior Kindergarten (SK): 5-year-olds

Student Name: **Date of Birth:**   M F   **Home Language:**

Oral Language

Understanding	Oct	Feb	Oct	Feb	Using	Oct	Feb	Oct	Feb
Words					Words				
Sentences					Sentences				
Story/ Paragraph					Story/ Paragraph				

I = Independent   S = With support   N = Not yet

Date: JK Talk Sample 1 (Assessment SET 1) Context:	Date: JK Talk Sample 2 Context:	Date: JK Talk Sample 3 (Assessment SET 2) Context:	Date: JK Talk Sample 4 Context:
Date: SK Talk Sample 1 (Assessment SET 1) Context:	Date: SK Talk Sample 2 Context:	Date: SK Talk Sample 3 (Assessment SET 2) Context:	Date: SK Talk Sample 4 Context:

Developed by Armadale PS Literacy Leadership Team

Know-ability: "Walking and Talking"

In between data conferences with teachers, Jill walked with intentionality, daily, in the school to see how the students were doing. She always checked in on the six Kindergarten classes with a predetermined focus for the Learning Walks and Talks (LWTs). Specificity could mean that the focus of the LWT was looking for evidence of shared or interactive writing, for example (Figure 4.2); Jill made a point of walking with a purpose to one wing of this very large school each day.

Reeves (2010, p. 59) says that it is "essential that school leaders distinguish evaluation—a process bounded by the constraints of legal precedent and collective bargaining—from assessment"—a process to promote growth through learning. For us, this relates to the monitoring and modeling stance that principals take by engaging in LWTs, wherein they walk in classrooms to observe and learn daily and have focused follow-up conversations (after many walks) with teachers about assessment and instruction.

Figure 5.15 demonstrates the relationship between the 5 Questions for students during LWTs and the Assessment Waterfall Chart (AWC) in Chapter 3. Students who can answer the 5 Questions with clear depth of understanding indicate the specificity of the assessment that has driven the instruction in their classrooms and their ownership of their learning. As Figure 5.15 shows, the 5 Questions for Teachers in their planning also directly relate to the AWC. The ultimate is student and teacher ownership of their learning and their clearly articulated next steps.

Leaders monitor their school's improvement plan by Walking with purpose and Talking with students daily, asking the 5 Questions (Figure 5.15 and Glossary). Leaders, like Jill and James, champion the importance of ongoing assessment practice by ensuring a *consistent, persistent, insistent* school-wide focus on student learning and quality teaching by using classroom, school, and system data to monitor progress and plan for actions going forward.

Does monitoring student progress using the Venn diagram process make a difference?

Assessments at Armadale PS (Chapter 3) showed that 31 of 75 Kindergarten students were at risk of not reading at the expected level. With focused literacy intervention, through ongoing Case Management

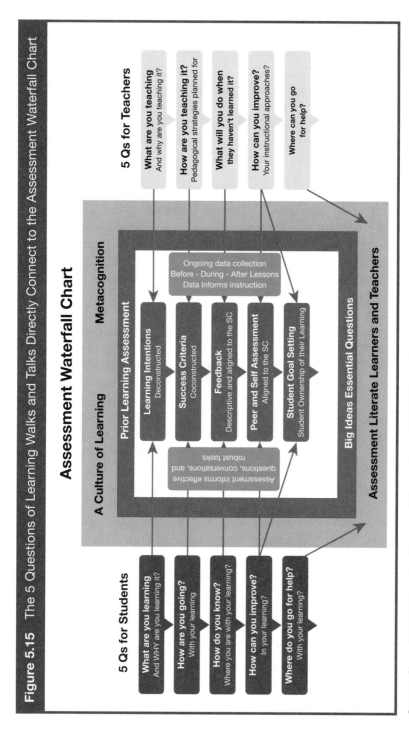

Source: Sharratt (2019); Graphic: Diocese of Lismore Central Office Team, Nov 25, 2021

Meetings, Jill and the Kindergarten teachers reduced the at-risk population to only 8 of 75 students by year end, and with all the remaining 8 reading above a Level 0. This is an outstanding example of the principal and leadership team as Knowledgeable Others, and the leadership team's sharing that Knowledgeable Other role throughout the school, in both data-informed and hands-on practitioner modes. As in the case of both Armadale and Kingsthorpe, it is also an example of leaders setting high expectations and simply not permitting any child to be left behind.

Deliberate Pause

- How is the impact on student learning monitored?

- Who models and monitors student learning?

- Are Learning Intentions aligned to standards or curriculum expectations? How do you know?

- How are Success Criteria aligned to Learning Intentions, and how are they differentiated for students? Are they used for Summative Assessment?

- Is feedback to students and teachers factual, objective, immediate, and aligned with Learning Intentions and Success Criteria?

- What examples do you have of putting FACES on the data at the district, region, network, school, and classroom levels? What PL is in place to learn from it?

According to our research respondents, principals' deep structural understanding of successful literacy practices in classrooms is KEY. Therefore, principals must be committed to conducting LWTs in classrooms daily—**not** to *visiting* or *wandering around*, but to walking in classrooms to observe, collect data, note successful practices, and confer with students and teachers. We often make assumptions about what is going on in classrooms unless, as principals and system staff, we make a conscientious effort to Walk and Talk in classrooms to ask students the 5 Questions. Learning Walks and Talks (Sharratt,

2011–2022) is a way of monitoring expected, effective practices in all classrooms.

Learning Walks and Talks not only give principals the opportunity to see what is being taught but also provide them with the opportunity to address the issues they observe or that teachers may ask about by offering ongoing PL at staff meetings and by pairing up teachers who need some assistance with other teachers who are delivering the expected practices; that is: Teachers teaching Teachers—the most powerful PL delivery vehicle! Focused daily Walks and Talks in all classrooms make monitoring progress enjoyable and celebratory and are a habit worth acquiring. The ultimate is teachers and leaders walking together to observe effective, expected classroom practices, as outlined in Chapters 3 and 4. Hey, and when it is done well, the kids love it and look forward to seeing their school leaders and teachers in their classrooms taking an interest in their learning.

Narrative From the Field

We got to know the FACES work when we translated the entire book into Spanish in 2017 so we could share it with many teachers and principals in Chile. Sharratt came to work with us in 2015 and again in 2017. In a district in the south of Chile she modeled and shared with many principals and teachers how to do Learning Walks and Talks (LWTs). We learned a lot, and then we taught many other teachers how to do LWTs. I think the most important thing is that we introduced that very powerful tool to support and refine the work teachers were doing in their schools. They are using it now to get evidence, to sharpen improvement cycles, and to learn and improve together. Principals with their teachers now know how students are improving, what's working, and what is not working by using the 5 Questions. For us all, the LWTs have become our means of inquiry and improvement in our focus.

As one principal said, "I believe learning to do LWTs was a huge contribution to student improvement for us that we are actually applying. Before we learned that, our support focused on teachers, now it is focused on students and how they are learning by using the 5 Questions as our evidence."

Another Principal said, "We really like the LWT tool. It helps us know what is happening with students and how to optimize our learning time. It also helps in finding the school focus and in giving direction

> to our work." We think this learning experience is for all students as our leaders begin to think that quality teaching promotes high quality expectations for our students. Leaders and teachers work and learn together because they are across all classrooms, inquiring and sharing the work done. So I think LWTs in Chile continue to be a tool to develop leaders as learners. (Isidora Recart, CEO, Arauco Foundation, Chile, personal communication, January 2022).

Learning Walks and Talks relate to what Senge (1990) reminds us so eloquently:

"[L]eader as teacher" is not about "teaching" people how to achieve their visions. It is about fostering learning for everyone. Such leaders help people throughout the organization to develop systemic understandings. Accepting this responsibility is the antidote to one of the most common downfalls of otherwise gifted leaders—losing their commitment to tell the truth. (p. 356)

Principals model leadership and learnership by being committed to the truth and by sharing responsibility, accountability, and ownership for student learning. In that way, they must "mobilize" teachers into action.

2. Mobilize-ability

Jill Maar and James Leach mobilized and galvanized their staff and community to focus on all students. They did this skillfully by getting teachers to collectively scrutinize their data, develop a plan of action, and seek input from the parents in the community before moving forward together. As the U.K. Office for Standards in Education, Children's Services and Skills (Ofsted) report aptly concludes, "[A]ll staff members need to be 'aboard the bus' when the school embarks on its journey of improvement" (cited in Calman, 2010, p. 25). *All staff buy-in is crucial to moving the improvement agenda forward in every school.*

Mobilize-ability: Magic Happens!

As one of our principal interviewees expressed,

> Support and encouragement are crucial. Pushing too hard never works. Magic happens when teachers take initiative within a framework which has been developed by the system, like the 14 Parameters. Incorporating PL into network, staff and division/year-level meetings needs to be led by staff not just the principal. When teachers are given time routinely to share their best practices, things happen.

Providing both time and resources for mentoring, coaching, and co-teaching (see Chapter 4) ensures that literacy, in the broadest sense, becomes and remains a focus. Walking the fine line between push and pull is always an exciting challenge and worth the time it takes to build strong leaders in a school (Fullan & Sharratt, 2007). Such leaders put FACES not only on student data but also on teacher performance data. They mobilize teachers in a positive, unthreatening manner by knowing their personal and professional goals, aspirations, and motivations.

As with students, leaders build teachers' capacity to accurately self-assess their teaching abilities and to seek collaborative learning opportunities when needed to ultimately benefit both teachers and students. When teachers become leaders, in *distributed leadership* roles (see Glossary), everyone benefits from the capacities of more of its members. Distributed leadership develops a fuller appreciation of interdependence and how one's behavior affects the organization as a whole (Harris, 2014; Leithwood et al., 2009; Louis et al., 2010). As Harris and Jones (2019) add poignantly,

> Policy makers also need to listen far more to those within the education systems, to the professionals who are so often excluded from substantive policy debates and decisions. They need to hear the voices of those teachers, leaders, and support staff on the front lines who are dealing with the brutal and heart-wrenching consequences of inequity and inequality. These education professionals are the true leaders of equity and excellence (p. 108) who can mobilize their teams into action.

Mobilize-ability: De-privatizing Practice

Leaders de-privatize practice, making teaching and learning transparent to all and debatable by all. How does that happen? EQAO research (Rogers, 2009) reported that

> a school culture that focuses on learning for *all* students was repeatedly described as an important factor in enabling each student to experience some measure of success. . . . Principals mobilize stakeholders by openly
>
> - holding and sustaining high academic, social and behavioral expectations;
> - using a variety of teaching methods to meet, in real ways, the needs of different students;
> - creating a consistently positive and caring school community;
> - encouraging positive role models to whom students can relate;
> - ensuring strong and effective educational leadership from the principal; and
> - maintaining ongoing active engagement of parents in the school. (p. 4)

Sounds a lot like our 14 Parameters of System and School Improvement!

The mobilization of these factors and the de-privatizing practice happens naturally when system and school leaders organize an annual Learning Fair—a culminating celebration and live report of evidence related to students' growth and achievement. This is not an exercise in bureaucratic accountability reporting. Put one way, we did not *start* with accountability but rather *ended* with it. Put still another way, after all schools were steeped in capacity-building, we sought a natural reinforcer that integrated "responsibility and accountability" (Parameter #14 in action!) and fed more positive energy into the improvement cycle at the school level (Sharratt & Fullan, 2009, pp. 90–92).

Interdependent leadership practice and the 14th Parameter are evident in annual Learning Fairs held now in many of the jurisdictions with which we work. For these culminating events, all elementary and secondary school teams prepare a half-hour multimedia presentation based on the following:

1. What the school set out to achieve that year

2. Evidence to support their students' increased literacy and numeracy achievement

3. What assessment and instructional strategies they used

4. Lessons learned

5. Challenges they are currently experiencing and next steps planned

What is most impressive about Learning Fairs is how articulate, consistent, and specific educators become when they discuss the what, the why, the how, and the assessed impact of their work (Parameter #1). Every school in the system participates perhaps in clusters, networks, Professional Learning Communities, or independently. There are, in other words, many change agents spread across all schools, all engaged in the same phenomenon—all using precise language, all pushing practice to the next level (Parameter #14).

Every school leader and teacher team prepares an evidenced-based report (focused on student data) and then submits it to their system leaders. The reports show their improved school results and their intentional next steps for the following year that are to be incorporated in their updated school improvement plans. Low-performing leaders are supported, "pulled along," and energized in this process by strong leaders who reach out—because the 14th Parameter is about shared responsibility and accountability for all our students. The annual reporting serves as a collaborative dialogue across schools and deepens participants' understanding of their own individual and collective learning that leads to the generation of additional next steps to be taken in their schools.

As well as generating new teaching strategies, it also broadens the interdependency from intraschool to interschool with one critical result being a reduction in the overall performance gap between schools—definitely an energizing way to de-privatize practice across schools in a system, network or state (see the Narrative From the Field at the end of this Chapter). It should be noted that in the communication of the description of Learning Fair participation is an absolute expectation that every school will participate. There are no "passes"; everyone participates, gives back, and learns as a result.

Mobilize-ability: Having an Urgent Craving

As Bill Gates (1995) says, "to be highly productive, we should introduce a sense of urgency into our lives." To us, it is urgent to get serious about putting FACES on the data and executing what we call the three tiers of instruction (see Chapter 4) in support of ALL students' growth. In our view, strategic leaders throughout the system—from elected officials to superintendents, principals, teacher-leaders, and teachers—energize and mobilize by doing the following:

- "Walking the talk" that models our shared beliefs and understandings, even when things are chaotic and budgets are pressed

- Remaining focused and staying the course on supporting evidence-proven classroom practices

- Having a laser-like focus on targeted high achievement levels

In our work these are recurring themes; however, here they are even more precise. Shared beliefs and understandings (Parameter #1) are more an outcome of a quality process than a precondition. Put differently, one condition for mobilize-ability involves working on defining, shaping, and refining the school's sense of shared moral purpose, using relevant data sources in relation to student improvement.

The more that beliefs are shared, the greater the ongoing effort, and the efficiency of the effort. As one principal reported, "[W]hen we reflect on the impact of our instructional decisions and what the data tell us about students' increased learning, it creates 'intellectual energy'" (Fullan & Sharratt, 2007). It becomes a craving to impact the learning of every student. This resonating quote leads us to think about how we sustain the intellectual energy created in Putting FACES on our Data and in mobilizing and sustaining subsequent actions.

3. Sustain-ability

Achieving and sustaining substantial improvement for all students all the time is complex. Sustain-ability at James Leach's and Jill Maar's schools will be experienced when students continue to achieve, decisions continue to reflect caring about students and teachers, and parents continue to feel part of the fabric of school life—no matter who is the principal. Leach and Maar have strong starts toward what

Louis et al. (2010) say that instructional leadership is: both climate and actions. The former relates to the steps that principals take to establish a culture that supports ongoing PL of research-informed instructional strategies; the latter refers to the explicit steps that principals take to engage with individual teachers about their own growth. According to this measure, James and Jill have done very well in ensuring the sustain-ability of their improvement work.

Some time ago we worried about the conditions in which school leaders can sustain reform efforts individually and collectively (Fullan & Sharratt, 2007), because state- and district-wide reform relies heavily on mobilizing leadership at all levels of the system.

Sustain-ability: We–We

We believe that intentional leadership models must unfold in a way that all schools benefit. The spirit underlying such approaches attempts to create a "we–we" mindset at every level. As a result of purposeful interaction within and across schools, school leaders become more aware of, and indeed more committed to, the success of other schools in addition to their own.

Although individual leaders, like James Leach and Jill Maar, can and must work on sustaining their own energies, the conditions for sustaining large numbers of people can be fostered only if the organization as a whole is working in this direction (Fullan & Sharratt, 2007). Moreover, we maintain that focusing on sustain-ability must become more deliberate and precise. Synergy is created when sustain-ability is worked on in a self-conscious and organizationally conscious manner.

Sustain-ability: Energy Creates Synergy

Sustain-ability conditions are those that motivate people to continue to invest their energies in working with others to accomplish greater student improvement. In 2007, we asked almost 100 elementary and secondary principals, "How do you as leader sustain your schools' literacy approach?" We found that most responses reflected the themes in our 14 Parameter research at the time and could be categorized into five major areas:

Shared beliefs, goals, and vision (Parameters #1, #6, #14—the nonnegotiables)

1. Distributed leadership and Professional Learning cultures (Parameters #2, #4, #7, and #8)

2. Data-based decisions/impact measures/celebrating success (Parameters #3 and #13)

3. Resources (Parameters #9 and #10)

4. School-community/home relations (Parameter #12)

These early findings parallel our 2012 research that identifies the top three leadership skills necessary to put FACES on the data—know-ability, mobilize-ability, and sustain-ability.

Successful sustain-ability is often related in the literature to what we have come to call the presence of dedicated *second change agents* or what is sometimes referred to as *distributive leadership*—a critical mass of middle leaders led by the principal working on establishing a culture of ongoing learning. The principal is the first change agent—the lead learner. Having one or more second change agents is crucial—for example, a teacher-leader or embedded instructional coach (Parameter #2) with direct responsibility and time during the school day to work alongside other teachers in their classrooms, to link teachers with each other internally and across schools, to help set up data management systems, and to work with the principal on the school improvement agenda. One principal summed this up by saying,

> Sustaining the momentum within the school is possible because of the many levels of support available to our school. The staffing made available for literacy coaches has been critical. This has given our school a teacher-leader who is working to increase the knowledge of all those around her. (Fullan & Sharratt, 2007)

Sustain-ability: Waste Not

Human and material resource management is part and parcel of continued success, provided that the resources selected are part of a focused cycle of success. Kick-start your improvement processes with new resources and then have your success "chase the money"—this year's success is next year's additional resources. For example, Armadale Public School received a grant from retailer Indigo Books for $176,000 to purchase resources for their library—the largest grant to be awarded to a school in Canada at the time of writing! This grant followed on tremendous initial success and honors the amazing work the entire staff has done. Bravo to Jill and her accomplished team including her parents and community!

Publicly elected officials and system and school leaders must agree to allocate funding for just-right resources aligned to the priority and continue to fund them through tough economic times (Parameter #10). Consideration for human and material resources must focus on equity of outcomes for all students and learning for all teachers (Parameter #9). However, wasted time and material resources are also equity issues that cause leadership frustration at every level.

Once leadership teams have a vision for each and every graduating student, anything that helps students achieve that vision is value-added. On the other hand, any action that does **not** help students move closer to that expectation is considered **waste.** For example, time can be a waste when it's lost due to inefficient transitions from class to class; undifferentiated instruction can be a waste if it causes many students to be retaught what they already know. Another type of waste is lack of knowledge- or skills-sharing, when students or staff members don't work collaboratively and share ideas to increase all students' growth or achievement.

When these *wastes* plus the many other forms of waste are reduced, students are able to add more value to their learning as they work toward the desired Success Criteria. James Leach encourages his staff to look at any school or system approach in the same manner, which helps his school staff become more precise and aligned toward the expected outcomes. What is the principal's role in determining waste in reaching the desirable goal of every student excelling?

Sustain-ability: Developing Other Leaders

It is well-known that one dimension of the leader's job is to focus on developing other leaders. However, as Reeves (2010) points out, "[S]ustained capacity-building for high-impact learning depends upon the development of teacher-leadership as well—those teachers who provide feedback to help their colleagues [see Chapter 4] and who receive feedback on the impact of their coaching" (p. 71). Teacher leadership must be a co-leadership endeavor with principals—establishing trusting relationships and equal partnerships as the work progresses (M. Sharratt, 2004). According to Davies and Davies (2011), "[I]t should be a mindset of 'doing with' and not 'doing to' that enables us to build engagement with others" (p. 174) to co-lead in the work of explicitly putting FACES on the data—what great leaders and teachers do!

Careful attention must be given to ensuring that aspiring principals have opportunities to learn the necessary skills. System leadership is challenged in today's context to find, train, and keep young leaders who are motivated to continue the work of FACES given its very public pressures and its considerable personal and professional demands. We note that leaders selected for the role of school principal should be able to create the conditions under which other leaders will flourish. There is no more neglected topic in research policy or practice. ***Supports and opportunities must be available for leaders who show the way to greater understanding of how they can bring these conditions about in their schools.*** We know that if these processes are not effective, schools pay a considerable price. Ineffective leadership can sabotage school reform processes in many different and subtly defiant ways. A positive example of how leaders can move, grow, and improve from within follows.

Narrative From the Field

Celebrating Learning in Western Canada

Prior to COVID-19 the Seine River School Division, in Manitoba, successfully held two division-wide Learning Fairs. School leadership teams, known as Learning Growth Teams (LGTs) after our ongoing work with Sharratt, gathered to share their year-long Collaborative Inquiry (CI) journeys. We believed that it was critical that school leaders be able to articulate our collective Learning Goal: to develop a theory of action and to document a path to increased student and teacher learning by being concise, intentional, and reflective on the impact of their practice on learning. Preparing for and presenting at our annual Learning Fair allowed LGTs the opportunity to share the wins and challenges of practice that they experienced in targeting deepened learning for teachers and leaders.

At the system level, we observed a strong increase in the level of complexity of the schools' work presented at the Second Annual Learning Fair as compared with the first one. The ability of LGTs to present data, evidence, and their learnings then to receive Descriptive

(Continued)

(Continued)

Feedback from their peers pushed CI and Professional Learning to new levels in our school division. This process was essential in assisting all staff involved in the FACES work to become more concise in their inquiries and more precise in their practice.

We realized that our Learning Fairs extended the thinking and learning of the staff as they moved from surface learning and expression to deeper thinking and finally to transferable use of knowledge. We see evidence of this transference when the CIs (Parameter #11) are demonstrated across all staff in one school and then across all staff in all schools. We also see the benefit of Learning Fairs when schools' Annual Improvement Plans begin to use the common language of improvement, such as Learning Intentions and Success Criteria in the Assessment Waterfall Chart (Chapter 3). We have determined that when language shifted in schools, due to the Learning Fair protocols, and a common language emerged across the school division, we were even more successful in generating a whole-system approach to improvement (Parameters #1 and #14).

Our Learning Fairs provided a venue for schools to share their findings, challenges, and next steps with other leadership teams in other schools and also with our valued partners—community members, politicians, parents, and other education partners. These exchanges have opened authentic and ongoing dialogue with our diverse community. Feedback from community members has been amazing; the Learning Fair is a true celebration of the work that our school teams are doing. School leaders and teachers can articulate the changes in teaching and learning that build stronger community support and a deeper understanding of the challenging work that LGTs are accomplishing.

Intentional precision-in-practice has developed using the vehicle of school CIs, beginning with the FACES of data. Because of the exchange of "learning," the Learning Fair has been a strong catalyst for change in the collective efficacy of LGTs, teachers, and students. Efficacy that has helped teams weather the difficulties of COVID, school shut-downs, and forced hybrid approaches as well as changes in education policy. The remarkable results through the consistent use of the Learning Fair template for collaborative sharing, indicated "good" work—and now we realize it is "THE WORK"—the only work that we need to sustain. (Michael Borgfjord, Chief Superintendent, Pembina Hills School Division, Alberta, Canada; and Elaine Lochhead, Chief Superintendent, Seine River School Division, Manitoba, Canada, personal communication, January 2022)

It is not so much that leaders need to believe that know-ability, mobilize-ability, and sustain-ability are possible, but rather that the only way to move forward is to be "in the game"—to be skilled (knowledgeable), empowered and empowering (mobilizing), and committed to (sustaining) the FACES of improvement. For an example of this from Vail, Arizona, click on QR Code 5.2.

QR Code 5.2:
Vail Unified
School District
Case Study

The benefits of principals' understanding the impact of know-ability, mobilize-ability, and sustain-ability on their all-inclusive approach to leadership is critical to their success in putting FACES on the data and making every student count as we witness in the following case study from Kentucky, USA.

A USA Case Study

Jefferson County Public Schools (JCPS) is the largest school district in Kentucky with 96,000 students and 150 schools (Fullan & Edwards, 2022). The majority of students are nonwhite and poor. In 2017, the State Board of Education was about to take over the district because of persistently low performance and failure to improve. Under the threat of state takeover the JCPS school board appointed one of its successful high school principals, Marty Polio, to the position of district superintendent. Here, we zero in on the question of "FACES."

Polio had written his doctoral dissertation on the topic of standards and grading practices. He considers existing grading practices, and the follow-on punitive accountability, one of the most detrimental components of K–12 education in the United States. "It's a matter of racial equity," he says. Following our change principle of "joint determination" (Fullan, 2019), Polio formed and helped lead a task force on designing a new system for assessment of learning.

The new system was designed to support authentic learning where students could pursue topics in more depth and be assessed in a different way—a way in which their individual FACES could come to life. JCPS designed what they called "A Backpack of Success Skills" that framed the learning:

1. Persistence and resilience

2. Communication

3. Collaboration

4. Innovation

5. Globally and culturally competent citizens

Polio elaborates:

> We want kids to practice and become proficient (in the skills). We want them to take artifacts of learning and, throughout their time in school, assemble artifacts on specific themes. Then in Grades 5, 8, & 12—the transitional years—all kids present [are formally assessed on] what they have done, presenting to a panel of three or four relevant teachers. Each student shows what he or she has done and provides examples. What this has enabled teachers to do is to authentically assess kids. (Fullan & Edwards, p. 81)

Within 3 years students (and their families) became more engaged, learning became more obvious, graduation rates moved up 4%, and students and teachers became more collaborative. Literally large numbers of students, teachers, and families came to *know* each other more personally.

In short, large numbers of students went from being anonymous (in some cases infamous) failures to being recognized and mutually valuing their successes. Our point is that as we move toward deeper learning goals, a golden opportunity is presented to transform assessment systems to those that are based on important new competencies. In a phrase, students FACES become more in focus and learning flourishes (Fullan & Edwards, 2021, pp. 72–83).

Deliberate Pause

- Who is in my class? (Note: Everyone has "a class" to teach and learn from—state leaders, school leaders, teachers, elected officials, and community members.)

- Whose learning is my responsibility?

- How do we ensure that the use of data considers emotional connectedness and cognitive insights?

- Are we using all the potential data points we have available—standards-based assessments, new, alternative forms of measurement?

As we have said in our Motion Leadership work, leadership is about causing positive movement in individuals, schools, and systems (Fullan, 2010b). Stated more dramatically, leadership stimulates large numbers of people to put in the energy to get better results even when at the outset they are not motivated to do so. *This is the magic of FACES.*

Sir John Jones (personal communication, November 2011) commented on the power of leaders who know and understand the relevant data so that all FACES may be put sensitively and skillfully on the data:

> Data is a clever seductress and those who are fixated by it often hide behind phrases like "What gets measured gets done." That may or may not be true. What is certain is that a leader who merely cognitively connects with numbers on a page or dots on a graph can never fully grasp the truth behind that detail. At best, the data tell half a story and, at worst, become a dangerous weapon in the leader's hands. It is only through emotional connectedness with the dots and the digits that the whole tale can be told and the data understood. Behind every dot and digit is a story of triumph over adversity, heroic failure or missed opportunity.

Behind every dot and digit is a FACE waiting to be revealed.

In Chapter 6, we look to how these three dimensions of leadership—Know-ability, Mobilize-ability, and Sustain-ability—extend to taking ownership (Driver 4), for putting FACES on the data at the school, district, region, state, and national levels.

CHAPTER 6

Ownership—Of All the FACES

A Focus on Equity and Excellence

Our culminating task is to represent all our research and the many hundreds of participants in our work across the globe in a single, reflective question: Who "owns" the FACES? We begin with a case study that scrutinizes that question from a nation's point of view. You may also be interested in an earlier case study centered on The Australian Capital Territory (ACT)—see QR Code 6.1.

QR Code 6.1:
Australian Capital Territory Case Study

A National Case Study: Wales

Education in Wales: Our National Mission (ADDYSG CYMRU, 2017) outlines that in November 2016, the OECD recognized the noticeable shift that had taken place in Wales' approach to school improvement— away from piecemeal and short-term policy toward one guided by a long-term vision. They found that the Welsh reform journey was increasingly characterized by close working relationships between government and the education sector, with a commitment to improvement "visible at all levels of the education system."

QR Code 6.2:
Curriculum for Wales

At the heart of this reform journey is the new curriculum for Wales (see QR Code 6.2) developed

(Continued)

(Continued)

QR Code 6.3:
Successful
Futures

through a process of co-construction and planned for first delivery in September 2022. The new curriculum is centered around four core purposes as proposed by Donaldson (2015). To read the full review click on QR Code 6.3. The four core purposes are these:

1. Ambitious, capable learners ready to learn throughout their lives.

2. Enterprising, creative contributors, ready to play a full part in life and work.

3. Ethical, informed citizens of Wales and the world.

4. Healthy, confident individuals, ready to lead fulfilling lives as valued members of society.

Welsh leaders recognized two factors that were required to launch and support the new curriculum: a culture representative of Schools as Learning Organizations (SLO), and an understanding of strong pedagogy. The SLO model consists of seven dimensions (2018) school-learning-organisation.pdf (oecd.org):

1. Developing and sharing a vision centered on the learning of **all** students.

2. Creating and supporting continuous learning opportunities for **all** staff.

3. Promoting team learning and collaboration among **all** staff.

4. Establishing a culture of inquiry, innovation, and exploration.

5. Embedding systems for collecting and exchanging knowledge and learning.

6. Learning with and from the external environment and larger learning system.

7. Modeling and growing learning leadership.

In "Successful Futures," Donaldson (2015) highlights the importance of a sound understanding of pedagogy in order to realize the "core purposes" of the new curriculum for Wales. In the summer of 2019, the regional consortia approached the Welsh Government with a proposal to engage with the evidence-informed work in the *FACES* and *CLARITY* texts to build that sound "common" understanding in Donaldson's report. In Phase 1, 32 secondary schools from across Wales would focus on the 14 Parameters of System and School Improvement (Sharratt, 2019; Sharratt & Fullan, 2012) that align closely with the Professional Learning (PL) requirements that would facilitate developing SLO while also supporting them in exploring a learner-centered approach to pedagogy and practice.

Schools with the leadership capacity to not only engage but also prepare to begin the school improvement journey with Sharratt were identified with the aim they would interpret and adapt the thinking to meet their own local needs. Professor Alma Harris (2022), Zoe Elder (2022), Dr. Angela Cooze (2022), and Professor Michelle Jones (2022) from Swansea University were engaged by the Welsh Government to evaluate the impact of this work.

The *CLARITY-FACES* PL approach was founded on collaboration, continuity, Knowledgeable Other input and active engagement leading to empowerment. The plan consisted of bringing together the leadership teams from across the schools for sessions led by Sharratt and a team of facilitators from the four regional education consortia two times per year, over the course of 2 years, each time for 5 days. A Learning Walk and Talk on the 5th day of each week contextualized the learning immediately in a real school Welsh context. Inter-sessional tasks were introduced; homework for the school leaders was to introduce and engage their school staffs with the learning, applying it and further contextualizing it within their own settings to ensure a whole-school approach to improvement. Regional staff supported schools to remain engaged with the work between the sessions with Lyn, visiting schools to support with intersessional task completion.

At the start of the first in-person session some schools felt that a number of the strategies in the 14 Parameter approach might already be taking place in schools and leaders were familiar with them. For example, a number of schools used the concept of a Data Wall to help identify underachievement in relation to working toward qualifications (GCSE) at 14–16. However, by the end of the second session a consensus was formed that the strategies people felt were in place were not being used holistically and with the same sense of purpose as exemplified by the Putting FACES on the Data approach set out in Parameter #6. By the end of the second initial 2-day session there was increasing confidence in and commitment to the strategies being developed as a result of the interactive nature of the sessions; there was visibly increasing ownership

(Continued)

(Continued)

being taken by the participating secondary schools, and it was clear that they were personalizing the learning to their own needs. Anecdotal evidence of the improvement journey follows here from three schools involved in the Leading Collaborative Learning (LCL) across Wales.

1. Bishop Hedley Catholic School—South Wales

Bishop Hedley Catholic School in South Wales has developed shared beliefs and understandings (Parameter #1) arising from a strong moral purpose and shared vision founded on fairness and equity. Engaging with the work of CLARITY has fundamentally changed the school's thinking in relation to assessment to meet the needs of every individual (Parameter #3). The holistic approach taken to the use of data—at the heart of co-constructed Data Walls—captures students' attitudes, attendance, and attainment (i.e., putting FACES on the data). That coupled with regular Case Management Meetings (Parameter #6) has allowed for earlier identification and intervention to meet individual student needs. An example of the approach's impact is increased engagement of disaffected mid-ability girls seeing an impressive 7% increase in the assessment outcomes over a 6-week period.

Discussion arising at the Data Walls at the whole school, department, and individual pupil levels have influenced pedagogical decisions resulting in more deliberate practice (Parameters #3, #6, #13, and #14). This has been coupled with Collaborative Assessment practices (Parameter #8) where teachers have been able to think deeply together around pupils' work samples and apply the principles set out in the Assessment Waterfall Chart (AWC) (see Chapter 3). The use of collaboration to address next step feedback has developed capacity within the school while supporting PL (Parameters #7, #8, and #11). The feeling is that this focused work has not only aligned pedagogical choices but also has made them more precise. It has also developed a shared responsibility and accountability (Parameter #14) while lowering individual teacher workload. The approach is a win-win within Wales. (Dr. Beverley Timothy-Webber, Assistant Headteacher, Bishop Hedley Catholic High School, Wales, personal communication, January 2022)

2. St. Joseph's Roman Catholic High School—South East Wales

St. Joseph's RC High School had a similar experience with Data Walls and assessment literacy. Two impressions changed:

1. The initial "We do this already" perception became a question—"Do we do this properly in a meaningful way?"; and
2. staff members recognized that the power of putting FACES to the data "lies in its sim-plexity" (Chapter 3). Data is now being seen in a different way and is being used to "bring children to life" in teacher conversations. The selection of individual pupils who are reflective of different groups of learners—called 'marker students'—is also helping the school meet the needs of these different groups in a bespoke or more tailored way. Data Walls have supported the school in honing its approaches to grouping pupils for intervention work.

The Case Management Approach (Parameter #6) is enabling a strategic analysis of pupils' skills to inform the design of bespoke interventions for specific groups of learners and individuals. The Case Management Meeting also provides precision-in-practice regarding evaluating the impact of the intervention swiftly, leading to an interactive process of designing interventions outside the classroom. Collaborative Assessment of Student Work (CASW; Parameter #8) is resulting in more meaningful discussions as teachers interrogate anonymous student work samples together and consider the implications for their practice, collectively.

CASW (Parameter #8) has been particularly impactful in the Welsh Department (of Education) where it has enabled intentional discussion of assessment and feedback and has led to detailed professional discussions focused on the pedagogical approaches needed to improve skill development evidenced in the pupils' work. Department staff have been able to co-construct effective examples of Diagnostic Feedback, DIRT (Dedicated Improvement and Reflection Time) tasks, and have begun to share ideas for modeling excellence. This process is building teacher confidence in their own subject knowledge and in their use of pedagogy to improve pupils' skills across Wales.

At St. Joseph's, "Big Ideas and Essential Questions" from the Assessment Waterfall Chart (AWC) (see Chapter 3, page 94) have been used to formulate Learning Intentions and drive forward curriculum design. Teachers have met in Area of Learning Experience

(Continued)

(Continued)

(AOLE) groups to discuss the Big Ideas and Essential Questions in their separate disciplines. Following a detailed exploration of the natural connections, these connections have been used to formulate Learning Intentions for units of work across the AOLE. This has been a useful approach as this ensures that learning is driving curriculum design and remains the focus. The use of "I can" statements in co-constructed Success Criteria supports this and brings a specificity to the learning (Parameters #3 and #13). This approach is particularly useful as this mirrors the language of the descriptions of learning in the Curriculum for Wales curriculum documentation. St Joseph's reports, "It is specifically this work on curriculum design which will be the focus of a professional Collaborative Inquiry (Parameter #11), as part of our School Development Plan (SDP), to answer the question, 'How far can the use of Learning Intentions and Success Criteria be used to structure a collaborative approach to curriculum design to create a curriculum which achieves the Four Purposes and the Catholic Virtues?'" (Jane Morgan, Deputy Headteacher, St. Joseph's RC High School, personal communication, January 2022)

3. Ysol Y Grango—North Wales

A similar experience at Ysgol Y Grango in North Wales resulted in the realization that "It is the FACES that matter and not the rows and columns on the spreadsheet." Once again, the school has started to change the way that it approaches the use of data. In two of the departments, the approach has promoted greater discussion around individual pupils and it is felt that the "kinesthetic nature" of the co-constructed Data Wall process—actively moving while talking at the Data Wall—is an important part of the process. The movement of pupils as a record of their achievement and/or growth on the Data Wall is leading to enhanced conversations about all students' progress (Figure 6.1).

Adopting the 14 Parameters at Ysgol Dyffryn Aman (YDA) is supporting the school in working toward its vision that focuses on students' growth and achievement. Data sources are used by educators to proactively personalize the learning experience for students, and the resulting pedagogical approaches ensure that assessment and feedback lead to adaptive and responsive teaching. Data about

Figure 6.1 Photos of a Data Wall

Source: Steve Garthwaite, Head Teacher

individual learners is collated through a range of methods, including questioning and oral participation in class, collaborative *book looks* and Learning Walks and Talks (Parameters #1, #3, and #14). These are all utilized as opportunities to adapt and grow.

The Case Management Meeting (Parameter #6) has ensured that staff have time together to identify strengths, diagnose learner needs, and jointly devise strategies that are unique to the pupil. These collaborative discussions lead to powerful outcomes through a holistic approach that supports well-being and allows potential to be fulfilled by students and staff.

Precision teaching and fine-tuning practice have been encouraged through collaborative PL that capitalizes on the skills and experiences of the school staff, and through that collaboration, all staff members are developing a shared understanding of learning (Parameters #1 and #11). The YDA Pedagogical Directory has been developed so that staff can see who the Knowledgeable Others are and make enabling and encouraging learning connections across the school (Parameter #2). These connections have led to a range of activities including joint planning (the 4 Cs in Chapter 4; Parameter #2), Collaborative Assessment of Student Work (Parameter #8) and Learning Walks and Talks (Parameters #4 and #14). (Stephen Garthwaite (Headteacher) Ysgol Y Grango, personal communication, January 2022)

As a result of the pandemic, PL with Sharratt quickly pivoted: shifting from face-to-face, to a series of 10 virtual, participatory webinars. A digital video recording of each session was provided for educators' reference to support the full implementation of the newly implemented Curriculum for Wales. The last of these sessions took the form of a Learning Fair during which schools shared aspects of their work and learned a great deal from each other.

It is evident that the FACES approach has positively influenced thinking and impacted on practice across the schools making up the first LCL network of secondary schools. Many of the schools reflected on how it was very positive to be part of a wider network, across Wales, working together to explore, reflect, and adapt strategies that are supportive in working toward the implementation of the new curriculum.

Through discussion, the Welsh government and Regional Leaders are co-developing Phase 2 of the work for 2022, and beyond that will allow the Secondary Schools and, in some cases, their Primary cluster partners to work together and have more time to engage in shared reflection and Collaborative Inquiry (Parameter #11) to further deepen their understanding and practice in relation to the implementation of the 14 Parameters.

It is felt that putting FACES on the data through the use of Data Walls and Case Management Meetings (Parameter #6) will ensure that the learner remains at the heart of their work moving forward with this expanded group of schools from across Wales as they explore the realization of their four core purposes. This next phase of the work will continue to support schools in their exploration of pedagogy and the realization of the new curriculum while developing schools as learning organizations. (Representatives from the Welsh Government, personal communication, December 12, 2021)

Professor Alma Harris (personal communication, July 7, 2021) and the research team from Swansea University added the following to the above account, saying:

> It's a huge privilege to be part of the Leading Collaborative Learning (LCL) work in Wales. The FACES-CLARITY work has been system-wide in the sense that it has embraced schools, regions, and government. At Swansea University, we've been very honored to be the research team. We've looked at the Leading Collaborative Learning program and its outcomes. Our team has spent 2 years collecting data on the processes, the intentions, and the outcomes of the work. I'm hugely

grateful to Zoe Elder as her work has been both forensic and methodical. Our data is due to be analyzed, but there are some themes already strongly emerging from the data sets, such as, the importance of Pedagogical Change, Capacity Building, Collaboration, Consistency, and Clarity.

Lyn Sharratt and the members of the regional teams have risen to the COVID challenges of 2020 and 2021 in amazing ways. The project has progressed in ways that we didn't anticipate, but in some sense, it's progressed in better ways for our schools through the provision of constant support. It has been remarkable. I think that this is not the end of the project; it's the start of a new phase of work around pedagogy in Wales. We in Wales know the importance of pedagogical change, and this has been a huge impetus to send us on our way. We are a system on the move, and this will help us move even further. For the complete report from the University of Swansea Research team to the Welsh Government, see www.lynsharratt.com.

Public Policy Implications

The Case Study from Wales demonstrates what it takes as a nation, state, region/diocese, network, and school to put FACES on the data—and to know how to teach each FACE. The process is the essence of public education—the very core. Education systems were not designed to be nor are they passive entities developed to warehouse children. Governments must spend big tax dollars on education—the education portfolio should be the largest component of a public budget. The underlying rationale is to educate all students to become contributing citizens. Specific mission statements between systems may differ, but the expense is not divided by child—it is universally available for *all* children in every jurisdiction to provide the very best pedagogical practices for everyone—that is *Equity and Excellence* for us. That is, governments support education financially because they believe it a right for **every child** to be educated, purportedly equally.

As Harris and Jones (2019) add poignantly,

Policy makers need to listen far more to those within education systems, to the professionals who are so often excluded from substantive policy debates and decisions. They need to hear the voices of those teachers, leaders and support staff on the front lines who are dealing with the brutal and heart-wrenching consequences of inequity and inequality. These education professionals are the true leaders of equity and excellence who can mobilize their teams into action. (p. 108)

What are our roles in advocating for every student to receive the support they require to achieve the highest possible growth and achievement they can? Leaders in schools must not only believe but also act to demonstrate that **they believe all students can learn and thus commit to having every teacher equipped with precision-in-practice and intervention skills so that each student does indeed learn to reach—or go well beyond—their predicted potential.** Known FACES is what that should that look like in all schools, in all nations!

In a presentation in Japan, Andreas Schleicher (2011), head of the Indicators and Analysis Division of the OECD Directorate for Education (PISA), stated:

[T]here is no question that most nations declare that education is important. But the test comes when these commitments are weighed against others. How do countries pay teachers, compared to other highly-skilled workers? How are education credentials weighed against other qualifications when people are being considered for jobs? Would you want your child to be a teacher? How much attention do the media pay to schools and schooling? What we have learned from PISA is that in high performing systems, political and social leaders have persuaded citizens to make choices that show they value education more than other things.

But placing a high value on education is only part of the equation. Another part is belief in the possibilities for *all* students and teachers to achieve success. In some countries, students are separated into different tracks at an early age, reflecting a notion shared by teachers, parents, and citizens that only a subset of the nation's children [FACES] can or need to achieve world class standards. Our analysis shows that systems that track students in this way, based [on] differing expectations for different destinations, tend to be fraught with large social disparities.

By contrast, the best performing systems deliver strong and equitable learning outcomes [for all FACES] across very different cultural and economic contexts. PISA 2015 and 2018 results (OECD, 2016, 2019) demonstrate that in Canada, Finland, Japan, Singapore, Shanghai-China, and Hong Kong-China, parents, teachers, and the public at large share the belief that **all** students are capable of achieving high standards and need to do so, and they provide great examples for how public policy can support the achievement of universal high standards (Parameters #1 and #14).

We have written here that it is imperative that there is a commitment to education and the belief that competencies can be learned and therefore **all** students can achieve (Parameters #1, #6, and #14). High-performing education systems share clear and ambitious standards across the board. Everyone knows what is required to get a given qualification, both in terms of the content studied and the level of performance needed to earn it. Students cannot go on to the next stage—be it in work or in further education—unless they show that they are qualified to do so. They know what they have to do to realize their dreams, and they put in the work that is needed to do it.

As Schleicher (2011) emphasizes,

> The most impressive outcome of world class education systems is perhaps that they deliver high quality learning consistently across the entire education system [and own all students' achievement] so that every student benefits from impactful learning opportunities. To achieve this, they invest educational resources where they can make the greatest difference, they attract the most talented teachers into the most challenging classrooms, and they establish effective spending choices that prioritize the quality of teachers hired. Some of the most successful systems are also actively looking outward, realizing that the benchmark for success is no longer simply improvement by national standards, but it is the best performing systems internationally.

"Last but not least, in high performing systems these policies and practices are aligned across all aspects of the system, they are coherent over sustained periods of time, and they are consistently implemented . . . And PISA shows," insists Schleicher, "that success is within the reach for nations that have the capacity to create and execute policies with maximum coherence in the system . . ." So, for us, this is all about focus on commitment to the whole data story that leads to increasing and owning *all* students' achievement—an *equity and excellence* issue for us as researchers and practitioners.

Increasing students' achievement is the core business of institutional education and of professional educators. Ownership of student improvement at all levels ensures that high expectations are set and students, parents, and staff are clear about the expectations and standards. Leaders must go beyond face value by example, demonstrating high standards for teaching and learning themselves, then monitoring high expectations for all students and teachers by *Walking and Talking* daily to look for and to celebrate examples of success against the high expectations (see Chapter 5) and to look for areas of potential improvement.

Parents and Communities Are "Owners," Too!

Remember the example of Luis in Chapter 1? Luis graduated—note that we didn't say "he was graduated"—no, Luis graduated, he earned it! The vice principal, his literacy coach, and his teachers "owned" Luis as an opportunity for which they *had to find* an elegant solution. They engaged his parents honestly and brought them into the solution; Luis took the opportunity and ran excitedly with it to the finish line.

Just as the school staff worked with Luis's parents, it is imperative that parents (each student's first teacher), become our valuable resources as partners in learning at all grade levels, not just in primary schools.

We know from our research respondents that making a connection with parents was a strong reason for putting FACES on the data, and we know from our research for Parameter #12 (parental and community involvement) that families who are involved in their students' schooling significantly increase their students' performance (Epstein, 1995; cited in M. Sharratt, 2004). By taking a collaborative approach to the development of family involvement programs, schools can form successful partnerships with families and community groups to improve the educational achievement of all students. "With frequent interactions among school, families, and communities," notes Epstein, "more students are more likely to receive common messages from various people about the importance of school, of working hard, of thinking creatively, of helping one another, and of staying in school" (p. 701). As a result, school-family-community partnerships enable students and families to produce and own their own successes.

Some commentators on public education make a point that student performance in any school is the direct effect of socioeconomic measures in the school area—the higher the status, the higher the scores. *__This myth has been shattered many times__*, often by results from schools in challenging circumstances, where leaders' and teachers' knowledge of each learner, precise assessment and instruction, and concerted efforts to involve parents and community have made remarkable differences for all students (see Sharratt & Fullan, 2009, pp. 68–90).

As we noted in Chapter 3, student-led conferences engage and inspire parents and the community to become active participants in schools' safe and supportive learning environments. Inviting local media to share in school celebrations such as these is a powerful way to share students' achievement with the broader community. Using social media platforms (safely) offers another opportunity to celebrate successes. On an ongoing basis, students, principals, and teachers need to be able to confidently articulate to parents and the community the why, what, and how of what they do in the classrooms (Parameter #1).

Finding relevant ways to invite parents and community members into schools to be an integral part of the focus on students' learning is critical. COVID has taught us all that learning environments can and must be redesigned by the use of new technologies to ensure continuous communication so that student learning at home and at school is seamless; however, there are limits to what can physically be supported and ethical responsibilities to ensure *all* students have equal access to the technologies required.

Successful system leaders and school principals find ways to involve social agencies to support families and hire community liaison workers to focus on bringing parents and community members into schools to contribute to the learning environment. In those ways, parents and students see schools as a collection of resources for their own learning. Teachers and leaders who work diligently on open communication with parents bring about a change in attitude toward parents who must be seen as important contributors to their children's education. Then we experience a strategic and necessary paradigm shift from blaming parents for their children to celebrating *all* the children whom parents send us.

In Ontario, the Toronto District School Board's (TDSB) Multi Year Strategic Plan (MYSP) calls for the centering of student identities and lived experiences. How can educators and school leaders do so in a meaningful manner and with communities that historically have not seen themselves reflected in their own learning experiences? How can educators walk in the shoes of the communities they serve when they don't reflect the identities of those in these very classrooms and schools? Listening to and walking alongside communities are important initial steps for educators to embark on in the spirit of true allyship and a shift forward from tokenistic practices.

This thinking also serves a critical purpose in honoring the rich cultural capital of such communities where immigrant stories are assets in colonial institutions and not deficits. Educators who situate themselves authentically into the community they serve shift from being just mere tourists (Brown, 2008).

Whether through Community Outreaching with parent leaders to get a glimpse into a day in the life of students and families or through Faith Walks at places of Prayer, much is to be learned when one steps beyond the school walls. Such authentic interactions with families and community members cultivate an enhanced cultural sensitivity among educators and further broadens their perspectives of the people they serve. This supports a positive intersection and exchange of belief systems in schooling experiences that may have an even more profound impact on educators than it does on students. This may indeed be their most critical PL in how it is that they proceed in centering and honoring the very lived experiences and identities of students with respect and care.

TDSB's Model Schools for Inner Cities initiative is another systemic approach where the school functions as the "heart of the community." This honoring of student and parent voices validates the lived experiences of those we serve and reflects a continued shift toward authentic community engagement. Educators are richer for serving in community when stepping beyond the school and exploring the capital of those who inhabit their classrooms. (Harpreet Ghuman, Superintendent of Education, Toronto District School Board, Ontario, Canada, personal communication January 2022)

We now bring together the work we have both done in the past 10 years in a final Case Study showing the intersection of the

14 Parameters of System and School Improvement and the 6 Deep Learning Competencies.

Case Study: Bringing Together the 14 Parameters and NPDL

A. Precision-in-Pedagogy at Wellington Point State High School

Driving improvement in pedagogy to lift students' learning and well-being is a key improvement strategy for schools across South East Region (SER), Queensland, Australia. The kind of teaching SER leaders believe works is linked closely to the leadership and capability development of school staff using Sharratt's (2019) refined 14 Parameters in *CLARITY: What Matters MOST in Learning, Teaching and Leading*, and using Fullan et al.'s (2018) 6 Deep Learning Competencies in *Engage the World, Change the World*. Our goal by focusing on the fully compatible high-impact practices of both texts is improvement.

For the last 2 years, SER leaders and teachers have connected with schools through the Leading Learning Collaborative (LLC) and Deep Learning. This work will continue in 2022 and, as a regional team connected together, SER will continue to partner with schools bound by our moral imperative that "illiteracy is unacceptable" (Sharratt, 2019, p. xix). Furthermore, by focusing on excellence, equity, engagement and well-being, SER will ensure that that every student succeeds and becomes "good at life." Practically, this means SER leaders are partnering with schools on improving literacy results by developing expertise in pedagogy.

As this work has progressed over the past 2 years, the staff at Wellington Point State High School (WPSHS) continued to apply Parameters #1, #6, and #14—the nonnegotiables of the LLC work—as well as taking a deeper dive into implementing the 6 Deep Learning Competencies (Character, Citizenship, Communication, Collaboration, Critical Thinking, and Creativity). The leadership team understood that both the 14 Parameters and the 6Cs were not add-ons but rather were mechanisms for sharpening the focus on the lens of learning—a lens used to view the achievement standards of the Australian National Curriculum and a refinement of the learning processes that engage learners, amplify the students' knowledge and skills, and drive thinking.

(Continued)

(Continued)

Deep Learning was introduced to develop and strengthen pedagogy and curriculum design at WPSHS. It involved the integration of the 6Cs and the 14 Parameters. This ensured they were developing and delivering learning that "sticks for life" by designing curriculum that was engaging, authentic, and enabled their students to develop as adaptable, flexible, resilient, situationally responsive learners for life.

Specific steps included

1. Analyzing whole cohort data to identify disengaged and under-achieving *marker* students (Parameter #3)

4. Holding a Data Day—teachers create Data Walls for *marker* students, taking a deep dive into data for selected students (Parameter #6)

5. Interviewing students to learn more about their learners (Parameter #1)

6. Creating a "Learning Design Day"—using the data and knowledge about the students, teachers design curriculum to cater to these students' needs and focus on developing the *whole student* (Parameter #6)

7. Meeting with stakeholders: student, parents, teachers, department heads, and other stakeholders to discuss unit design, assessment, and goals for the following term (Parameter #12)

8. Implementing units, gathering data of progress and success throughout a unit using teacher observations and deep learning competency rubrics (Parameters #3 and #13)

After completing two successful trials in 2020 with our new Deep Learning process and integrating the Case Management Approach (Parameter #6) and curriculum design, leaders and teachers have seen improved outcomes for their *marker students* and now have a process that they believe can be upscaled to ensure greater student outcomes and success for *all* students (Parameter #14).

At the beginning of the 3rd year of implementing Deep Learning and integrating the LLC CLARITY work, their focus and objectives were to:

✓ consider sustainability and scalability—delivery of deep learning units for whole cohorts of students, not just for the marker students; and

✓ focus on the least-served learners by introducing Parameters #1, #6, and #14 concepts into their deep learning work.

This heralded a new stage in the WPSHS Deep Learning journey. Beginning with shared beliefs and understandings (Parameter #1), bookended with a strong focus on collective responsibility and accountability (Parameter #14) and enriched by knowing our students through a Case Management Approach (Parameter #6), the culture of high expectations and improvement has been elevated. Leveraging Collaborative Inquiry (Parameter #11) within a powerful, proven evidence-base, WPSHS staff members have shown how precision-in-pedagogy "Deep-ens" Learning. (Brian Ragh, Assistant Regional Director; Simone Ivey, Deep Learning Project Officer; Dr Robyn Burton-Ree & Tara Nathan, Teachers, Wellington Point State High School, personal communication, January 2022)

Case Studies Reveal "Ownership by *All*"

The case studies we have presented in this book define "ownership"—specifically shared beliefs and understandings (Parameter #1), putting FACES on the data (Parameter #6), and shared responsibility and accountability (Parameter #14)—as the non-negotiable core of our work—the central components of system and school improvement. They have reflected what we have learned throughout our years as researchers and practitioners. Evidence of improvement on a large scale is tangible, visible, and audible. Using the words of teachers, leaders, and students, we summarize the ten ways to describe what it means to put FACES on our Data and take action.

1. **Data Use at Every Level:** Data keeps us grounded and focused. We identify the strengths of the student(s), and the concerns, share expertise and ensure that we reach out to the relevant Knowledgeable Others (KOs) for support if needed.

The answer is often in the room as we build an expert teaching force to teach all students! Our conversations do not get stuck on factors outside the school gate, so to speak, but rather are focused on our instruction—what is within our control if we connect the right people in the room. If we don't have the answer in the room, we are now searching for the right people to assist (James, Year 5/6 Teacher, Lismore Diocese).

2. **The Right People and Right Approaches:** We see more evidence of shared responsibility. This was evident in the collaborative assessment of our writing samples. Our teachers have a greater sense of cross-stage empathy. Stage 3 teachers can empathize with the data in Kindergarten and vice versa. We have staff teaching Grades 4–6 who are K–2 trained and share invaluable knowledge. The process is leading to getting the right people in the room and the right strategies in place for Case Management Meetings, for example. *Everyone owns the learning; everyone owns the data.* We will be fully committed to this work, with a sharp focus on the targeted Parameters #1, #6, and #14 but not losing sight of **all** 14 Parameters. These three words that will keep coming up again and again—*precision-in-practice*. It's not an acronym to be said but the phrase of doing (Brendan, Principal, Lismore Diocese)!

3. **A Robust Framework:** As the knowledge grew, the staff could easily identify the connections between the 14 Parameters with what they were already doing. They could see how their current structures and practices of Professional Learning Teams (PLTs), age-appropriate pedagogy, and co-teaching models would support the FACES and CLARITY Collaborative work (Dan, Grade 2 Teacher, Lismore Diocese). There is a common language across our school. All teachers use it and all students understand it. There is consistency for the students when they move from Stage to Stage (Tracey, Year 4 Teacher, Lismore Diocese). I feel that students have much more voice in this way of learning (Sophie, Year 9 Student, Armidale Diocese).

4. **Alignment From System to Schools to Classrooms:** The work aligned with previous work and was an opportunity to do something as a whole staff, to build something together (Andrew, Grade 6 Teacher, Lismore Diocese). The biggest impact is asking the 5 Questions (for students) . . . if we go into another classroom, we ask the 5 Questions. If a student comes to show me a piece of work, I ask the questions. *All* teachers are also doing the same thing (Dan, Grade 2 Teacher, Lismore Diocese).

5. **Hear ALL Students' Voices:** When we started pulling apart the 14 Parameters, we could see our work in supporting *all* students. The biggest impact is that the students are becoming independent learners. It is giving them a good understanding of what they are learning and how they learn. It has helped teachers support the learning through things like planning to use precise Learning Intentions and to co-construct Success Criteria (Dan, Grade 2 Teacher, Lismore Diocese). I find Success Criteria really helpful because I can just look on the board and I know what I am up to or what I need to get better at. If I am away, I just come back and look at the Success Criteria and I know what I have to do (Grade 2 Student, Lismore Diocese). I now feel that **students have more ownership of their learning.** We know what we are learning about (Learning Intentions) and how to be successful (Success Criteria) (Heidi, Grade 11 Student, Armidale Diocese).

6. **Precision-in-Practice**: We needed to change because students weren't really grasping the why and what they were learning. When we changed to deconstructing Learning Intentions (LIs) and co-constructing Success Criteria (SC), **students were able to clearly articulate their learning**. So we are now experiencing more student ownership of their learning. In fact, when our LIs and SC got wet, students were really upset because they had put so much work into them (Bradley, Secondary Science Teacher, Armidale Diocese)!

7. **Go Slow to Go Fast:** There were times where we had to slow down and go deeper. There were other times when we had to slow down and **make sure others were on the journey with us**. There were also times where we had to stop as a whole school, discuss and reflect before moving forward (Brendan, Principal, Lismore Diocese). We knew that we had to ensure ownership of staff and build consensus in decision making. With this in mind, we were intentional in our processes and needed to be comfortable with not knowing where our staff discussions could take us. We also needed to be very reflective as a team and to *use the data we had based on staff discussions, wonderings, and feedback to determine our direction.* At certain points we had to loop back to prior learning to go deeper to support staff to determine our direction and secure continued staff buy-in. We had to get our *why* right (Katie, Assistant Principal, Teaching and Learning, Lismore Diocese).

8. **Collaborative, Open-to-Learning Stance:** We support each other and have shared ownership over the work. We have robust conversations about student outcomes now. There are so many positive outcomes for the students. I think the Case Management Meetings (CMMs) have had the biggest impact. *They are a team approach to individualizing student needs.* I have had six CMMs, and I can see the growth in the learning of each student. For both the staff and the students, there is a consistent approach (Andrew, Grade 6 Teacher, Lismore Diocese). The students have really surprised me with what and how they can contribute to their learning. I know we have to have high expectations; however, *the students who I thought would struggle have really surprised me.* It is still fresh for them, and it will take time, but they are able to explain their learning (Nicole, Grade 1 Teacher, Lismore Diocese). We now have *more effective collaboration and are not operating in silos.* By sharing information, knowledge, and skills, we are focusing on the learning needs of individual students (Katie, Secondary Leader of Learning, Armidale Diocese).

9. **Leadership at Every Level Matters:** I see the positive impact of this work as being:

- ✓ Greater student engagement;

- ✓ Teachers co-planning units of study and developing common assessment tasks;

- ✓ Teachers co-assessing anonymous student work samples; and,

- ✓ Teachers and leaders reflecting on practices across faculties (Camilla, Secondary Leader of Learning, Armidale Diocese).

10. **Learning is Growth AND Achievement:** When leaders and teachers see growth in a student's learning, the staff are excited and we share this *with parents* as evidence of all students' learning (Brendan, Principal, Lismore Diocese). We developed our own leadership adapt-ability and built the capacity of the leadership team through *our reflective conversations*. We really value the opportunity and time to meet before and after staff meetings to plan and reflect on the learning and build our own capacity to lead learning together (Belinda, K–2 Instructional Leader, Lismore Diocese).

The FACES work is best embedded in our school cultures where the elements of *collaboration, curriculum design, assessment literacy, instructional intelligence, teacher development (job-embedded learning), and the community* are working together. A bit like the warp and weft of a mat. To deepen our learning, we need to consider the links, or as we often say, "join the dots" in the hearts and minds of our staff to keep the momentum of change going. This is NOT "one more thing to do"! (Michele McDonald, Director of Teaching and Learning, Lismore Diocese, NSW, AU, personal communication, January 2022)

System leaders in the Diocese of Armidale add to McDonald's comments about what it takes to lead our FACES improvement work:

A strong school and system vision for learning is the use of the 14 Parameters in our jurisdiction. The work of Sharratt and Fullan in deriving the 14 Parameters leads to System and School Improvement; our starting point is the Shared Beliefs and Understandings of Parameter #1. This belief underpins everything we do in our system. The belief that everyone can learn to high standards is essential to leading a learning agenda that authentically engages and includes all key stakeholders. A strong belief needs actions and strategies to bring the belief to fruition. We have challenged ourselves, and others to enact a plan to achieve the vision that every student can learn to high standards and every teacher can teach to high standards with the right support. With this comes shared responsibility to and accountability for every learner in our system (Parameter #14) enhanced through the sharing of each other's learnings and monitoring student progress as an authentic Professional Learning Community. **As leaders we have "consistently, persistently and insistently" articulated this vision**. "Systemness" for us has been achieved through a set of non-negotiable based on the 14 Parameters. Growth and achievement have been measured through the consistent collection of agreed-upon data sets that really have put "FACES on our Data." (Chris Smyth, Director of Education, and Regina Menz, Principal, O'Connor Collegiate, Armidale Diocese, NSW, Australia, personal communication, January 2022)

Leaders at all levels within and across many jurisdictions have adopted the student improvement approach in FACES and are rightfully proud of their learning gains in improving all students' growth and achievement. Not because of the gains but by putting FACES on the data, leadership teams and their networked school staff teams have begun to create a strong tradition of *owning* success for ALL their students, as the new Case Studies in this revised *FACES* edition show so clearly.

Deliberate Pause

- Who owns the responsibility for all your students' growth and achievement?

- What is your strategic leadership style in calm and crisis?

- How do you support parents and the community to take ownership for students' learning?

- What supports are in place to encourage *all* staff members to own *all* students' growth and achievement with emotional connections and cognitive insights to each FACE?

- If you were not able to continue to lead at your level tomorrow, would the caring and ownership of *all* student and teacher success continue?

Leadership in Calm and Crises

Our work with different jurisdictions with their unique and similar challenges, and the many varying change agendas keeps returning to *uplifting leadership* in various forms. It is always about: spiritual or moral leadership; leaders as lead learners (modeling and nurturing and spreading leading capacities); contextual literacy (understanding and having empathy for local culture); establishing cultures of continuous learning; and accountability with its many internal and external FACES. Harris and Jones (2020) affirm our thinking about leadership needed to do the work of FACES by considering "leadership in crisis."

> There is no neat blueprint for leadership in such times; and, no pre-determined roadmap, no simple leadership checklist of things to tick off. There are only highly skilled, compassionate and dedicated education professionals trying to do the very best they can and to be the very best they can be. (p. 246)

An excellent example of this leadership is the case study of Ben Adlard school in northern England.

Case Study: Ben Adlard School

Ben Adlard school was persistently at the bottom of all league tables when Marie-Claire Bretheron was appointed as a new principal in 2014 with a turnaround mandate. On arrival she said to the staff of over 30 teachers, " I am not going to sack [fire] anyone; and of the first 8 weeks I am just going to observe" (Fullan 2019, p. 35). Bretherton interviewed

(Continued)

(Continued)

every teacher, and 3 months into the journey she began to make some small-scale instructional changes (entirely compatible with our 14 Parameters). Six months into the change, the school gradually accelerated the changes including learning from each other. Two years later the culture of the school had for the first time changed for the better. It became an award-winning school (including new success in literacy achievement). No one—not one staff member—left during this turnaround. Parameters matter when they are coordinated and established by leaders who zero-in on joint determination, incremental adaptation, and cultures of internal accountability. Leadership and Parameters together (Fullan, 2019).

The Intersection of Our Work

The 14 Parameters continue to be a powerful and comprehensive framework for practitioners and other decision makers in the field of system and system improvement. The Parameters fit well with other related work such as the New Pedagogies for Deep Learning (Fullan et al., 2018), and with the CLARITY paradigm developed by Alma Harris (2022) (See QE Code 6.3). Never have these ideas been more critical than the current time of rebuilding public education beyond the COVID disruption. Sharratt's and Fullan's work has always been and continues to be seamless, building on the strengths of each other's thinking and writing.

FACING Forward

As we face forward in 2022 it seems like an appropriate time to take a wider perspective. In the first 2 decades of this century, a good deal of progress has been made in establishing the FACES and 14 Parameter models. The foundation work was done in the first decade starting in YRDSB's 150 schools. FACEs has since developed an international presence in more than 20 countries. As we take stock of the prospects for the 3rd decade, we see two possible scenarios in the work that we are personally involved in around the globe. One concerns that way in which COVID has stopped the world in its tracks—there is literally little energy in early 2022 to engage in serious system change. On the other hand, because we are both still very close to practice, we detect a murmur of a potential surge that could take over later in the current year. There are more people now who know the old school system (say in 2019) was not working, and certainly was not going anywhere, and they know they cannot defend the status quo. We know for sure that our physical and social problems (respectively climate, and group conflict/deteriorating social trust) are at rock bottom. We know that mental and educational health are linked, fragile, and both in jeopardy.

We also detect an ironic murmur: a desire for and knowledge of some of the new changes in learning that should be made, combined with (this is the ironic part) a state of "I am too tired to lead any change." Knowing humans, and especially the young (including the very young), we think that this low-lying exhaustion will be temporary. COVID took us down rapidly. New conditions such as proactive education that integrates learning and well-being and that positively addresses **equity** (both school and non-school dimensions) **and excellence** could mark a new era of positivism. It is true that we are optimists, but we are also good at reading the signs.

Ownership is not an end product; rather, it is a new foundation for going further. In fact, we have found that while moral purpose can drive implementation, the reverse causal sequence is a more powerful driver. To be crystal clear, realizing success may continue to form or deepen a leader's and teacher's sense of moral imperative (Fullan, 2011b). As one of us proved in practice (Sharratt) and we discussed together in Realization (2009), Putting FACES on the Data is very powerful motivator indeed. As systems and schools recover from COVID, the timing is perfect to begin or to continue implementing this full-time, continuous work by taking ownership of the FACES, now. It's time to give FACES an uplift in the service of system change—to the benefit of our students and teachers and societies.

FACES is our 'forever work'!

(G. Mowbray, CEO, Diocese of Maitland–Newcastle).

EPILOGUE

In this book we have used a range of case examples. Each case has its own context, but the message of success is remarkably consistent. Every situation of success has focused leadership. Such leadership sees the assessment-instruction nexus as the core work. They mobilize all others toward this task. They want to impact the whole system whether that is a school, a district, a province or state, or a country. But they do it in a way that pinpoints each and every individual. The only way to make this memorable is to conjure human FACES out of what are otherwise impersonal, and therefore meaningless, statistics. FACES make the whole enterprise meaningful. A leader's most significant measure of success is evidence-proven impact, including individual success stories that are part and parcel of a larger story line: success stories of students; success stories of positively changed and continuously improving classroom practices; and success stories of leaders who are *consistent, persistent, and insistent* in ensuring quality teaching in every classroom, K–12.

This ability to focus and mobilize is crucial these days when there is so much contentious noise in the larger context. In the first edition we examined this work from the perspective of what one of us called the *right* and *wrong* policy drivers (Fullan, 2011a). As coincidence would have it Fullan (2021) just released the 10th Anniversary update of the drivers paper. If we pair the drivers we come up with the following framework (note also that instead of calling the less effective ones *wrong* we now refer to them as *less prominent*). The pairs are:

"Well-being and Learning" (Academic Obsession)

"Social intelligence" (Machine intelligence)

"Equality investments" (Austerity)

"Systemness" (Fragmentation)

A driver is a policy and set of related strategies that is intended to affect the whole system positively. Less effective policies (those in parenthesis above) have that intention but fail to have an impact; right drivers have positive intentions and *do* have an impact. The leaders we have featured in this book are all on the side of the right drivers. In our broader system we have also concluded that the existing paradigm serves an increasingly smaller and smaller percentage of students (see Fullan & Gallagher, 2020). As you go up the grade levels only 25% of students find that regular schooling has a clear sense of purpose for them, noting also that success is skewed in a highly inequitable way (Fullan, 2021, reviews the evidence).

It is revealing how the experience with COVID-19 has dramatically reinforced the requirement to pay attention to FACES. The pandemic has revealed even more transparently that the pre-existing system was ineffective and has highlighted that *well-being and deeper learning* must become the foundation of future public education. This is more than a simple extension of the case for *FACES*. It means that the case for focusing on individual students is now even more obvious for the much deeper goal of fostering the well-being and learning for students to survive and thrive in this century. Including literacy and numeracy but going beyond into global competencies (character, citizenship, collaboration, communication, creativity, and critical thinking) the new public education system must enable all learners to *engage the world change the world* (Fullan et al., 2018).

As we write this 10th Anniversary edition the pandemic has brought the world, and education as we knew it, to a standstill. We predict as the pandemic lessens that it will be followed by a period of innovation and greater prominence of the young as learners and as "changemakers." This not only legitimizes our case for *FACES*, but propels it to a different level. Literacy yes, and also well-being and deeper learning for students and adults alike.

FACES was aways about the whole human being. In the next period, more than ever we will need both new ideas (innovation) and powerful systems of implementation. Both *CLARITY* (Sharratt, 2019) and its web-based partner, the Clarity Learning Suite (CLS), and Deep Learning are such strong, universally applicable examples of how to implement this work. The CLS focuses on the assessment-instruction nexus, building skills, and the capacity to learn to change. Deep Learning expands this focus on the 6Cs, again, offering educators the background knowledge and developing the learning skills to make the changes in systems and schools. The idea is to innovate in relation to more fundamental learning goals, to engage students, teachers, and leaders in irresistible learning experiences. We do this across the curriculum—arts, mathematics, science, and beyond. And also in relation to what we say in deep learning, "Become good at learning, and good at life."

Go back to the human roots of education—the human-emotional connections—make learning flourish on a grand scale. The next 10 years will be very different than the past decade. Make those FACES brighter, more knowing, and more active in improving their own and others' lives.

GLOSSARY OF TERMS

14 Parameters   An evidence-proven System and School Improvement Framework implemented globally by thousands of schools and systems (Sharratt, 2019; Sharratt & Fullan, 2012; CLARITY Learning Suite 2021: https://cls1.claritylearningsuite.com.au)

5 Questions   What are you learning? Why?; How are you doing?; How do you know?; How can you improve?; Where do you go for help?

Accountable Talk   Teachers and students engage in dialogue to understand their own perspectives and the perspectives of others in seeking clarity.

Anchor Charts   Classroom charts that prompt students to remember their learning, their work, and the processes they've explored. Most useful are those that are visible in the classroom and that are co-constructed by teachers and students to provide clarity. They are referred to as "The Third Teacher."

Assessment   A process that takes place between teachers and students so that students can understand where they are, how they are doing, and where they are going.

Assessment as Learning (Diagnostic)   Varied forms of assessment to determine the instructional starting points for each student at every grade level.

Assessment *for* and *as* Learning (Formative)   Seamless integration of information about a student's learning that informs the instruction needed in a timely way with multiple opportunities for students to demonstrate the new learning. During lessons, teachers instantly use the information given by students to clarify meaning, misunderstandings and go deeper into the demonstration and sharing of their learning. Assessment that drives instruction is a never-ending cycle in which one informs the other, daily.

Assessment becomes instruction that becomes assessment. Thus data today is instruction tomorrow—or the very next minute.

Assessment of Learning (Summative) Assessment at the end of a unit of study or a term—through observation; conversations with students; or an examination of products, comparing them against the established Success Criteria. The most powerful Summative Assessment informs Diagnostic Assessment and next steps in Instruction.

Authentic Learning Learning related to students' real-life experiences that are relevant to them, their context, and their culture.

Big Ideas "Educational leaders are coming to understand that the notion of teaching through 'big ideas' is about teaching the higher-order thinking skills of analysis, interpretation, evaluation and synthesis of a text or curriculum unit. The term 'big ideas' does not mean naming a theme unit such as 'Friendship' and selecting a bunch of books and activities that go along with the Friendship Theme, but rather providing students with the modeling of higher-order thinking skills and opportunities to think through text or essential questions critically, bringing them to levels of deep understanding, creativity and new learning. 'Big Ideas' can be addressed through the reading of individual texts or through a unit of study but they need to cause and stretch student thinking by highlighting what is essential in the text or learning experience and connecting these ideas meaningfully to students' lives and the world." (Melanie Greenan, doctoral candidate, OISE/University of Toronto, personal communication, January 2022)

Bloom's Taxonomy A system, developed by Benjamin Bloom at the University of Chicago in 1984, to describe thinking skills as a hierarchy with knowledge and memory as foundational skills, followed progressively by comprehension, application, analysis, and evaluation skills.

Bump-It-Up Walls (BIUWs) Help teachers communicate clear expectations and help students develop the thinking skills required to become evaluators of their own work. They provide students with a visual reminder of what the Success Criteria look like and how to get there.

Collaborative Inquiry A process in which a question, arising from data, is the focus for all staff for at least a year. It is often a conundrum-based question (not a "'problem"!) arising from an area of whole-school need to get focused on improvement, informed by data. Most successfully completed by whole staffs collaboratively inquiring after their *next best learning move* in their schools.

Comprehension The ability to draw meaning from written text, visual media, and the spoken word.

Critical Literacy A process of going beyond the literal text to realize an author's deeper meaning. Often focuses on issues of equity, fairness, and social justice. Critically literate students can determine if a point of view is justified from their point of view.

Cross-Curricular Literacy When literacy curriculum expectations, concepts and/or skills are specifically taught in the subject areas.

Developmental Learner Profile Student information is kept in files that show all aspects of the student as a learner: their social, emotional, and academic growth and achievement. Samples of current student work are kept and results of assessments housed for reference by students and teachers in setting new learning goals. They can be accessed readily by teachers for colleague discussions and transitioning to the next teacher(s)—so that instructional time is not lost in conducting diagnostic assessments with each new teacher.

Differentiated Instruction An approach to maximize each student's learning by assessing student need and designing instruction to match the need, thus moving the student forward. The content, teaching processes, resources, and product can be differentiated— not the curriculum expectations unless the student has been identified as special needs.

Distributed Leadership Leadership is the art of influence. Distributed leadership is when leadership is shared influence with the attached responsibility and accountability.

EQAO The Education Quality and Accountability Office (EQAO) assessment is the standardized test given to Ontario, Canada, students in Grades 3 and 6 in reading, writing, and mathematics and in Grade 9 in mathematics. The office also develops and administers the Ontario Secondary School Literacy Test (OSSLT) for all Grade 10 students, which is a diploma-bearing assessment, because students cannot graduate from an Ontario high school without passing this test.

Graphic Organizer A visual framework that helps students organize and chunk their ideas and thinking to make processes and content more easily understood.

Higher-Order Thinking (HOT) Skills The skills to be able to develop a critical stance through inference; by making connections and predictions; and by analyzing, synthesizing, and developing a supportable argument or opinion.

Independent Reading and Writing The ultimate goal in the gradual-release-of-responsibility model: readers and writers who can enjoy both reading and writing on their own. The primary responsibility for reading and writing is with the student when they are independent, which becomes the gradual-acceptance-of-responsibility model.

Inquiry-Based Learning Learning in which students ask questions and solve problems to develop knowledge and skills in their areas of interest, allowing them to find new areas of interest.

Instructional Intelligence Being consciously skilled in integrating the use of clusters of skills, strategies, tactics, and organizers. Often highly effective teachers work intuitively. Their work is exemplary, but they are not able to describe what they do. Instructional intelligence provides a language to describe instructional methodology. Teachers can then share their expertise as well as assess and refine their own practice. Instructional intelligence includes reflective use of such skills and strategies as effective (cooperative) group work, concept attainment, inductive thinking, thinking strategies, and framing questions. Instructional intelligence means weaving these tactics, skills, and strategies together into effective instruction for each student (Sharratt et al., 2002).

Learning Intention We have chosen to use Learning Intention in this book; however, other terms that are similar are Learning Goal or Learning Target. The Learning Intention is directly developed from the Curriculum Expectations. It can be several of the Curriculum Expectations clustered together for teaching purposes. Success Criteria for students are directly developed from the Learning Intention and most effective when co-constructed with the teacher. The Learning Intention must be in student-friendly language, be deconstructed with students and be visible in classrooms for students to reference.

Leveled Resources Teacher assesses a student's appropriate developmental level of reading unseen text and the readiness of a student to progress to the next reading level. This process allows for flexible groupings of students, K–12.

Literacy Begins with the basic skills of being able to read, write, speak, listen, view, represent, and do mathematics. It becomes the ability to comprehend, think critically, resolve problems, and use higher-order thinking skills independently. We have added higher-order, critical thinking skills to the list of basic literacy skills for twenty-first century learners.

Mentor Texts Rich pieces of literature that teachers can use to demonstrate or model the teaching points they are making, such as reading comprehension strategies. These teacher-selected texts create common conversations with students that result in students' becoming critical consumers of varied forms of texts.

Modeled–Shared–Guided–Interdependent-Application Model 5 progressions of learning about practice that is scaffolded (see below), beginning with *modeled* (demonstrated by leader) practice, then moving to *shared* (leader and learner) practice, scaffolded to *guided* (demonstrated by the learner) practice, and then self-actualized in *interdependent* practice and *application* of the new learning to other learning (learners and leaders flying together).

Multi-Literacies Include the traditional literacy definition (above) and may extend to include information, cultural, financial, critical, media, digital and environmental.

NAPLAN The Australian National Assessment Program for Literacy and Numeracy that is implemented each year for students in Years 3, 5, 7, and 9.

New Pedagogies for Deep Learning (NPDL) https://deep-learning.global Global partnership involving 12 countries focusing on implementing Deep Learning.

Oral Language   The foundational skill that underscores all learning to read, write, and comprehend. Oral Language morphs into Accountable Talk (above) as students progress through the grades.

PISA (Program for International Student Assessment) International assessment of the learning performance of fifteen-year-olds from over 65 countries, focused on literacy, math, science, and collaborative problem-solving. PISA is conducted every 2 years and operated by the Organisation for Economic Co-operation and Development (OECD).

PM Benchmark Assessment Tool Kit   An assessment tool produced by Nelson Publishers to provide comprehensive reading assessment resources using 30 unseen leveled texts.

Prior Knowledge   What students already know at the outset of a lesson. Should be assessed before teaching new information, to allow for differentiation of instruction.

Probe Level   Reading Comprehension assessment: A multiple-use reading probe (typically implemented as a one-on-one interview) designed to gain insight into a reader's comprehension skills and reading behaviors (https://comprehenz.com/wp-content/uploads/2020/10/PROBEBLUEMANUALSAMPLEPAGES.pdf)

Read Aloud   When teachers share rich literature with students by reading out loud to them and sharing their thinking about the lines, between the lines, and beyond the lines.

Reflective Practice   Ongoing habit of mind that teachers and leaders use to think critically about their work. Reflective practitioners ask, often, What worked? What didn't work? and What can I do differently? Students learn this habit as well from teachers who make this practice explicit.

Responsive Literacy   Composed of oral language and modeled, shared, guided, independent reading and writing, and application of skills learned includes media literacy.

Scaffolding   Supported progressive learning during which knowledge is built up. New knowledge is brought into play and is connected with prior knowledge. Each layer is built on a solid foundation created by previous learning.

Self-Assessment Students' assessment of their own work against the Success Criteria to determine their next steps in their learning.

Success Criteria Criteria tied directly to Learning Intentions, which are developed from (clustered) curriculum expectations. Should be visible and available in classrooms so that students can use them as a reference while they are doing their work and against which they can measure progress toward their own goals for improvement. They are most effective when co-constructed by teachers and students.

Teacher Moderation (Better known as Collaborative Assessment of Student Work [CASW]) Parameter #8 A process of teachers working together to collaboratively assess commonly developed assessments to ensure not only consistency of practice across a grade or subject area but also give teacher feedback on changed classroom practice needed and discuss what the feedback with be to the student of this piece of work. Through CASW, teachers work together to share beliefs and practices, enhance their understanding, compare their interpretations of student results, and confirm their judgments about each student's level of work. The student work samples are anonymous.

The Third Teacher The culture of learning established when attending to thoughtfully co-created learning spaces at every level of the education system.

Think Alouds (Modeled Reading) Teachers make their thinking "visible" as they read a text out loud to students modeling their thinking so that the students can gather information, develop insights, solve problems, or correct any confusion about how a good reader reads and thinks about the text during the process. Using Think Alouds, teachers draw out and explain the inferences made in texts being shared.

Word Study Systematic exploration of the patterns and irregularities in working with words. Teachers often use Word Walls to work with word patterns or families of words or to introduce words that will be used in a new learning unit.

APPENDIX A

*Matrix of Scaffolded Learning
Using the Gradual-Release-of-
Responsibility Model: From Modeled
to Shared to Guided to Interdependent
Practice and Application for Practitioners*

Appendix A 14 Parameter Matrix of Scaffolded Learning Using the Gradual-Release Model

Parameter	Modeled Practice	Shared Practice	Guided Practice	Interdependent Practice	Application
1. Shared Beliefs and Understandings					
a. *All students can achieve high standards given time and the right support.*	System and school leaders and teachers can articulate vision everywhere, at any time (PL sessions, staff meetings, official board of trustee meetings).	Leaders and teachers work in smaller clusters or networks using "accountable talk" protocols (i.e., teachers can articulate why and how they teach what they do).	All teachers receive intensive, ongoing PL focused on classroom practice (e.g., Learning Walks and Talks, Collaborative Inquiry, 3-part lesson for Mathematics, 4 C's and Lesson Study).	Special education and regular education assessment and instruction practices are seamless; all students are engaged and achieving, and all parents are involved.	Whole-System-wide Approach with examples that show K–12 students can and will learn.
b. *High expectations and early and ongoing intervention are essential.*	They use data in the system and schools to set targets; intervention practices are in place in all schools.	They discuss how to use data to differentiate instruction; intervention techniques are discussed and in place at every level.	Teachers collaboratively assess student work; performance targets are visible in every classroom.	The case management approach (CMA) is used for each student who may be struggling, stuck, or needing extending; all students can articulate performance targets and their work to be done.	Teachers are teaching teachers!

Parameter	Modeled Practice	Shared Practice	Guided Practice	Interdependent Practice	Application
c. *All teachers can teach to high standards given time and the right assistance.*	■ Leaders and teacher-leaders model and work alongside classroom teachers.	■ They use video clips to discuss best practices and build on clips.	■ KOs, now embedded, demonstrate assessment and instructional approaches/ strategies and model co-constructing Success Criteria and giving and getting Descriptive Feedback.	■ Teachers and leaders co-teach, question as critical friends, and examine students' thinking.	■ Practice begets even better practice when co-planned, co-taught, co-debriefed, and co-reflected on, using the 4 C's model.
d. *Leaders, teachers, and students can articulate what they do and why they teach the way they do.* (Adapted from Hill and Crévola, 1999)	■ Leaders and teachers can articulate to colleagues and parents why they are instructing as they are, what they are expecting to see from their students.	■ Leaders support teachers to share practice through demonstration class visits, opening doors in their own school, watching others work with purpose, knowing what to look for.	■ Leaders and teachers plan together and watch each other teach (lesson study) and demonstrate student improvement by using samples of student work.	■ Students can articulate why and how they learn, using the same common language and evidence from their work.	■ Alignment of the vision and voices of leaders, teachers, and students.

(Continued)

(Continued)

Parameter	Modeled Practice	Shared Practice	Guided Practice	Interdependent Practice	Application
2. Embedded Knowledgeable Others (KOs)	■ Partial staffing (for a KO) is allocated during school day to model successful assessment and instruction practices in every school. ■ Selection is critical: they must be evidence-proven "Knowledgeable Others," (KOs) credible, supportive, approachable.	■ Ongoing dialogue with principal and leadership team focuses on system, school, and student data. ■ KO is contributing member of the leadership team	■ Systems find funds to hire and carefully select KOs in every school ■ KOs work alongside classroom teachers in planning with data and implementing approaches that meet the needs of every student. ■ They demonstrate assessment and instruction practices in all subject areas. ■ They demonstrate technology use as a basic, integral instruction tool.	■ Step back—lead from behind. ■ Students consistently use high-impact strategies and skills; teachers and KOs support when necessary. ■ KOs co-teach (4 Cs: Co-Planning, Co-Teaching, Co-Debriefing, Co-Reflecting) with teachers across all divisions to refine practice and focus on students' thinking.	■ Use their own classrooms to show small groups of teachers explicit examples of high-impact approaches in action. ■ They demonstrate their diplomacy in every setting, working from where teachers and leaders "are," to where they can be!

Parameter	Modeled Practice	Shared Practice	Guided Practice	Interdependent Practice	Application
3. Quality Assessment Informs Instruction	■ Minimum 100-minute block is time-tabled for use of high-impact instructional approaches, K–12. ■ Minimum 75-minute blocks are time-tabled for literacy and mathematics instruction. ■ Interruptions are eliminated during instructional blocks. Time is protected for instruction.	■ All instruction is planned using GRR to progress from modeled to shared to guided to interdependent to application. ■ Using data, teachers move from whole- to small-group to individual differentiated instruction.	■ Ongoing diagnostic and formative data determine which students need more daily guided practice in every subject area. ■ Ongoing, daily assessment practices informs all instruction. ■ Literacy and Mathematic Literacy skills are observed and demonstrated through PL, such as Lesson Study sessions. ■ Higher-order questions promote critical thinking.	■ Students' voice is heard frequently. ■ Students work independently using explicit, timely, formative feedback from teachers' assessments (e.g., minimum one praise point and two instructional points *with examples* [Year-Level dependent]). ■ Students use multiple forms of technology to demonstrate their thinking and learning and their facility with technologies.	■ Assessment Waterfall Chart (AWC) is evidenced in all K–12 classrooms.

(Continued)

(Continued)

Parameter	Modeled Practice	Shared Practice	Guided Practice	Interdependent Practice	Application
4. **Principal as Lead Learner**	◾ Principals can articulate deep, structured understanding of assessment that drives instruction for *all* staff. ◾ They use technology for effectiveness and efficiency. ◾ They have a KO if needed.	◾ Principals are part of Teaching and Learning teams attending PL with staff; no other priority is more important to spend time on. ◾ Superintendents, curriculum staff, and principals lead PL sessions.	◾ Principals and staff use data to drive school plans and guide selection of resources and instructional approaches/ strategies. ◾ They provide focused PL mobilizing resources that reflect system vision and guidelines.	◾ Principals and teachers support **all** students' learning through frequent, nonevaluative LW&Ts and follow-up reflective conversations with staff about practice. ◾ They ensure that all teachers and students have opportunities to learn with and through appropriate technology.	◾ Principals are KOs who attend and are "present" at all PL sessions. ◾ Principals and leadership teams use technology to gather data on the 5 Questions for students asked during LWTs.

Parameter	Modeled Practice	Shared Practice	Guided Practice	Interdependent Practice	Application
5. **Early and Ongoing Intervention**	◾ Data used to identify struggling students' strengths and areas of need early in each school year at every grade level to put interventions and monitoring tools in place immediately.	◾ System, school, and classroom assessment data are shared with all teachers to make collaborative decisions about how to move all learners forward who may be struggling, stuck, or need extending.	◾ Guided instruction training, in evidence-proven interventions is provided for some teachers who form first cohort, and a systematic plan is developed to provide PL and resources for *all* teachers in system over a five-year period.	◾ *All* students are actively engaged in relevant and appropriate learning using high-impact assessment and instruction approaches. ◾ Students use technology to support their individual differentiated learning.	◾ Wait lists are a thing of the past— no students wait! Intervention is urgent. ◾ All students receive the support and precise instruction they require because all teachers know their students' instructional starting points. ◾ *All* teachers are intervention teachers—and can teach *all* students.

(Continued)

(Continued)

Parameter	Modeled Practice	Shared Practice	Guided Practice	Interdependent Practice	Application
6. Case Management Approach (CMA)	◼ Leaders and teams gather, triangulate, and report data for system, schools, and students. ◼ Display performance data privately on a co-constructed Data Wall. Data folders, Venn Diagrams, Excel Spread sheets of Student or Class profiles are an important part of the work with data but are not "instead of" Data Wall and must be also be private (not for students or parents). Data is used for staff to initiate rich discussion and take collective responsibility for all students' improvement.	◼ Teachers identify the students with whom they need instructional support. ◼ Timetables reflect that specialist teachers in the school provide instruction in classroom teachers to engage in data conversations at the Data Wall and to attend Case Management Meetings (CMM).	◼ Principals, KOs, and classroom teachers come together in regularly scheduled Case Management Meetings (CMMs) during the school day. ◼ Classroom teachers present students' work for collective problem solving. ◼ The team recommends instructional strategies to try; whole team, takes ownership for supporting teacher and student.	◼ Teachers implement instructional strategies recommended in CMMs. ◼ They return to follow-up meetings with the CMM team until student improvement is achieved. ◼ Many or all students benefit from the strategies tried for one student: *"Necessary for one; good for all!"*	◼ Data Walls demonstrate "Putting FACES on the Data"; ALL staff own *all* the FACES and take intentional action! ◼ Data conversations and CMMs are routinely scheduled into the school day and "data conversations" at the Data Wall begin every meeting.

Parameter	Modeled Practice	Shared Practice	Guided Practice	Interdependent Practice	Application
7. Focused Professional Learning (PL) at Staff Meetings	■ Principals and leadership teams, as lead-learners, model key system messages and embed PL at all staff meetings—and during every learning opportunity.	■ Principals, KOs, assessment and instruction leaders, and teachers, using diagnostic data and observations from Learning Walks and Talks (LW&Ts), determine staff learning needs and lead differentiated PL. ■ Teachers use technology to access personal PL 24/7 certainly beyond the scope of in-person PL provided at staff meetings.	■ Principals and KOs use school data to identify the Parameters that need focused PL. Parameters #1, #6, and #14 are non-negotiable, are most challenging, and are always 'givens' to review frequently in new ways. ■ They develop a key CI question that reflects the Parameters chosen (see Parameter #11) and may work all year on finding and improving answers in a never-ending CI cycle.	■ Beliefs match practice and become a habit of mind. ■ School and classroom learning environments are characterized by high energy and teaching spaces where the "Third Teacher" is evident and being used as a teaching tool. Staff room conversations focus on students' improvement, and students use common language modeled by K–12 teachers.	■ "Learning" is the focus of all meetings where staff gather—Operational issues are relegated to admin email.

(Continued)

(Continued)

Parameter	Modeled Practice	Shared Practice	Guided Practice	Interdependent Practice	Application
8. **In-School Meetings—Collaborative Assessment of Student Work (CASW)**	■ Teacher-leaders and department heads model what strong practice looks like in all curriculum areas at every large- and small-group teacher and leader meeting; operational issues are reduced to email/memo format.	■ Weekly discussions of <u>anonymous</u> student work samples at grade, division, or department meetings lead to development of a common language, deep understanding of curriculum expectation and explicit assessment that informs instructional approaches/strategies.	■ Leaders and KOs build and share an expansive repertoire of high-impact assessment and instructional approaches to support teachers—this is often actualized at CMMs.	■ Students benefit from immediate, explicit feedback from teachers about their work and are given on-the-spot instruction to move them forward. Teachers must record feedback given so they can expect to see it used in the next piece of students' work.	■ CASW demands that teachers examine their own practice in light of colleague discussions and also pursue what might be the feedback to the student of this piece of work.

Parameter	Modeled Practice	Shared Practice	Guided Practice	Interdependent Practice	Application
		Teachers have common planning time to collaboratively assess anonymous samples of student work and reach consensus through rich dialogue on the level and needs improvement of each piece of work.	Teachers learn from each other by modeling what is working for them; they walk in other classrooms together to see others' practice and discuss refining their own.		
9. Centralized Resources	Leaders, teacher-leaders, and teacher-librarians collect current print and digitized resources for teachers' and students' use and locate them in a central location for all teachers to use.	Teachers share the use of leveled texts and multi-dimensional, multi-modal resources, all labeled appropriately according to learners' stages.	KOs and teachers collaboratively plan and teach lessons using a variety of resources and instructional approaches that meet *all* students' needs.	Students see themselves reflected in the classroom resources used. Students know how to use web-based technology to find resources and information and know how to apply them.	All staff share the use of collected resources—this becomes obvious and actioned at CMMs where teachers' capacity is built to teach ALL students.

(Continued)

(Continued)

Parameter	Modeled Practice	Shared Practice	Guided Practice	Interdependent Practice	Application
	▪ Analyze gaps in resources to determine what further resources are needed.	▪ Resources are also categorized by authors, genres, and publishers, and include graphic novels, science journals, bibliographies, software, and so on. ▪ Leaders and teachers select professional readings (focused on their priority or CI) and discuss at voluntary book studies.	▪ Teachers use technology to discuss, share, and guide use of exemplary resources with others.	▪ Students share their resources in collaboratively designed group work processes with built-in individual student accountability.	

Parameter	Modeled Practice	Shared Practice	Guided Practice	Interdependent Practice	Application
10. Allocation of System and School Budgets for Learning	■ Senior leaders and elected officials (trustees) continue to fund needed resources (human and material) in tough economic times by finding operational areas in which to cut costs; they are united in "staying the course" and live in Parameters #1 and #14.	■ System curriculum consultants share how to use resources and assessment and instruction al approaches, using blended learning model (face-to-face time and interactive technology time) to reach *all* teachers. ■ Teachers in small groups are expected to try out resources and apply their new skills to refine their practice.	■ KOs support the selection and use of resources for classrooms and book rooms. ■ Carefully selected resources mirror the diversity in classrooms and enable *all* students to relate to and 'see' themselves in the resources.	■ Equity of outcomes for *all* students is experienced and acknowledged through data— *all* students are meeting the high performance targets set for them. ■ Students, parents, and the community see schools as resources for their own learning; schools find many contextually unique ways to accomplish this.	■ When budgets are tight, funding for learning remains intact.

(Continued)

(Continued)

Parameter	Modeled Practice	Shared Practice	Guided Practice	Interdependent Practice	Application
11. Collaborative Inquiry (CI)—A Whole-System Approach	▪ Principals and leadership teams model the exploration of system, school, and student data to determine areas of students' strengths and needs.	▪ Principals and leadership teams share system and school data with *all* staff and discuss teaching outcomes necessary to increase growth and achievement for *all* students. They use data to determine their CI.	▪ System PL is provided to guide staff to focus on developing one CI question re what they need to know more about, based on multiple data sets. ▪ Time is set aside throughout the year for discussion focused on finding answers to the CI question—an example of accountable staff talk.	▪ The system gives money for in-school PL days to consolidate findings to answer and write a report on the CI question. ▪ *All* teachers are committed to applying discussed assessment and instruction approaches needed to answer the CI question to ensure that *all* students are learning and progressing.	▪ Whole-System and Whole-School approach to CI becomes "the norm" as investigations not only unpack high-impact strategies but are interpreted and applied in every classroom by every teacher—an "open-to-learning stance" is needed to make this happen.

Parameter	Modeled Practice	Shared Practice	Guided Practice	Interdependent Practice	Application
12. Parental and Community Involvement	■ Everyone models the belief that parents are students' first and most important teachers whom parents are trusting us to ensure that their children reach their full potential.	■ Principals and teachers reach out to the community to bring parents in to schools. ■ Schools host adult learning sessions day/night. ■ Use of technology and software to learn at home is supported through take-home technology and teacher-prepared work designed for each student.	■ Principals and teachers are able to confidently articulate to parents and the community why, what, and how they do what they do in *all* classrooms.	■ Parents and students know what, why, and how students are doing and have a clear understanding of learning expectations and what students need to do to reach the next learning level.	■ Parents see themselves as vital members of the school community who have contributions to make—and are frequently asked to make them.

(Continued)

(Continued)

Parameter	Modeled Practice	Shared Practice	Guided Practice	Interdependent Practice	Application
13. **Cross-Curricular Literacy Connections**	■ The language of the discipline is modeled in every subject area. ■ The modeled, shared, guided, independent and application of the GRR approach is used to differentiate instruction and scaffold Critical Thinking as the outcome of learning in *all* subject areas.	■ Discussion groups, demonstration classrooms, video streaming, and web technologies are used to share examples of cross-curricular instruction for all teachers' PL.	■ Curriculum consultants and KOs work alongside classroom teachers to integrate literacy skills and concepts into *all* subject areas.	■ Students experience that the taught, learned, and assessed curriculum align. ■ Students make connections to text as media and media as text. ■ Students work collaboratively online, building projects together.	■ Bump-It-Up Walls become Learning Walls in every subject area, including Learning Intentions and Success Criteria, so that students can self-assess and know their next steps for learning and goal-setting.

Parameter	Modeled Practice	Shared Practice	Guided Practice	Interdependent Practice	Application
14. Shared Responsibility and Accountability	■ The focused literacy priority of the nation, state, system, school, and classroom is aligned, clear, precise, and intentional. ■ Everyone knows and can articulate the aligned priority.	■ All elementary and secondary school teams participate in evidence-proven precision-in-practice. Presentations from every school occur at system-wide annual Learning Fairs.	■ All schools host their own Learning Fairs for parents and community members. ■ Teams of teachers present their CI findings' evidence that shows increased students' growth and achievement at their system and school Learning Fairs.	■ The CMA (Parameter #6), with time during the day, is available to any teacher who is struggling to reach a student; teachers and leaders, assisted by colleagues, find assessment and instructional strategies that work with each student brought forward to a CMM and continue until they find an approach that works—never giving up on one student thus all becoming responsible and accountable for *all* students and supportive of all teachers.	■ System improvement is an outcome of a line-of-site to exemplary classroom practice. ■ Staff and students are supported with "just right" resources and "just-in-time instruction" and PL directed at each student's "point-of-need."

(Continued)

(Continued)

Parameter	Modeled Practice	Shared Practice	Guided Practice	Interdependent Practice	Application
	■ The priority is clearly reflected in the CI question developed (Parameter #11) in every school using triangulation of data.	■ Principals and teachers conduct non-evaluative, focused LW&Ts together to ask reflective questions about practice that go deeper and cause reflection on their own practice ■ Classroom teachers open doors to each other, making practice public.	■ Streaming technology is used to make the Learning Fairs accessible to the broader community. ■ All teachers use assessment data to drive differentiated instruction. ■ Assessment data are delivered to leaders' and teachers' desktops, making everyone responsible and accountable for putting individual student FACES on the data and taking action on behalf of *all* students.	■ Students, facilitated by teachers, present at Learning Fairs in their schools and can articulate to parents and the broader community why they have improved in their learning and what their next steps will be. Teachers and leaders show how their work is connected to the system work at the Learning Fairs as alignment is KEY. ■ Students and teachers develop Sharepoint or other technology locations to communicate their achievements	■ All teachers become/are intervention teachers. ■ All teachers and leaders can teach ALL students using evidence-proven approaches. ■ Everyone is a leader.

Parameter	Modeled Practice	Shared Practice	Guided Practice	Interdependent Practice	Application
			▪ Principals and teachers conduct non-evaluative LW&Ts together, which result in coaching conversations that go deeply into practice to support *all* students' growth and achievement.	continuously to those beyond their schools (such as, superintendents, community members, trustees, and so on). ▪ Data conversations focused on increasing students' growth and achievement occur spontaneously throughout the school day by *all* staff and students who make classrooms public places of learning.	

Why are Parameters #1, #6, and #14 non-negotiable?

APPENDIX B

Data Collection Placemat for Research

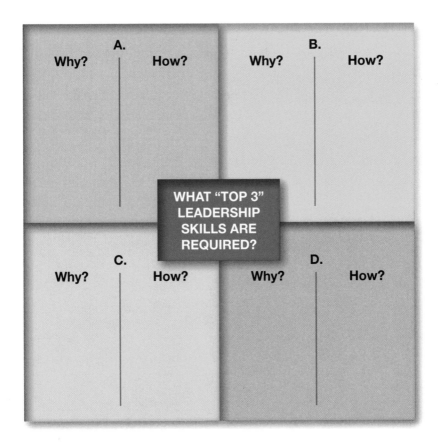

Instructions for using the placemat:

1. Divide your group into fours and divide your chart paper into four equal quadrants/sections and letter them A, B, C, and D.

2. Individually write in your section the answers to these questions:

   a. Why do we put FACES on the data?

   b. How do we put FACES on the data?

3. As a team, reach consensus on what leadership skills are required to put the FACES on the data.

4. Record your top three leadership skills in the center of the paper.

5. Give us some concrete examples or stories of where this is happening.

APPENDIX C

*Initial Case Management
Meeting Template*

Begin by reviewing the co-constructed Operating Norms to establish a "Culture of Learning."

Student's Name: _____

Grade: _____ Date: _____

Teacher's Name: _____

Focus of Teacher's Request for Support: _____

Student's Background Information:
Interests:
Strengths:
Identifications/Accommodations:
Other Important Learning Information:

(Continued)

(Continued)

Observation:

Background Info (Understanding of Learning Intentions and Success criteria; teacher observations, assessments administered):

Analysis of current work sample:

What are the strengths of this student?	What are the areas of need for this student?

Which area is critical to student's growth and achievement?

How can we build on this student's strengths?

What instructional approaches/strategies has teacher already tried?

Plan:

What is a reasonable next short-term goal for this student? Why?

What instructional approaches and/or strategies will you try, and WHY do you think they will work?

Strategy/ Rationale	Modeled	Shared	Guided	Independent	Application

(Continued)

(Continued)

Group suggests various approaches/strategies not tried using above grid.

Teacher selects one and determines how long it will take to implement the strategy with student before determining if successful or not.

What resources will teacher need to implement this plan?

Evidence and Follow Up:

What kind of work samples from this student will you bring to the next meeting?

Next Meeting Date (3 weeks later with same teachers and leaders around the table):

THINK ABOUT: What other instructional practices from our
Responsive Literacy Program might this student respond to?

READING

Modeled	Shared	Guided	Independent	Application
☐ Read Aloud	☐ Book Talks	☐ Instructional Level Reading	☐ Self-Selected	**Can read other text of increasing difficulty**
☐ Think Aloud	☐ Story Theatre	☐ Focus: Comprehension	☐ Literature Circle	
☐ Different Genre/ Reading	☐ Reader's Theater	☐ Before Reading	☐ Reading Workshop	**Can read other genre with fluency and comprehension**
☐ Whole Class	☐ Paired Reading	☐ During Reading	☐ Conferencing	
☐ Broaden Interests	☐ Choral Reading/ Speaking	☐ After Reading	☐ Buddy/ Partner Reading	**Can read and interpret accurately other subject area texts, information**
☐ Thinking and Problem Solving	☐ Whole Class (same reading material)	☐ Small Flexible Groups	☐ Book Club	
☐ Student Engagement/ Motivate	☐ Build Skills and Strategies	☐ Groups Based on Needs	☐ Pursue Areas of Interest	
☐ Students Develop Appreciations	☐ Framing Questions	☐ Reinforce Strategies Taught	☐ Books Easily Accessible	
	☐ Student Engagement/ Motivation		☐ Diversity	

WRITING

Modeled	Shared	Guided	Independent	Application
☐ Teacher Write-Aloud	☐ Teacher and students write story together with the teacher as scribe	☐ Focused Mini-Lessons	☐ Journal	**Can write using a variety of genres for a variety of purposes in every subject area**
☐ Show Process in mini-lesson		☐ Small Flexible Groups (needs)	☐ Constructed Response	
☐ Thinking/		☐ Reinforce Strategies Taught	☐ Writing Workshop	
☐ Problem Solving	☐ Students share the pen to complete a story after talking about a shared event	☐ Groups Based on Needs	☐ Conferencing	
☐ Whole Class			☐ Process Writing	
☐ FOCUS (week, month, term)			☐ Flexibility of Topic	
☐ Use of Resources			☐ Pursuit of Interests	

(Continued)

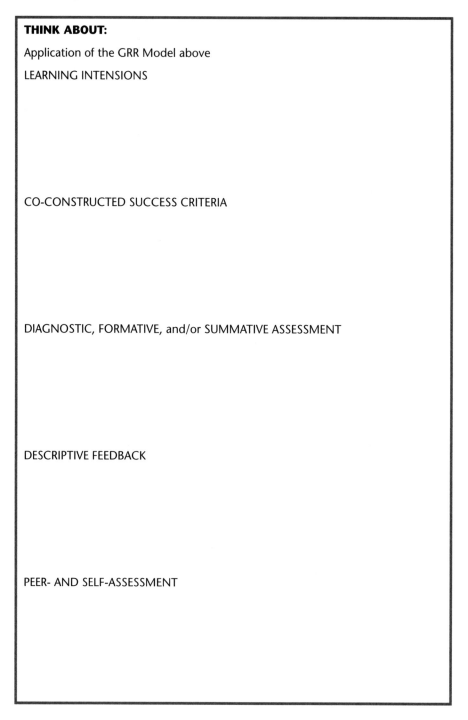

THINK ABOUT:

Application of the GRR Model above

LEARNING INTENSIONS

CO-CONSTRUCTED SUCCESS CRITERIA

DIAGNOSTIC, FORMATIVE, and/or SUMMATIVE ASSESSMENT

DESCRIPTIVE FEEDBACK

PEER- AND SELF-ASSESSMENT

INDIVIDUAL GOAL SETTING

CO-CONSTRUCTED ANCHOR CHARTS

EXEMPLARS

RICH TASKS

OTHER:

Source: Adapted from York Region District School Board (2007).

Case Management Follow-Up Meeting Template

Review co-constructed Operating Norms before meeting begins.

Student's Name: _____

Grade: _____ Date:_____

Teacher's Name: _____

ACHIEVEMENT STANDARD

Learning Intention:

Success Criteria:

Evidence Brought Forward From Previous Case Management (CM) Meeting

Hear teacher's voice as teacher presents the evidence.

Scrutiny of New Student Work Sample(s)

What teaching approaches and strategies have been used?

What can this student do?

What progress has this student made?

Plan

What is the short-term goal now for this student? Why?

Where do we need to provide ongoing support for this student?

What pedagogical strategies will you use next? Such as:

Modeled:

Shared:

Guided:

Independent:

Application:

(Continued)

(Continued)

Evidence and Follow-up

What are the Next Steps in support of this student?

If unsuccessful, what other approaches are recommended?
What will be the evidence brought back to next meeting?
We are not giving up!

How can we support you (the classroom teacher) until the next meeting?

Is there any external support that we all need?

Is there any current research that we all need to read?

If this case is successful, which other students in your class might benefit from this strategy? ("Necessary for some – good for all," says Lyn.)

On what date will we all return?

APPENDIX D

The Teaching-Learning Cycle

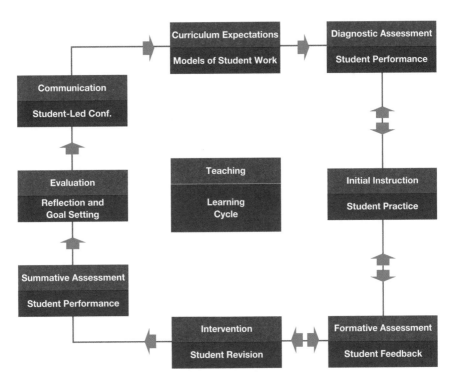

Source: Printed with permission from York Regional District School Board (2007).

APPENDIX E

Weekly Literacy Block Planner

Week of: _____

Literacy Focus: _____

Suggested Weekly Literacy Block Planner

Time	Component	Monday	Tuesday	Wednesday	Thursday	Friday
Suggested Guidelines	Entry: Welcome students into classroom and promote polite and respectful interactions. Support students as they get organized for the literacy block.	Literacy Learning Intention: ☐ Clustered curriculum expectations and big idea	Literacy Learning Intentions: ☐ Clustered curriculum expectations and big idea	Literacy Learning Intentions: ☐ Clustered curriculum expectations and big idea	Literacy Learning Intentions: ☐ Clustered curriculum expectations and big idea	Literacy Learning Intentions: ☐ Clustered curriculum expectations and big idea

Time	Component	Monday	Tuesday	Wednesday	Thursday	Friday
10–20 min.	Modeled or Shared Reading	Text:	Text:	Text:	Text:	Text:
	☐ Comprehension strategies					
	☐ Author study/ genre study					
	☐ Think aloud with focus	Focus:	Focus:	Focus:	Focus:	Focus:
	☐ Critical literacy analysis					
	☐ Poem/cross-curricular					
	☐ Article/poster/ graphic text					

(Continued)

305

(Continued)

Time	Component	Monday	Tuesday	Wednesday	Thursday	Friday
10–20 min.	Language & Word Study/Book Talks	Text or Comprehension or Critical Literacy Focus:	Text or Comprehension or Critical Literacy Focus:	Text or Comprehension or Critical Literacy Focus:	Text or Comprehension or Critical Literacy Focus:	Text or Comprehension or Critical Literacy Focus:
	☐ Word sorting/ making words					
	☐ Fix-up strategies					
	☐ Phonics					
	☐ Phonemic Awareness/ Alphabetic Knowledge/ Phonics. Word Study					
	☐ Grammar					
	☐ Fluency and phrasing					
	☐ Word wall					

Time	Component	Monday	Tuesday	Wednesday	Thursday	Friday
20–30 min.	<u>Independent Reading</u> ☐ Phonemic Awareness/ Alphabetic Knowledge/ Phonics. Word Study ☐ Book talks ☐ Reading response ☐ "Just right" books ☐ Reading logs ☐ Current events	Students to one-on-one conference with: ☐ ☐ ☐ ☐ ☐ ☐ ☐ ☐	Students to one-on-one conference with: ☐ ☐ ☐ ☐ ☐ ☐ ☐ ☐	Students to one-on-one conference with: ☐ ☐ ☐ ☐ ☐ ☐ ☐ ☐	Students to one-on-one conference with: ☐ ☐ ☐ ☐ ☐ ☐ ☐ ☐	Students to one-on-one conference with: ☐ ☐ ☐ ☐ ☐ ☐ ☐ ☐
20–30 min.	<u>Guided Reading</u> ☐ See resources (i.e., guided reading folders in Realization, 2009) for student groupings, focus, prompting questions, and assessment	GR Group # — Text: Focus: GR Group # — Text: Focus:	GR Group # — Text: Focus: GR Group # — Text: Focus:	GR Group # — Text: Focus: GR Group # — Text: Focus:	GR Group # — Text: Focus: GR Group # — Text: Focus:	GR Group # — Text: Focus: GR Group # — Text: Focus:

(Continued)

(Continued)

Time	Component	Monday	Tuesday	Wednesday	Thursday	Friday
10–20 min.	Writer's Workshop Mini-Lessons: ☐ Modeled writing ☐ Shared writing ☐ Interactive writing (primary) Practice: ☐ Independent writing and Application	Form and Focus of Writing:	Form and Focus of Writing:	Form and Focus of Writing:	Form and Focus of Writing:	Form and Focus of Writing:

Time	Component	Monday	Tuesday	Wednesday	Thursday	Friday
20–30 min.	<u>Guided Writing</u> ☐ Writing form, feature, and genre ☐ Writing traits (ideas, organization) ☐ Structure ☐ Grammar, Spelling, Phonics, and Punctuation ☐ Details and descriptive vocabulary ☐ Review and Track Writing Process used	Guided Writing Focus: Names of Students in Small Group: ☐ ☐ ☐ ☐ ☐	Guided Writing Focus: Names of Students in Small Group: ☐ ☐ ☐ ☐ ☐	Guided Writing Focus: Names of Students in Small Group: ☐ ☐ ☐ ☐ ☐	Guided Writing Focus: Names of Students in Small Group: ☐ ☐ ☐ ☐ ☐	Guided Writing Focus: Names of Students in Small Group: ☐ ☐ ☐ ☐ ☐

(Continued)

(Continued)

Time	Component	Monday	Tuesday	Wednesday	Thursday	Friday
Next Steps or Congress when whole class gathers to refer back to Learning Intention and co-construct the "I Can" statements of the Success Criteria	Reflection from today's literacy block and whole-group, small-group, and individual instruction to plan for tomorrow Draw out Success Criteria	Reflection:	Reflection:	Reflection:	Reflection:	Reflection:

- Important to note that oral language, media literacy, critical literacy, and higher-order thinking skills are all interwoven throughout the literacy block and in all other subject areas
- The focus and order of the literacy block will change depending on student need—more time may need to be given for modeled practice and learning styles, social-emotional skills, and student voice and interest will be taken into account when planning.

APPENDIX F

Task-Oriented Question Construction Wheel Based on Bloom's Taxonomy

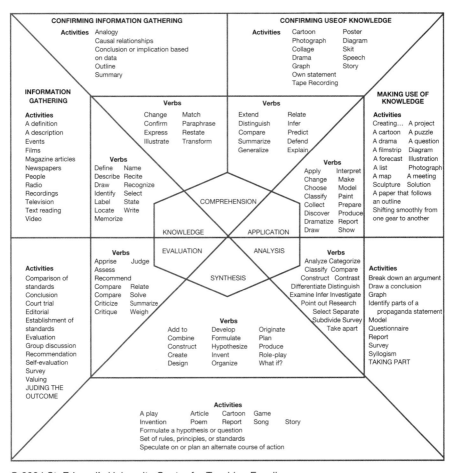

APPENDIX G

*Cross-Curricular Literacy
Indicators of Success*

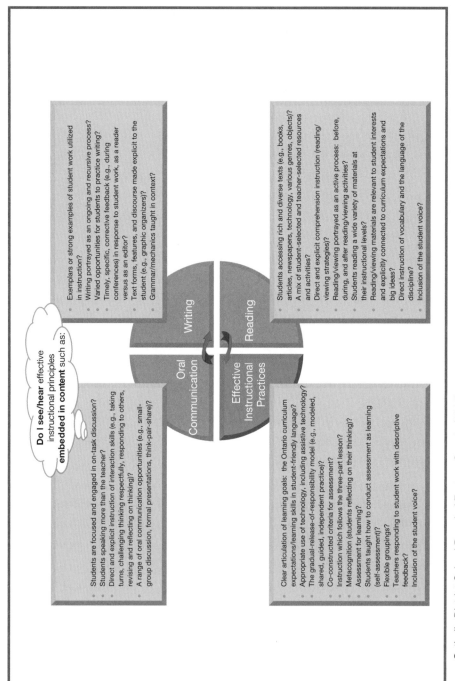

Do I see/hear effective instructional principles **embedded in content** such as:

Writing

- Exemplars or strong examples of student work utilized in instruction?
- Writing portrayed as an ongoing and recursive process?
- Varied opportunities for students to practice writing?
- Timely, specific, corrective feedback (e.g., during conferences) in response to student work, as a reader versus as an editor?
- Text forms, features, and discourse made explicit to the student (e.g., graphic organizers)?
- Grammar/mechanics taught in context?

Reading

- Students accessing rich and diverse texts (e.g., books, articles, newspapers, technology, various genres, objects)?
- A mix of student-selected and teacher-selected resources and activities?
- Direct and explicit comprehension instruction (reading/viewing strategies)?
- Reading/viewing portrayed as an active process: before, during, and after reading/viewing activities?
- Students reading a wide variety of materials at their instructional levels?
- Reading/viewing materials are relevant to student interests and explicitly connected to curriculum expectations and big ideas?
- Direct instruction of vocabulary and the language of the discipline?
- Inclusion of the student voice?

Oral Communication

- Students are focused and engaged in on-task discussion?
- Students speaking more than the teacher?
- Direct and explicit instruction of interaction skills (e.g., taking turns, challenging thinking respectfully, responding to others, revising and reflecting on thinking)?
- A range of oral communication opportunities (e.g., small-group discussion, formal presentations, think-pair-share)?

Effective Instructional Practices

- Clear articulation of learning goals: the Ontario curriculum expectations/learning skills in student-friendly language?
- Appropriate use of technology, including assistive technology?
- The gradual-release-of-responsibility model (e.g., modeled, shared, guided, independent practice)?
- Co-constructed criteria for assessment?
- Instruction which follows the three-part lesson?
- Metacognition (students reflecting on their thinking)?
- Assessment for learning?
- Students taught how to conduct assessment as learning (self-assessment)?
- Flexible groupings?
- Teachers responding to student work with descriptive feedback?
- Inclusion of the student voice?

Source: Catholic District School Board of Eastern Ontario (2011).

314

APPENDIX H

Guiding Questions for
Collaborative Team Book Study

Chapter 1: From Information Glut to Well-Known FACES

- Create an inventory of the data-generating tools used by your teachers, by your district, your school, by your network, and by your state.

- Of all the data available, which are most critical? Justify your thinking.

- In putting FACES on your data, analyze and discuss how useful your data have been to system leaders, principals, KOs, and teachers.

- Examine what is available and what your staff members want to know more about. List the data that might be useful to you for determining students' FACES that your state, districts/regions, networks, and schools are missing or that appear to be missing.

- Give examples from your data that demonstrate that *all* students are learning to their maximum potential—and that *all* teachers are teaching to their maximum potential.

- Determine how many FACES—not the percentages, but the actual number of students—are exempted from assessments. Why were these exemptions granted? Is the reasoning for these exemptions legitimate? How do you know?

- What percentage of students (in your state, school, or classroom) can read with fluency and comprehension by the end of Grade 1? How do you know? What determines the reading standard?

- Define literacy in your context. What does cross-curricular literacy look like, K–12? What criteria do you use to measure a responsive, flexible literacy program that is a cross-curricular?

- What is the collective plan for improvement—how do you build consensus so that all staff commit to improvement? How can the 14 Parameter Framework help you?

- What resources are available to you to implement this focused improvement?

- Critique your implementation of value-added support for *all* students' learning. How are your Knowledgeable Others offering added value to the Professional Learning of leaders and teachers?

- Review the 14 Parameter framework in Appendix A. Identify your strengths and areas of need. Develop a plan to implement Parameters #1, #6, #14 (the non-negotiables) and one additional Parameter. Build this into your improvement plan, thinking about how you will scaffold the learning from *modeled* to *shared* to *guided* and ultimately to achieve *interdependent* practice by all staff. Will they be able to *apply* this learning alone or together at your school, system, or in another school or system?

- Develop your own comparison chart, using the gap analysis that St. Bridgit's did in this chapter.

- Explain why you think Parameters #1, #6, and #14 are non-negotiable and must be revisited frequently.

Chapter 2: The Power of Putting FACES on the Data

- Think about the three research questions presented in FACES. How do your answers compare to the research data? How do they fit into the chart and summary responses in this chapter?

  ○ Why do we put FACES on the data?

○ How do we put FACES on the data?

○ What are the top three leadership skills needed to put FACES on the data?

- Relate how state and system reviewing of and knowledge about the performance data affect your leadership and what teachers teach and what students learn?

- Do teachers know what data sets look like for the whole school and system—beyond their class? In other words, consider how all teachers get to see and understand the big picture in your school (and district or region), too.

Chapter 3: Making It Work in Practice–Assessment Literacy

- Construct a Mind Map of the processes involved in knowing each and every learner.

- How do you determine what is to be taught and who needs to be coached and about what?

- How do you make a Learning Intention easily understood to all students? To all teachers? Explain why it is critically important to identify big ideas and essential questions with students. How do teachers engage in "Prior Learning Assessment" so they are not teaching what students already know?

- Point out and visit all classrooms where teachers display Success Criteria that have been co-constructed with students.

- Explain all the components of assessment—check for understanding by consulting the glossary. Use the Assessment Waterfall Chart as your guide.

- Are all students and teachers improving? How do you know? Examine the Data Wall process that Principal James Bond uses. How can you adapt that process to your situation? Data Walls are **private** places for teachers and leaders to discuss the growth and achievement (or not) of each student. Where can the confidential Data Wall be located in your context? Define the implementation process for using a Data Wall. List the steps involved. What will you consider strategically in implementing the Data Wall process in your state? System? Network? School? Classroom?

- Take a moment to think about yourself as leader and what you can do to improve as a leader by looking at and comparing your work to the mythical cohort described in the chapter. Select a group of students for which a snapshot of each grade score across all grades in your school could represent a cohort of students going through all grades in your school. Calculate the students' scores across disciplines (e.g., reading, writing, math or numeracy, and other literacy measures). Do they increase as the grades increase, do they decrease, or are they sustained at a high level from the early years? Is there fluctuation at certain grade levels? Predict and discuss how that fluctuation will represent leadership opportunities for you with teachers who may require additional support.

- Confirm with evidence that your teachers and leaders give Descriptive Feedback directly against the Success Criteria that is factual and objective and that outlines and gives examples of how to improve as a student or as a teacher.

- Recommend to others where you could go for help as an instructional leader or a teacher. Reflect and give evidence of whether students in your system, school, and classroom

  - Set their own individual goals and monitor progress toward achieving them

  - Seek clarification or assistance from others when needed

  - Assess and reflect critically on their own strengths, needs, interests, and next steps

  - Identify learning opportunities, choices, and strategies to meet personal needs and achieve goals

  - Persevere and make an effort when responding to challenges

- Compare the Ballarat Clarendon College case study and lessons learned to your situation. What will you add or delete from your improvement plan after discussing this case study? How will you become more focused on assessment that improves instruction?

Chapter 4: Making It Work in Practice–Instruction

- In your school, does everyone believe that every student can and will learn?

- How do you know that your collective expectations for all FACES are high enough? Is there planned and purposeful literacy learning in kindergarten?

- Defend oral language as the foundation of all instruction, K–12?

- Do all teachers *model, share,* and *guide* reading and writing beginning in kindergarten? What strategies do we recommend to ensure that these happen? Is there time for *independent* practice and reflection? How do you know that students can *apply* what they have learned?

- Research to discover if your teachers can answer these five fundamental questions:

  1. What am I teaching?

  2. Why am I teaching it?

  3. How will I teach it?

  4. How will I know when all students have learned it? What then?

  5. Where do I go for help?

- Define and list the characteristics of your literate graduate.

- Identify the components of an impactful K–12 literacy program by referring to Appendix E. How does your program compare?

- Explore if students in your school are required to use new ways to think about and solve problems. Make a list of these new ways—what they look like and sound like in classrooms. What evidence do you have that higher-order, critical thinking verbs (Appendix F) are embedded in performance tasks?

- Are tasks relevant to and authentic for students? How do you know?

- Do disciplines come together, and can they be explored together in the performance tasks that teachers and students select?

- Examine if teachers in the subject disciplines use a common language and common assessments of written work and thinking skills so that students can transition readily from year to year and across all disciplines.

- Collect evidence that all learning tasks prompt thinking and creativity and stimulate curiosity.

- Give examples that support students' ability to confer, consult, and communicate with others.

- List all the ways your teachers make their students' thinking visible.

- Assess if your students are required to write down and reflect on their thoughts and learning each day. Explain how and when that happens.

- Reflect on how Principal Joanne Pitman and her staff use Case Management Meetings to support all students and all teachers. How would you make this work in your context? What operational issues need to be considered in making this approach successful?

- Role-play a Case Management Meeting with your staff using the template in Appendix C(a) and then the follow-up template in Appendix C(b) 3 weeks later when the same group reconvenes.

- If we were to watch you teach over a 2-month period, elaborate on what we would see that would increase the learning and life chances of *all* your students.

- If we were to watch you lead as principal over a 2-month period, reflect on what we would see that would increase the Professional Learning of your teachers.

- When a teacher is having difficulty making progress with a specific student, how does the teacher come to you with a statement of need, or how would you notice the apparent difficulty? Assess the attributes of the Case Management Approach (Data Walls and Case Management Meetings) to instructing each student, then implement by embedding in the timetable.

- Defend or negate the following statement (provide reasons for your point of view): Inquiry is driving the learning and thinking of all students at this school.

- Are multiple data sources driving instruction in classrooms? How do you know?

- Are Collaborative Assessment of Student Work (CASW), time with Knowledgeable Other, Co-Constructed Data walls, Case Management Meetings, and collaborative inquiry the operating norm in your system? School? How do you know? What successful learning interventions do you deploy in your school? What is the success rate in bringing underachieving students to acceptable or above acceptable levels of performance? Do the interventions enable your teachers to close the gap between lower performers and higher performers on assessments? What criteria are used to evaluate successful interventions?

- Make a list of conclusions that Lyn and Michael came to in determining the powerful advantages of the co-teaching model. Explain the cycle. Discuss how this can be set in motion in your context.

Chapter 5: Leadership–Individualizing for Improvement

- Is the Professional Learning that you are leading making a difference to improved student learning? How do you know on a daily, weekly, and monthly basis?

- As leader, how do you monitor your impact on student learning? Explain how your thinking about the monitoring of students' growth and achievement is transformed into action.

- Who monitors students' growth and achievement across the entire school? Network? System? Who reports that improvement or no improvement in a timely fashion to the teacher, looking for answers, not to the question "why aren't they learning?" but rather to the question "how can we help you to improve all students' achievement?" How early in the semester or learning cycle do you have this progress information so that you can offer interventions when required? Compare your actions to those used by Principal Jill Maar at her school and Principal James Leach at his school.

- What examples do you have of putting FACES on the data at the system, region, network, school, and classroom levels? What

Professional Learning is in place for leaders to learn from data? How do you define instructional leadership? What Professional Learning is in place for principals and deputy principals to become instructional leaders?

- Who is in my class? (*Note:* Everyone has "a class" to teach and from which to learn: system leaders, principals, KOs, teachers, elected officials, and community members.)

- Whose learning is your responsibility?

- Summarize the strategies that you use to ensure that the use of data considers emotional connectedness and cognitive insights?

- How does your leadership compare to the strategies used by James Leach and Jill Maar?

- Do you conduct Learning Walks and Talks regularly to ask students:

  ○ What are you learning? Why?

  ○ How are you doing?

  ○ How do you know?

  ○ How do you improve?

  ○ Where do you go for help?

- Do you take teachers on Learning Walks and Talks with you, as leaders, and ask yourselves the above questions?

Chapter 6: Ownership—Of All the FACES

- Discuss who owns the responsibility for all your students' growth and achievement.

- Deconstruct the support you give to parents and the community so that they can assist in taking ownership for student achievement. Compare and contrast your work to the strategies we discuss for enhancing parental and community involvement.

- Formulate a to-do list after discussion about the Wales Case Study and how they achieved improvement across their entire nation.

- Reflect and collate what supports are in place to encourage *all* your employees—not only teachers—to own *all* students' growth and achievement with emotional connections and cognitive insights? In your opinion, what is missing? Who needs to know what is needed?

- What are your narratives from the field?
- Write your own case study of improvement in putting FACES on the data. Then publish it! Congratulations, you have contributed to the learning growth of your colleagues.

REFERENCES

ADDYSG CYMRU Education Wales. (2017). *Education in Wales: Our national mission*. Author. https://gov.wales/sites/default/files/publications/2018-03/education-in-wales-our-national-mission.pdf

Allen, R. (2003). *Expanding writing's role in learning.* Curriculum update. Association for Supervision and Curriculum Development.

Australian Curriculum, Assessment and Reporting Authority. (2010). *NAPLAN achievement in reading, writing, language conventions and numeracy: National report for 2010.* Author.

Australian Curriculum, Assessment and Reporting Authority. (2009). *NAPLAN achievement in reading, writing, language conventions and numeracy: National report for 2009.* Author.

Australian Curriculum, Assessment and Reporting Authority. (2008). *NAPLAN achievement in reading, writing, language conventions and numeracy: National report for 2008.* Author.

Barber, M. (2021). *Accomplishment: How to achieve ambitious and challenging things.* Penguin House.

Barber, M., Moffit, A., & Kihn, P. (2011). *Deliverology 101.* Corwin.

Bennett, B., & Rolheiser, C. (2001). *Beyond Monet: The artful science of instructional integration.* Bookation.

Bennett, B., Sharratt, L., & Sangster, S. (2001). *Systemic change: A focus on instructional intelligence . . . two and one-half years into a five-year journey.* OISE.

Brown, L. (2008, May 21). Where teachers learn diversity. *Toronto Star.* https://www.thestar.com/life/health_wellness/2008/05/21/where_teachers_learn_diversity.html

Calman, R. C., for the EQAO. (2010). *Exploring the underlying traits of high-performing schools.* Queen's Printer.

Chambers, A. (1985). *Book talk.* Bodley Head Limited.

Chappius, J. (2007). *Learning team facilitator handbook.* Educational Testing Service.

City, E., Elmore, R., Flarman, S., & Teitel, L. (2009). *Instructional rounds in education.* Harvard Education Press.

Cornelius-White, J. (2007). Learner-centred teacher-student relationships are effective: A meta-analysis. *Review of Educational Research, 77*(1), 113–143.

Davies, B., & Davies, B. (2011). *Talent management in education.* SAGE.

Donaldson, G. (2015). *Successful futures: Looking at the curriculum and assessment arrangements in Wales.* Corwin. https://gov.wales/sites/default/files/publications/2018-03/succesful-futures-a-summary-of-professor-graham-donaldsons-report.pdf

Dufour, R., & Marzano, R. J. (2011). *Leaders of learning: How district, school, and classroom leaders improve student achievement.* Solution Tree Press.

Duke, C., & Duke, P. (2006). Special education: An integral part of small schools in high schools. *High School Journal, 89*(3), 1–9.

Earl, L., & Katz, S. (2006). *Leading schools in a data rich world: Harnessing data for school improvement.* Corwin.

Elder, Z. (2022). *An exploration of schools as learning organisations as a catalyst for school and system change* [Unpublished PhD Thesis].

Elmore, R. F. (2004). *School reform from the inside out: Policy, practice, and performance.* Harvard Education Press.

Epstein, J. (1995). School/family/community partnerships: Caring for the children we share. *Phi Delta Kappan, 76*, 701–712.

Feldman, J (2018). *Grading for equity: What it is, why it matters, and how it can transform schools and classrooms.* SAGE.

Fountas, I. C., & Pinnell, G. S. (2001). *Guiding readers and writers: Teaching, comprehension, fluency, genre, and content literacy.* Heinemann.

Fullan, M. (2021). *The right drivers for whole system success.* Centre for Strategic Education. https://michaelfullan.ca/wp-content/uploads/2021/03/Fullan-CSE-Leading-Education-Series-01-2021R2-compressed.pdf

Fullan, M. (2019). *Nuance.* Corwin.

Fullan, M. (2013). *Stratosphere: Integrating technology, pedagogy and change knowledge.* Pearson.

Fullan, M. (2011a). *Choosing the wrong drivers for whole system reform.* CSE.

Fullan, M. (2011b). *Moral imperative realized.* Corwin.

Fullan, M. (2010a). *All systems go.* Corwin.

Fullan, M. (2010b). *Motion leadership: The skinny on becoming change savvy.* Corwin.

Fullan, M., & Edwards, M. (2022). *Spirit work and the science of collaboration.* Corwin.

Fullan, M., & Gallagher, M. J. (2020). *The devil is in the details: System solutions for equity, excellence, and student well-being.* Corwin.

Fullan, M., & Knight, J. (2011). Coaches as system leaders. *Educational Leadership, 69*(2), 50–53.

Fullan, M., & Sharratt, L. (2007). Sustaining leadership in complex times: An individual and system solution. In B. Davies (Ed.), *Developing sustainable leadership.* SAGE.

Fullan, M., & Watson, N. (2011). *The slow road to higher order skills.* Report to Stupski Foundation.

Fullan, M., Quinn, J., & McEachen, J. (2018). *Deep learning: Engage the world change the world.* Corwin.

Galileo Educational Network. (2008). *Evidence of learning in the 21st century classroom: Classroom observation rubric and leadership for learning by instructional leaders.* Author.

Gates, W. (1995). *The road ahead.* Viking Press.

Greenan, M. (2011a). The secret of success criteria. *Principal Connections, 14*(3), 10–13.

Greenan, M. (2011b). *Teaching "big ideas" to little kids.* Dufferin-Peel Catholic District School Board.

Hanson, R., & Farrell, D. (1995). The long-term effects on high school seniors of learning to read in kindergarten. *Reading Research Quarterly, 30*(4), 908–933.

Hargreaves, A. (2019). Teacher collaboration: 30 years of research on its nature, forms, limitations, and its effects. *Teachers and Teaching Theory and Practice, 25*(5), 603–621. https://doi.org/10.1080/13540602.2019.1639499

Hargreaves, A., & Fink, D. (2006). *Sustainable leadership.* Jossey-Bass.

Hargreaves, A., & Shirley, D. (2006). *The fourth way.* Corwin.

Harlen, W. (2006). *Teaching, learning and assessing science 5–12* (4th revised ed.). Chapman.

Harris, A. (2014). *Distributed leadership matters: Principles, practicalities and potential.* Corwin.

Harris, A., Elder, Z., Jones, M., & Cooze, A. (2022). *Leading collaborative learning: Final report.* Welsh Government.

Harris, A., & Jones, M. S. (2019). *System recall: Leading for equity and excellence in education.* Corwin.

Harris, A., & Jones, M. (2020). COVID 19—school leadership in disruptive times. *School Leadership & Management, 40*(4), 243–247.

Harste, J. C. (2003). What do we mean by literacy now? *Voices from the Middle, 10*(3), 8–12.

Hattie, J. (2012). *Visible learning for teachers: Maximizing impact on learning.* Routledge.

Hattie, J. (2009). *Visible learning: Synthesis of over 800 meta-analyses relating to achievement.* Routledge.

Hattie, J., & Timperley, H. (2007). The power of feedback. *Review of Educational Research, 77*(1), 81–112.

Hill, P. W., & Crévola, C. A. (1999). The role of standards in educational reform for the 21st century. In D. D. Marsh (Ed.), *ASCD Yearbook 1999: Preparing our schools for the 21st century* (pp. 117–142). Association for Supervision and Curriculum Development.

Hopper, K., & Hopper, W. (2009). *The puritan gift: Reclaiming the American dream amidst global financial chaos.* Tauris.

Horizons of hope: An education framework for the Archdiocese of Melbourne. (2018). Melbourne Archdiocese Catholic Schools (MACS).

Leithwood, K., Mascall, B., & Strauss, T. (2009). *Distributed leadership according to the evidence.* Taylor & Francis.

Lent, R. (2017). *Disciplinary literacy: A shift that makes sense.* https://www.ascd.org/el/articles/disciplinary-literacy-a-shift-that-makes-sense

Louis, K. S., Leithwood, K., Wahlstrom, K., Anderson, S., Michlin, M., Mascall, B., Gordon, M., & Thomas, E. (2010). *Learning from districts' efforts to improve student achievement: Final report of research to the Wallace Foundation.* Wallace Foundation.

Love, N., Stiles, K. E., Mundry, S., & DiRanna, K. (2008). *The data coach's guide to improving learning for all students.* Corwin.

McCormick Calkins, L. (2001). *The art of teaching reading.* Heinemann.

Meek, M. (1991). *On being literate.* Heinemann.

Millar-Grant, J., Heffler, B., & Mereweather, K. (1995). *Student-led conferences.* Pembroke.

Moss, C., & Brookhart, S. (2009). *Advancing formative assessment in every classroom—A guide for instructional leaders.* Association for Supervision and Curriculum Development.

OECD. (2019). *PISA 2018 results (Volume I): What students know and can do.* Author. https://doi.org/10.1787/5f07c754-en

OECD. (2016). *PISA 2015 results (Volume I): Excellence and equity in education.* Author. https://read.oecd-ilibrary.org/education/pisa-2015-results-volume-i_9789264266490-en

Ontario Ministry of Education. (2010a). *Growing success.* Queen's Printer.

Ontario Ministry of Education. (2010b). *Ontario language arts curriculum.* Queen's Printer.

Ontario Ministry of Education. (2004). *Literacy for learning: Report of the expert panel on literacy in grades 4 to 6 in Ontario.* Queen's Printer.

Ontario Ministry of Education. (2003). *A guide to effective instruction in reading: Kindergarten to grade 3.* Queen's Printer.

Ostinelli, G. (2008). *The school improvement advisor/researcher SIA: Helping the individual school in the self-management of improvement.* Research paper presented to the Admee Meeting, Geneva, Switzerland.

Quinn, J., McEachen, J., Fullan, M., Gardner, M., & Drummy, M. (2020). *Dive into deep learning.* Corwin.

Reeves, D. B. (2010). *Transforming professional development into student results.* Association for Supervision and Curriculum Development.

Reeves, D. B. (2011). *Elements of grading: A guide to effective practice.* Association for Supervision and Curriculum Development.

Robinson, K. (2009). *The element.* Viking.

Rogers, W. T. (2009). *Towards an understanding of gender differences in literacy achievement.* EQAO Research Bulletin #5. EQAO.

Schleicher, A. (2011). *OECD presentation to world education ministers in Japan.* Tokyo, Japan.

Schön, D. (1983). *The reflective practitioner.* Basic Books.

Senge P. M. (1990). *The fifth discipline: The art and practice of the learning organization.* Doubleday.

Sharratt, L. (2019). *CLARITY: What matters MOST in learning, teaching, and leading.* Corwin.

Sharratt, L. (2011–2022). *Learning walks and talks* [Training materials].

Sharratt, L. (1996). *The influence of electronically available information on the stimulation of knowledge use and organizational learning in schools* [Doctoral dissertation]. University of Toronto, Canada.

Sharratt, L., & Fullan, M. (2012). *Putting FACES on the data: What great leaders do!* Corwin.

Sharratt, L., & Fullan, M. (2009). *Realization: The change imperative for deepening district-wide reform.* Corwin.

Sharratt, L., & Fullan, M. (2006). Accomplishing district wide reform. *Journal of School Leadership, 16,* 583–595.

Sharratt, L., & Fullan, M. (2005). The school district that did the right things right. Annenberg Institute for School Reform, Brown University. *Voices in Urban Education, Fall,* 5–13.

Sharratt, L., Ostinelli, G., & Cattaneo, A. (2010). *The role of the "knowledgeable other" in improving student achievement, school culture and teacher efficacy: Two case studies from Canadian and Swiss perspectives and experiences.* Paper presented at the International Congress for School Effectiveness and Improvement, Kuala Lumpur, Malaysia.

Sharratt, L., & Harild, G. (2015). *Good to great to innovate: Recalculating the route to career readiness, K–12+.* Corwin.

Sharratt, L., & Planche, B. (2016). *Leading Collaborative Learning: Empowering Excellence.* Corwin.

Sharratt, M. (2004). *The impact of teacher leadership on students' literacy learning* [Master's thesis]. University of Toronto, Canada.

Shulman, R., for the EQAO. (2010). *Strategies that work for schools: Thinking globally in a postmodern world.* Queen's Printer of Ontario.

Teddlie, C., Reynolds, D., & Sammons, P. (2000). The methodology and scientific properties of school effectiveness research. In C. Teddlie & D. Reynolds (Eds.), *The international handbook of school effectiveness research* (pp. 55–133). Flamer.

Temple, J. A., Reynolds, A. J., & Miedel, W. T. (1998). *Research on Chicago child-parent centers.* Sector and Charles Stewart Mott Foundation.

UNESCO. (2006). *Education for all global monitoring report.* www.unesco.org/education/GMR2006/full/chapt1_eng.pdf

Wiliam, D. (2011). *Embedded formative assessment.* Solution Tree.

Willms, J. D., Friesen, S., & Milton, P. (2009). *What did you do in school today? Transforming classrooms through social, academic, and intellectual engagement: First national report.* Canadian Education Association.

York Region District School Board. (2007). *Guidelines for curriculum implementation: A curriculum expectations document.* Author.

York Region District School Board. (2004). *The literate graduate.* Author.

INDEX

A SAGE Publishing Company

CORWIN HAS ONE MISSION: to enhance education through intentional professional learning.

We build long-term relationships with our authors, educators, clients, and associations who partner with us to develop and continuously improve the best evidence-based practices that establish and support lifelong learning.

ACEL's vision is to contribute to a vibrant professional learning community founded on a shared commitment to improve the quality of learning for all. As one of the largest cross sector professional associations in the education sector in Australia and the wider Asia-Pacific region, ACEL partners with like-minded organisations to ensure that educational leaders get access to most current research and best practice in their field.

THE PROFESSIONAL LEARNING ASSOCIATION

Learning Forward is a nonprofit, international membership association of learning educators committed to one vision in K–12 education: Excellent teaching and learning every day. To realize that vision, Learning Forward pursues its mission to build the capacity of leaders to establish and sustain highly effective professional learning. Information about membership, services, and products is available from www.learningforward.org.